UNION-CASTLE LINE
PURSERETTE

COVER ILLUSTRATION
PRETORIA CASTLE and CAPETOWN CASTLE at Port Elizabeth in the late 1940s.
PRETORIA CASTLE was sold to Safmarine in 1966 and re-named S. A. ORANJE.
(A. S. Mallett collection)

UNION-CASTLE LINE PURSERETTE

by
ANN HAYNES
(née WILLIAMS)

MALLETT & BELL PUBLICATIONS
THE CABINET
HIGH STREET
COLTISHALL
NORFOLK
NR12 7AA

This book is dedicated to
the memory of my beloved
husband David, who died
on 29th June 1997

British Library Cataloguing in Publication Data
Haynes, Ann
  Union-Castle Line Purserette

ISBN 0 9509453 4 X

Computer typeset by Ann Haynes
Printed and bound by Page Bros, Norwich

CONTENTS

ODE TO MISS A. WILLIAMS
ON GOING TO SEA

When you sail away this week
In your uniform so chic
We shall think of you and, maybe, shed a tear.
But we'll hope the sea's not frisky
When you reach the Bay of Biscay
(You'll get your sea legs soon, never fear.)

May you quite forget what care is
As you head for the Canaries,
With the Line to cross and lots of fun in store.
While we roam these streets suburban
You'll be on your way to Durban -
How I wish that I could meet you on that shore!

We know you'll be hard-working,
With little chance of shirking -
Such a lot of work, and little time for fun;
But don't get in a tiz.
When you reach Port Eliz.,
You'll have time to soak up all that lovely sun.

We'll keep our jealousy in check
When we think of you on deck
In bikini and a simply stunning tan.
And when you're in Mid-Atlantic
With the moonlight so romantic
Like the Mounties may you always get your man!

When you're home again and dry
You must come to I.C.I.
And relate to us what you have seen and done.
But until that happy day
There is little left to say
Except good luck, God speed - and do have fun!

Doreen Stammers
October 1965

FOREWORD

APPLICATIONS are invited for appointment as PURSERETTE on the sea-going staff of a well-known shipping line, from young ladies between 23 and 28 years of age; a good G.C.E. plus first-class secretarial qualifications and experience are required; a good appearance and the ability to deal pleasantly and tactfully with a wide range of clerical and social activities are essential. Please write, giving full particulars, to Box AA 381, care of Streets, 110 Old Broad Street, E.C.2.

That was how it all began, with an advertisement in the Personal column of THE TIMES newspaper in March 1965. As Miss Ann Williams I applied and went for numerous interviews, and was offered a job as a Purserette with Union-Castle Line. It wasn't until a long time later I discovered that hundreds of applications were received and fewer than a handful of us were offered a position. I joined Union-Castle Line in October 1965 and "worked by" on STIRLING CASTLE (with QUEEN MARY berthed nearby) and PRETORIA CASTLE in Berths 102 or 104, opposite the Flour Mills in Herbert Walker Avenue, Southampton, before sailing on my first lavender-hull vessel - TRANSVAAL CASTLE - at 1 o'clock on Friday 12th November 1965.

I wrote home to my parents regularly and frequently during the two years I was at sea, and they kept all my aerogrammes, letters and photographs, which I still have with my memorabilia. Some time after my late husband David's death in June 1997, I decided to re-type the letters onto the computer so our grown-up children (Philip and Caroline) could enjoy reading about my time at sea.

Now, as a Director of the re-launched Union-Castle Line, with our Centenary Voyage leaving Southampton on 11th December 1999, it has been suggested to me that this might be an appropriate time to share "a laugh on the ocean wave" with others. Union-Castle Line has been part of my life for a long time now, so share and enjoy a little bit of nostalgia for one of the greatest shipping lines ever - The Union-Castle Mail Steamship Company Limited.

Ann Haynes (née Williams)
August 1999

They that go down to the sea in ships, that do business in great waters

These see the works of the Lord, and his wonders in the deep

For he commandeth, and raiseth the stormy wind, which lifteth up the waves thereof.

They mount up to the heaven, they go down again to the depths: their soul is melted because of trouble

They reel to and fro, and stagger like a drunken man, and are at their wit's end

Then they cry unto the Lord in their trouble, and he bringeth them out of their distresses.

He maketh the storm a calm, so that the waves thereof are still

Then are they glad because they be quiet; so he bringeth them unto their desired haven

Extracts from the Log . .

Voyage Twenty-Six of R.M.S. "Transvaal Castle"

CAPTAIN N. M. LLOYD. R.D., R.N.R.

LAUNCHED 17-1-61 CLYDEBANK 32,697 TONS

SOUTHAMPTON   TO   CAPE TOWN

Date	Distance Run	Lat. | Long.	Wind Force	Temp. at Noon Air	Sea	Itinerary
12-11-65		Southampton	NE 2	48°		1.00 p.m. Departed Southampton Cloudy & clear 2.54 p.m. Departed Needles Pilot 11.20 p.m. Passed Ushant Is., entered Bay of Biscay Tombola Dancing
13-11-65	494	44°24N 08°35W	WNW 5	56°	58°	Moderate sea, heavy swell Cloudy & clear 3.30 p.m. Passed Cape Villano, left Bay of Biscay Captain's Cocktail Party Welcome Dance Cinema -"How to Murder Your Wife"
14-11-65	528	36°05N 12°15W	SW 3	64°	64°	Slight sea, heavy swell Fine & clear 10.30 a.m. Divine Service conducted by Captain 4.45 p.m. "The Bridge and the Ship" Illustrated Lecture by Captain Cinema - Travel & Interest Song Guessing Competition Orchestral Concert Whist Drive
15-11-65	504	Las Palmas	Light Airs	70°	70°	Rippled sea, low swell Fine & sunny 11.00 a.m. Arrived Las Palmas 3.30 p.m. Departed Las Palmas Tombola Cinema -"Major Dundee" Dancing
16-11-65	476	20°45N 17°55W	NNE 5	68°	70°	Slight sea, low swell Fine & sunny Tournaments commence Childrens Cinema Dog Racing Dancing
17-11-65	535	11°52N 17°28W	NNE 4	80°	81°	Slight sea, low swell Fine & sunny 4.00 a.m. Passed Cape Verde & Port of Dakar Deck Sports Cricket Match - Passengers v Officers Transvaal Derby Late Night Dancing
18-11-65	516	05°03N 12°20W	SSE 2	81°	81°	Slight sea, low swell Fine & sunny Childrens Fancy Dress Party Tombola Beetle Drive Cinema -"Rotten to the Core" Dancing
19-11-65	512	01°35S 07°00W	SSE 4	75°	74°	Slight sea, low swell Cloudy with sunny periods 6.20 a.m. Crossed Equator in Longitude 8°18W 10.30 a.m. Crossing the Line Ceremony Fancy Dress Parade & Gala Dance - Midnight Supper
20-11-65	522	08°25S 01°37W	SE 3	71°	71°	Slight sea, low swell Cloudy & clear Cinema - "The Great Escape" Tombola Dancing Frog Racing
21-11-65	515	15°08S 03°48E	SE 3	67°	68°	Slight sea, low swell Cloudy & clear 10.30 a.m. Divine Service conducted by Captain Quiz Orchestral Concert
22-11-65	513	21°48S 09°24E	SE 4	64°	64°	Slight sea, moderate swell Cloudy with sunny periods Finals of Tournaments Childrens Cinema Tombola Dancing
23-11-65	498	28°23S 14°56E	SE 3	63°	62°	Slight sea, low swell Fine & sunny Hostess Half Hour Farewell Dance - Prize Giving
24-11-65	379	Cape Town				6.00 a.m. Estimated Time of Arrival in Table Bay 7.00 a.m. Estimated Time of Arrival in Berth

TOTAL DISTANCE 5992 MILES - - AVERAGE SPEED 21·99 KNOTS

Extracts from the Log . .
Voyage Twenty-Six of R.M.S. "Transvaal Castle"

CAPTAIN N. M. LLOYD. R.D., R.N.R.

LAUNCHED 17-1-61 CLYDEBANK 32,697 TONS

CAPE TOWN   TO   SOUTHAMPTON

Date	Distance Run	Lat. | Long.	Wind Force	Temp. at Noon Air	Temp. at Noon Sea	Itinerary
8-12-65		Cape Town		64°		4.00 p.m. Departed Cape Town — Cloudy & clear Tombola Cinema - "Big Job" Dancing
9-12-65	473	27°43S 12°46E	S 5	66°	64°	Moderate sea & swell — Cloudy with sunny periods Captain's Cocktail Party - Welcome Dance
10-12-65	561	20°12S 06°42E	S 4	68°	66°	Slight sea, moderate swell — Cloudy with sunny periods Tournaments commence Childrens Cinema Tombola Dancing
11-12-65	569	12°41S 00°43E	SE 4	69°	69°	Slight sea, moderate swell — Overcast & clear Deck Sports Cricket Match-Passengers v Officers Cinema -"None But The Brave" Whist Drive Frog Racing Dancing
12-12-65	550	05°20S 04°48W	SE 3	75°	75°	Slight sea, low swell — Fine & sunny 10.30 a.m. Divine Service conducted by Captain 4.45 p.m. "The Bridge and the Ship" Illustrated Lecture by Captain Quiz Orchestral Concert Crew Boxing Tournament
13-12-65	576	02°10N 10°46W	SE 3	79°	78°	Slight sea, low swell — Fine & sunny 4.42 a.m. Crossed Equator in Longitude 8°50W 10.30 a.m. Crossing the Line Ceremony Beetle Drive Cinema –"Dear Brigitte" Tombola Dancing
14-12-65	556	09°36N 16°18W	Light Airs	82°	82°	Rippled sea, low swell — Fine & sunny Childrens Fancy Dress Party Tombola Dog Racing Dancing
15-12-65	546	18°22N 17°54W	NE 4	72°	72°	Moderate sea, low swell — Fine & sunny 2.20 a.m. Passed Cape Verde & Port of Dakar Fancy Dress Parade & Gala Dance - Midnight Supper
16-12-65	505	26°25N 16°03W	NE 6	68°	67°	Rough sea, moderate swell — Fine & sunny Childrens Fair Childrens Cinema 6.00 p.m. Arrived Las Palmas 9.30 p.m. Departed Las Palmas
17-12-65	398	Madeira	NE 4	63°	66°	Moderate sea, low swell — Cloudy with sunny periods 12.00 noon Arrived Madeira 1.30 p.m. Departed Madeira Finals of Tournaments Tombola Transvaal Derby
18-12-65	476	39°30N 12°16W	SE 5	61°	60°	Moderate sea, heavy swell — Cloudy with sunny periods 11.45 p.m. Passed Cape Villano & entered Bay of Biscay Cinema - "The V.I.P.'s" Tombola Prize Giving - Farewell Dance
19-12-65	527	47°12N 06°27W	SW 6	55°	52°	Rough sea, heavy swell — Overcast with rain 10.30 a.m. Divine Service conducted by Captain 4.15 p.m. Passed Ushant & entered English Channel Cinema - Travel & Interest Quiz Carol Singing
20-12-65	341	Southampton				4.00 a.m. Estimated Time of Arrival Nab Pilot Station 7.00 a.m. Estimated Time of Arrival Southampton

TOTAL DISTANCE 6078 MILES   -   -   AVERAGE SPEED 22·40 KNOTS

R.M.S. "TRANSVAAL CASTLE"
CAPTAIN N. M. LLOYD R.D., R.N.R.
VOYAGE 26
LEAVING SOUTHAMPTON 12TH NOVEMBER 1965

14th November 1965
Sunday, 6.20 p.m. at sea
Dear Family

I am now sitting under a hairdryer, feeling quite pleased with life. But to start at the beginning. On Friday we sailed at 1.00 on time, of course, and we shut shop and waved from the Promenade deck to the crowds below. Back to work, passed the Needles, took a picture through the Bureau porthole. I had previously received a large box of flowers from the girls at I.C.I. Paints Division (Doreen, Pat, Marian, Marsha etc.) Wasn't that nice of them? A lady passenger also gave me some - she had been given lots, so thought I might like to take some of them off her hands. So I did. P.M. I felt a bit peculiar so retired early (11.00). Busy in Bureau until last minute. I had a small disaster and spilt pink typewriter correcting fluid all down the skirt of my one and only navy uniform dress too. Must be nervousness, but everyone is very kind.

Sat. a.m. tried to get up at 6.45, but couldn't. Felt dreadful, was sick, and couldn't walk, let alone work. Nursing Sister rushed in and fed me pills. Tried to get up for lunch, and felt better after walk in fresh air. Lunch (light) in cabin, then a little typing. Tea drink, then went to Captain's Cocktail Party. Two "sittings" - my feet started to ache because we actually stood the whole time. Felt better in company too. Then dinner, ate turkey, or was it steak, anyway had a little meat and enjoyed it and felt much better. Then some of us went to the pictures. Yes, we did. Saw "How to Murder your wife". Bed late again of course. This morning I didn't get up until 7.45, so felt better still. Now passed through the Bay of Biscay so the sea is calmer, and sky clearer and blue. Quite busy today, tried selling South African stamps but wasn't too successful - I can't learn which stamps for which places, and at which rates (air/surface). I hope it comes with time! Had a rest from 1-3 today. Should have been until 4, but we were busy in Bureau. I booked a hairdo yesterday, so rushed in here at 5.40 (late). Tonight is dinner, then an "entertainment" - "Name the Song" competition. Nice and quiet for a Sunday. Oh yes, this morning we attended Church service at 10.30. Enjoyed it. Quite short, but nautical. I wonder if we always have "For those in peril on the sea" .... ?

Tomorrow we arrive at Las Palmas at 11.00. Don't know whether I will get ashore, but fingers and legs all crossed. Crossing the Line Friday - should be interesting - and warmer. Start sunbathing Tuesday I reckon. Jealous?

Love, Ann xxx

Cape Town November 1965
Transcript of a tape I made and sent home as a surprise.

Hello, I thought you'd be interested in knowing what I've been up to since I left Southampton. I've done an awful lot, there hasn't been much time to write so I thought it best if I told you something about it. I've got beside me a Programme of Events which shows all the different days and times of things so I thought if I go through that I'll try and remember funny things. So much has happened it is almost impossible to remember everything but I'll bring all the papers home and tell you more then.

As I told you in my letter I was seasick ill on Friday night and Saturday morning and got better fairly quickly as the pills worked. On the Sat. we had the Captain's Cocktail party - 2 sittings - and had to go along there and make party talk, quite interesting, but a bit difficult sometimes. After dinner, and the food is very good, we went to the Dance in the Assembly Room. I think you probably saw that when you came on board. Sunday I worked the rest of the day after Church Service. Wore my hat and felt very new. In the evening there was a Song Guessing Competition and I sat at a table with others and asked pax. to draw title of song on a piece of paper., allocated them a number, and they had to go round and guess everyone else's. Some were a bit funny and some a bit peculiar but don't think I could have done any better myself.

Monday was Las Palmas and I went on a tour the Hostess organised for pax. - she asked me too. I jumped at it, taxi tour of island. Up to the garden city, saw camel, top of crater, ex volcano, farm right down in middle of it, the cave dwellers, visited the house Columbus stayed in, saw anchor, log books, interesting. Marvellous views. I was lucky to get ashore.

Monday was Tombola in the Golden room, my first bingo session. I was allowed to call one set of numbers, they said I had a good voice, although I felt rather nervous. Couldn't remember things like legs 11. Tuesday up early doing News, 5.30 for 6, rush to Radio Office to collect stencils, run off on the machine in the Bureau, quite a business. Swim in big pool before dinner, then on the Tote for Dog Racing.

Wednesday I was in the Doldrums - truly, because that is part of the Southern Atlantic Ocean. I've been looking out for dolphins etc. but never seem to be there at the right time. Cricket match on deck, fun for passengers; swim for me after work; p.m. TRANSVAAL CASTLE Derby , that was funny, and I wore a pretty crepe paper hat.

Thursday afternoon I helped to judge the Children's Fancy Dress Parade. The Captain judged too, Hostess and me, very enjoyable.

Friday - oh yes, woke up in the morning and they said 6.15 this morning we crossed the Equator - did you feel the bump? I said no; they said oh well, 10.30 you are in the Crossing the Line Ceremony, so I actually took part. I wore a bikini and a long grass skirt. We marched along the deck, the band, the Captain dressed as Neptune, the Hostess dressed as his fairy Queen, me as a South Sea maiden, and doctors and nurses and policemen, really funny. Then back to work for rest of day. It was a Tombola evening, so I had my hair done again. Then the Gala Dance, a very popular event, everyone has to wear a head dress if they want to enter the competition, long dresses, long gloves, good entries. Midnight they had an Egg and Bacon Supper so we were allowed to stay up for it as a special concession; normally we have to be off decks by 11.30 p.m. Down to the galley, get a tray, collect your food, bacon, egg and coffee (I was quite ready for it) then back into the Dining Room and candles in bottles on the tables - it looked really good. So of course that was me late to bed again.

Lost time on clocks again. On News again, machine went wrong again, but maybe third time lucky I'll get it done. Tombola again, no swim, hair done, tonight Frog racing. The Captain is very expert at this so is probably going to win. Whether he is allowed to I am not so sure. I will be on the tote again. We go back into blues tomorrow, a shame.

I've made a few odd notes of things to tell you. On sunny days we go up on the Funnel deck. Daddy told me about the Funnel Deck on his ship. Here, all the Officers have to go up there. We use the steamer chairs, that cost the passengers thirty bob, which are so comfortable. We have the free use of them until Cape Town. Last night I had to attend a private Captain's Cocktail party and announce the names of people as they arrived.

In the mornings I usually go for a walk after breakfast, fresh air, 10 minutes round the Promenade Deck. You probably remember that Deck from your visit; 6 times round is a mile, so I usually do 2. Food is very good and I keep trying something different every night.

I've now decorated my cabin - put my "Desert Island Discs" up, you know the ones, my Imperial Records from I.C.I. Paints Division, tee hee; I've got a big map of the world, and a big "Spain is different" poster. It's beginning to feel like home now, although I don't spend much time in here. I fly in and fly out, and wash my bits and pieces when there is time, every few days.

Oh yes, talking about washing. All my uniforms have been Christened. I got "boob" juice on my navy day dress - unusual expression I hadn't come across before. When you type a stencil and make a mistake you have to blot it out to be able to overtype it correctly so you use correcting fluid. I dropped it down my dress in two splurges. Had to take emergency action and send it to the Laundry. Very annoying. Same with white dresses, as managed to get odd marks on them but never mind.

Each of us Purser's Clerks has a till and this is quite a responsibility, I'm not very keen on this. But you have to take money for all sorts of things and change it and you have the responsibility for it all. I seem to be £1 down today, but I managed to wangle things so it's all right. Told you about swimming after work ends at 5.30, and you've no idea of how peculiar it feels, temp. around 80 odd degrees, November, swimming around, unbelievable. I keep saying this to everyone and they say oh yes, everyone's like this on their first trip. But it really doesn't seem possible that it's really happening to me. But it's marvellous.

It was the Gala Dance last night, and I had to start a Snowball Dance. I love dancing as you know and usually get invited to dance. We are only allowed to dance 2 consecutive dances with any one particular Officer, so we go around and it is quite fun and us girls are in our element of course. Last night the 2nd Purser said the Purser said we had to start a Snowball Dance so we did. With all the passengers looking, John (Bokor-Ingram) and I had to take to the floor, quickstep for 2 minutes, then choose another partner, nearest male to you. I got some man who was sitting there, 90 in the shade, dark glasses, could hardly walk, he clasped me so tightly I could hardly breathe and he said to me very confidingly "Of course you know I ought to be in bed really dear". No answer to that, rather wish he had been. Snowball turned into a Paul Jones. Everything is fun, I really am enjoying it.

I just live for the day. The only time you worry about the next day is if you are doing the News the next morning, making sure you have enough paper, and everything organised. I just lose track of the days of the week. We are in the South Atlantic at the moment, nearest land miles away, Ascension Island probably. We are steaming along, it's cloudy today, in blues tomorrow, warm 70 ish, not complaining. Sometimes I actually read the News and gather that you are having rain, fog etc. and really nasty weather. I couldn't care less mates! Well, I'm worried that you are all in the cold but England seems so far away and I look at the map on my wall and think they are all up there and I'm down here, and can hardly believe it.

I keep pinching myself but I am having a marvellous time, I really am, for my first trip and that's probably got a lot to do with it.

I'm actually in Cape Town, sideways on to Table Mountain. It's just like the picture in my geography book at Bishopshalt School. Oh, I'm so thrilled to see it. We arrived late because of fog, and the siren was on for half an hour. We docked a mile away this morning to wait for it to lift, an hour later than expected. Got in here and I was allowed to rush up on deck and there was the Mountain with the tablecloth on, marvellous. Something called Signal Hill is just near, a very sharp peak with cloud going up and round it, and I hope to go there this afternoon.

In the Bureau we are doing 3 shift days round the Coast, 8.30 a.m. - 9 p.m., so usually on for 1 or 2 shifts. This morning it seemed like absolute chaos on arrival so after a quick lunch one of the young men here suggested going to Cape Town so we changed and got a taxi. We wandered round Adderley St. which is the main shopping boulevard here, lovely, very enjoyable. Big stores, well planned and laid out, didn't buy anything but had a quick look round, with Table Mountain in the background. Clear sky and it really is flat, I keep having to look at it. Got back for work for 3 p.m., a quiet afternoon because we are in port.

Yesterday, Tuesday, there was a sort of anticipation all over the ship, getting ready for Cape Town arrival. I had to do some work for a passenger, 2 hours dictation. He had been on a grand tour and wanted 100 copies of everything so it took me 10 hours , so you can imagine what he was charged. As a gift he gave me a tiny purse from Seville. Yet another passenger, a nice old lady , gave us 3 girls a large tin of Quality Street chocs. so we are in the process of eating them. We just chatted with her, very friendly and I think she liked us.

Do you remember on telly a few months ago a programme called "Opportunity Knocks"? On one of them was a muscle man, with rippling muscles, which he moved in time to music. Well, he's on board, he's one of the pax. and he keeps giving private shows. Did one at the Crew Dance the other night on the Well Deck and us Officers were invited along. All the crew were there and the muscle man came on, all in gold paint, little hat painted gold, and he gave his demonstration in time to music. Beautiful muscle control but I thought it was rather revolting. I'm sure he was quite a nice man really but what an unusual act. Most pax. really nice, friendly and very chatty now because they are nearly home.

Had a little party before dinner the other night, just to return hospitality from others so that was good. I've had my first gin and tonic and enjoyed it. We met the SOUTHAMPTON CASTLE here, which left at 4 p.m. with flags and waves.

Think I've told you everything now. I have photos. to show you taken on board. I had 5 letters in the post this morning, lovely, thank you. I'm having trouble reading Daddy's writing, but I'll do it given time. I shall use aerogrammes for easiness if you don't mind in future.

I do hope you like this tape, and it's a nice surprise. This is something Doreen and I planned ages ago and thought it would be a good idea to send you a tape telling you exactly what is happening to me. I can just picture your surprise when you open it and listen to it.

Must finish, but thank you all so much for your letters and messages, they were ever so welcome. I had a little trouble reading Daddy's but I'll do it, but I really was grateful to everybody for writing, it's so nice to get the letters even though they are written a week or more ago. Thank you ever so much. See you soon, take care of yourselves, and love to everybody.
Ann

At Sea between Cape Town and Port Elizabeth

25th November 1965
Dear family

As I am again under the hairdryer, I thought I would try to write in answer to your letters. Thank you again for them, they were so welcome. It was such a surprise to think that my letter from Las Palmas only took one day. I am quite well and very happy. I felt homesick on Sunday morning in church, but that didn't last long. Not enough sleep, I expect! (If my writing keeps changing, it's because the dryer keeps rolling away; I have to hang on with one hand, write with the other, and hope and pray the letter doesn't slip! Difficult!)

We left Cape Town a.m. today and passed the "Cape of Good Hope" after lunch. We are now getting round towards the Indian Ocean, which should be warmer. Tonight it is Bingo again, Dancing and/or Cinema. Such goings on. But to business. The car - I hope you can get rid of my Austin Ruby as soon as it is convenient - I will keep my fingers crossed about the battery! Yes, I think it would be a good idea to hire a car from 21st to say 25th or 24th December. Thanks for the offer of the Consul too. Offer accepted with thanks. I think it would be best to get a car at home, don't you? There must be lots of reasonably-priced cars for hire in the district. I don't really want to drive up from Southampton. I would rather like a Mini, if you can fix it, but I leave it in your capable hands (n.b. I do not fancy a turquoise one, please.)

I hope you like the surprise I have arranged for you all. I wish I could be there to see your reactions. All carefully planned anyway! I got a letter from Aunty Doris too, yesterday. Raise the flags! Very pleased to hear from her anyway. Letters also from Doreen Stammers and Marian Paget. The Bureau gang all decided somebody must love me after all. Wait til they see me get a letter at every port! It is so comforting to know there will probably be a letter everywhere; just this first time especially. Oops, there goes the dryer again. Mummy, you will no doubt be delighted to know that I am sending cards to everyone I should send them to. I am keeping a list, so you can give me 10 out of 10 when I get home! Ha Ha. Elaine, I am glad about your job. Hope to hear from you about it. I remember us seeing it advertised. Good luck. Regards to Derek too - hope his car is O.K. Daddy, thanks for details of cars etc. and everyone for messages. Wish you were all here.
Love, Ann

Friday, Port Elizabeth
Dear Family

This is just going to be a short (joke!) note about last night's incident. You may hear in the next few days something about an accident aboard the ship on Thursday night. One of the members of the crew jumped overboard at 1.30 in the morning and the ship had to stop, the accident boats were launched and there were great goings-on.

We first knew of it when a loud klaxon hooter went off in the female Officers accommodation and we all woke up. I looked at the clock and couldn't believe it. It was dark outside. I was frightened for a moment, but immediately got out of bed, grabbed my life jacket and coat and rushed to Maggie Telford's room. She was in a similar state of panic but then one of the men Officers rushed in and said it was a Purser Patrol. I knew about this manoeuvre and knew I had to be outside the Bureau as soon as possible. We got dressed in a matter of seconds and rushed to the Bureau. All the crew had been called out and all the Officers. Lots of people had not dressed completely. There didn't seem to be any passengers around but this was because the alarms had not gone off in their accommodation. This was then about 1.40 a.m.

Next we heard that a Stewardette had jumped overboard but this was all extremely unofficial. We hung around our positions for ages and went back to our cabins at 2.45. We couldn't sleep so sat up (the 4 girls) drinking coffee etc. We heard one accident boat come back at 4.00 and then we heard that she had been picked up, drowned. It seems such a horrid thing to have happened. It was like a nightmare. We went back to bed at 4.30 and I couldn't get back to sleep for quite a while. She was buried at 8.00 a.m. at sea.

The worst part as far as I was concerned was when I had to go down to the girl's cabin and make a list of all her personal effects. Another of the Stewardettes came and sorted out her clothes and papers and I had to list them. It was a very unpleasant job. There was a feeling of tragedy all day yesterday. Apparently the girl had been very depressed and had just had news of a divorce. It was all very sad.

However, the rest of the day made up partly for this. Round the coast we have to work on shifts, so we get odd hours off. Yesterday of course this was all a bit disorganised, but I managed to get off after lunch and went out to the Oceanarium. This was a marvellous visit. I saw the performing dolphins and they were so clever. They perform twice a day and we saw the 3.30 show. First we walked round the snake garden and saw a coloured man handling snakes and he told us all about the different sorts. Nasty. Then we saw the crocodiles splashing around and a couple of parrots trying to get their mid-day snooze. Then we walked round the base of the a(c)quarium (sorry, cannot spell) and looked through windows into the water where there were two do(l)phins (sorry, cannot type either) one seal and two turtles swimming around. Then up to the seats and we saw the dolphins perform. They seem to be very intelligent. They played games, retrieved rubber rings, jumped up and rang bells, jumped even higher and grabbed fishes from a stick held above the water. And one even towed a little rubber raft round which had a South African flag flying on it, with a little penguin sitting inside with a tiny sailor cap on. Very amusing. It was a very good show and I took lots of pictures. It was a beautiful day - the sun shone down from a cloudless blue sky and the surf washed up on the sandy beaches while the palm trees looked on.

The city of P.E. is neither old nor new but there are a few really big shops. The big chain store equivalent of Woolworths is the OK Bazaar and this was quite interesting inside. It seemed so strange to be walking around in a thin summer dress and see Christmas decorations, cards and greetings everywhere. Can't really believe it is almost December and Christmas. They are just starting the summer season here.

Oh yes, just remembered something funny that happened on the way back from seeing the dolphins. I went with the 2nd Purser John Bokor-Ingram to see them, as we were both off duty at the same time. We caught a taxi out to the Oceanarium and arranged for him to call for us at 4.00. He arrived, and we got halfway to the town when he ran out of petrol! We were going down a hill at the time and only managed to get halfway up the other side. We jumped out and the driver flagged down one of his mates, who took us the rest of the way. When we told everyone else about this, when we got back, they all laughed and said they had heard of cars running out of petrol but this was ridiculous. It was very amusing actually. So that was yesterday more or less. I helped in the office during the evening and danced most of the night. I don't seem to get much sleep but I am still on my feet. Changing subject, did I tell you about the notice on my desk? It says "The hurrider I go, the behinder I get". Just hits the nail on the head sometimes in this chaotic office. But its all quite hilarious and I am having the time of my life. No doubt things will settle down some time but at the moment everything is very new and very exciting. I get a lot of teasing, but it is all fun. I am well and happy, and will not crack up just yet.

Love, Ann.

R.M.S. "TRANSVAAL CASTLE"

Captain N. M. Lloyd. R.D., R.N.R.

OFFICIAL RACE CARD

OF THE

TRANSVAAL DERBY

Meeting held on Wednesday, November 17, 1965

OWNERS TO ACT AS STEWARDS

TOTE by Hoppitt and Coppitt (*Port Said*) Ltd.
Motto " It Pays To Stay with The Firm That Stays To Pay "

RULES

1. The winner of each Race shall be eligible for the "Transvaal Derby".
2. The course consists of a length of tape which the horse must traverse by cutting from end to end, with the scissors provided for the purpose. Pipping is not allowed.
3. The Tape is to be held in one hand and the scissors in the other hand behind the back, until the Starter gives the word.
4. The Tape must be held in FRONT of the cutting scissors by the first fingers of the non-cutting hand until past the winning post.

Every horse shall, as far as possible, keep a straight course down the middle of the Tape, and, if it runs off the course *i.e.* cuts through the edge of the Tape, it will be disqualified.

6. A horse shall be disqualified and its owner keel-hauled, or hung from the yard arm, if:-

a. Eats its own bedding, drinks its bath water, bites, snorts, cavorts or is guilty of any practice unbecoming its pedigree.

b. If during the later days of training it fails to obey its owner's commands or has or will show any tendency or desire to change its owner (husbands excepted) or occupies any stable other than its own.

c. During the actual progress of the race if it hurls any unkind words or even thinks any unkind things about any other horse in the race.

d. It attempts in any way to influence the result, either by canoodling carousing, or in any way biassing the Judge.

7. Horses must parade and race in the registered colours of their owner but eyebrows, lips, hair, cheeks, toe-nails and finger-nails must not be coloured to match as this has a tendency to dazzle the Racegoers.
   Any rule not mentioned above will be strictly enforced

MARITIME POLICE NOTICE

The Public are warned to beware of Spivs, Tipsters, Pickpockets, Cardsharps, Vamps, Flappers, Flirts, Mermaids and Cavorting Horses, also the Treasurer of the Sports Committee. *Everyone present is under suspicion.*

1st Race   The Opening Time Handicap

Owner, Horse & Pedigree   *Jockey*

1 ....   BUBBLES
               by Champagne out of France
2 ....   MERRY WIDOW   ....
               by Husband out of Way
3 ....   PROPOSAL   ....
               by Girl out of Leap Year
4 ....   PUFF ADDER   ....
               by Accountant out of Breath
5 ....   BLONDIE   ....
               by Peroxide out of Bottle
6 ....   THROWN   ....
               by Rough Sea out of Bed

Winner.................................   Time.................

2nd Race   The Maidens Plate

1 ....   SLICK CHICK   ....
               by Egg out of Incubator
2 ....   DOLPHIN   ....
               by Fish out of Water
3 ....   BLENHEIM   ....
               by Apple out of Orchard
4 ....   GONE   ....
               by Run out of Town
5 ....   FLAT SPIN   ....
               by Plane out of Control
6 ....   VICTORIA FALLS   ....
               by Champerone out of Sight

Winner.................................   Time.................

3rd Race   The Equator Stakes

1 ....   NO NO
               by Small Voice out of Dark Corner
2 ....   YES YES   ....
               by Deep Voice out of Same Corner
3 ....   RED HOT   ....
               by Bearing out of Oil
4 ....   LOST WEEKEND   ....
               by Pub out of Beer
5 ....   MAY QUEEN   ....
               by Beauty out of Vote
6 ....   IN CLOVER   ....
               by Couple out of Sight

Winner.................................   Time.................

4th Race   Scissorwitch Cup

1 ....   THE VISIT
               by Mother in Law out of The Blue
2 ....   ROCK & ROLL   ....
               by Record out of Juke Box
3 ....   ON THE DOLE   ....
               by Man out of Work
4 ....   CIDER   ....
               by Juice out of Apple
5 ....   EXAGGERATION   ....
               by Mountain out of Molehill
6 ....   DUCKS   ....
               by Batsmen out of Practice

Winner.................................   Time.................

5th Race   The Owner's Handicap

(Open to Owners of Fillies who have won their Heats)

1 ....

2 ....

3 ....

4 ....

Winner.................................   Time.................

6th Race   THE TRANSVAAL DERBY

(Open to Winners of previous Races)

1st Race.................................   Time.................

2nd Race.................................   Time.................

3rd Race.................................   Time.................

4th Race.................................   Time.................

GRAND WINNER.................................

East London, 28th Nov. 1965 (Sunday)
Dear Family

This really is going to be just a short note, because the ship leaves here in just 35 minutes time. We arrived here at 7.00 a.m. this morning, and needless to say we were all up and working in the Bureau. I didn't receive any mail! As I said in my last letter, we work on a shift basis round the coast and I had this morning off. This meant working until 10.00, then as the ship sails off at 4.00 I had to be back here by 12.30 so that the rest of the crowd had an equal amount of time off. There were four of us off at the time (Tony, Ann and Godfrey) and we all went for a walk.

East London is just a port, but it has a beautiful beach. We all walked along the beach and the rocks, with the surf pounding up against the rocks. There were lots of people riding the crest of the waves, and it was all extremely hot. As we didn't have much time, we had all kept our uniform on. Thank goodness we went back into "whites" today so at least they were fairly cool to wear. The temperature must be quite high (up in the eighties) and the sun was blazing down. Came back in time for quick reviver (drink) before short period of work, then lunch. Then on duty for the afternoon. Did the urgent things and then decided I could take time off to write to you all.

Sorry if the letter is a bit disjointed: I am trying to look as if I am busy doing urgent office work, but this is only for the benefit of passengers. Most of the passengers round the coast are South African. We leave here at 4.00 today as I said and arrive in Durban tomorrow just after dawn, by the sound of it. We always have to be up early in port, to be in the office by the time the Immigration etc. people come aboard. If you are really unlucky, you have to be up in time for the arrival of the pilot, which is usually an hour before arrival in port, to sort the Mail which comes on board with him.

Tomorrow I hope to see the Indian Market in Durban and try and see some of the countryside. I have quite a lot of time off (fingers crossed) so there should be a good chance to see the different things. On the way back in Cape Town I aim to get up Table Mountain - I shall be very disappointed if I don't but very glad if I can. I also hope to be going out for the day down to Cape Point (I seem to remember I have said this before) and that should be very enjoyable. Not much more to report - had an enjoyable evening last night, Dog Racing and Dancing. In bed before midnight for a change. Hope you are all well - it is so nice to hear from you all at the different ports. Sorry about the weather - hope it improves.

Love Ann.

Durban, 30.11.65
Dear Family, I thought you would like these very lifelike pictures of Durban. We arrived at crack of dawn yesterday (Monday). Work til 10 a.m. Rest of day off - a.m. to Indian Market: lots of smells, curry, curios, lunch at hotel, excellent, Indian Ocean pounding on beach (miles of it). Extremely hot. P.m. out to see "Magnificent Men" film; then meal. Bed late. Marvellous evening. Durban is huge, quite a beautiful city. Beaches are huge and clean. After lunch walked along to see Ricksha men and took pictures. Very colourful. Didn't tell you about East London - it is on the River Buffalo and is surrounded by Pineapple Stations where they grow hundreds and hundreds of the things. Hope to order fruit on way home. Keep you going for weeks. Food still excellent (one-track mind) and plenty of wine and drink aboard. Oh yes, it rained yesterday evening. It was very humid too. They have put Christmas lights in the main streets of Durban and they switched them on for the first time last night. The only thing was that they forgot to tell anyone, so I think we were the only people to see them, when travelling to the cinema in the evening.

Picture of street reproduced in daily paper today so I kept it. Durban really is a lovely place to stay for 3 days, we all feel quite at home and everyone looks forward to getting here.

Lots of love, Ann.

East London
2nd December 1965

Dear Family

Here we are back in E.L. again and as I am on duty for both morning and afternoon, I thought I would get down to a letter to you. We are not very busy (yet). I got a letter from Daddy in Durban - did I tell you that - and one from Marian. I have come to the conclusion that I do not seem to be actually answering your letters as such, but simply reading them and enjoying them, then writing back to tell you what I have been up to. This time I will try and answer them.

Yes, it does seem rather peculiar to be in these places I have only dreamed about for so long. I cannot really take it all in, but I am making the most of every minute and opportunity of seeing places. I have been quite lucky with time off and have managed to be taken around to see the sights.

I am glad the Cheese & Wine party went off all right - you certainly made a lot of money I thought. The mauve waistcoat sounds a bit er, well, shall we say unusual.

I hope Mummy and Aunty had a good day in London and the weather was not too bad for them. Although it is almost Christmas it must be easier for you all to believe it than it is for me. Here we are in "whites", with lots of hot weather, blue sky and sea (not at the moment to be quite honest, but most of the time) and yet yesterday the agents in Durban wished us all Happy Christmas when they left the ship. Most peculiar. When you said that you may have repeated yourself, I know what you mean. I have several times wondered just how many times I have told you some things. But never mind. It think it bears repeating. I do hope you have got my surprise by now. It was such fun doing it, and I was longing to be there when you received it. I see that I posted it on 24th November so you should have it by now. Hope so.

So Austin Ruby has really gone now. Yes, we had great fun with her, I loved owning her. I thought it was funny that every time you hear the telephone, you expect it to be me, asking for help. Talking of telephones, I enquired about phoning home from the ship from here but it costs quite a lot, and they cannot guarantee a good reception, so I will not be ringing you.

Now to try and answer Mummy's letter. My hair costs me 10/6d. a time, reduced rate. I told you I had it cut short the first time I went. It seems very short to me and I like it very much. It is still in the same style with side curls coming forward in front of my ears, but it is much shorter at the back. It looks very smart I think. I need it away from my collars I think, as I usually wash my own dresses and I don't like giving myself extra work! I am having it trimmed again this evening after work, with shampoo and set of course, and this will probably cost me 16/6d. It is cut really well. It gets very sticky very quickly so I like to have it done often. We don't have to worry about "what shall I wear this evening" - the answer is always the same - uniform. So we can only go to town with things like make-up and hair.

Something I haven't mentioned before is the "Board of Trade Sports". This is not as much fun as it sounds. It is Lifeboat Drill while at sea, and happens once a week. We had the last one on Sunday after leaving E.L. southbound and it drizzled all the time. Not "Outspan" weather at all, except for the warmth. Never known Boat Drill be over so quickly.

The work is going well. We get up at 7.30 usually, to open the Bureau by 8.30 round the Coast. As I said, we are on shifts after 10.00 a.m. so meals are rather quick affairs, as we have to relieve each other at the counter. We stay open until 9.00 p.m. at night, again only round the Coast, so it makes a long day. But one person is never on for the whole day. Today I am on for the morning and afternoon, but I have a whole day off in Cape Town later on, so it all works out fairly. I certainly have no complaints anyway.

When we sail from a port, usually at 5.00 p.m., we close the Bureau at 5.30 which is normal closing time and then have to type furiously. We have to get the Passenger Lists done as soon as possible. There is furious activity going on behind the closed shutters of the Bureau, with people typing, others checking tickets, lists of figures being checked, people running off the stencils, and others putting sets of lists together, ready for immediate circulation. Tempers get a little frayed as you can imagine, but last night's big session went off quite well. We finished by 6.45 p.m., which was very good. The Durban embarkation list is usually the worst of the trip, and most of us expected to be working until 10.00 at night. After dinner at 7.30 (again round the coast only one sitting, and we do not "dress") I had to help sell Bingo tickets. Then back to my cabin, painted my nails, and fell asleep. So I accidentally got an early night.

That deals with the work. Now for the other girls. The other Purserette is very nice and I like her very much. I am learning a great deal from her about the job, and she is the sort of person who warns me about the various pitfalls, like certain officers/crew or the Captain's quirks. The Captain for instance is fussy that all notices on any of the notice boards should have 4 drawing pins to hold them up. Not just 2, but 4. He is also particular about the whole place being spick and span - quite right too. He "circulates" every morning, so we all have to be on our toes. All the people in the Bureau are great fun, and we have lots of laughs all day long. I suppose we are all so dependent upon each other, if you see what I mean, living and working in such close quarters for so long.

Now for the men. There are lots of gorgeous, handsome, suntanned, men around. I suppose the uniform helps a lot, but wow! The Officers are very well-mannered. It is so pleasant to have doors opened, chairs pulled out, everyone standing up when a lady sits down, and so on. There are 2 Purserettes, 1 Hostess, 1 Children's Hostess and 1 Nursing Sister, all Officers, so we have quite a time. The food is yummy, but you should all be here too though. So often in the last few weeks I have wanted to wave a magic wand and get you all here. You would enjoy it all so much. I think you would benefit so much from all the sunshine. It doesn't seem fair in a way. Mind you, I am making the most of it and feel extremely lucky. It still seems like a dream but it is beginning to feel a bit like a more permanent dream now. It doesn't seem possible that we are now on the homeward run. Once we get back to Cape Town and the last customers embark, we can start to relax and enjoy it all once more, especially up to Las Palmas. I really enjoyed that bit, and now we are going back the weather should improve. Although I keep saying that I sunbathe, don't expect to see me looking dark brown - we haven't had all that much time, or sunshine, for getting suntans, and working in the artificial light makes it difficult to tell whether it really is suntan or not. Then when you get up on the Funnel deck and bask in the sunlight it is so brilliant that I feel white. Oh well, 20th December will prove everything.

See you soon. Love, Ann

Cape Town, 6th December 1965

Dear Family
Here we are in Cape Town again and yesterday I had a wonderful day so I thought I would tell you about it while I have the chance.

It is now 8.45 a.m. on a Monday morning and I am waiting for my turn to go to breakfast. The Bureau opened at 8.30, and at the moment we don't have many customers.

Anyway, yesterday we arrived here at 7.00 a.m. I woke up at 5.30 a.m., suddenly thought I might see sunrise over Table Mountain so rushed up (dressed) on deck with camera. Sun was coming up to the left of the Mountain and it was quite a sight. Then I went down to the Bureau as we always have to be up early when we reach port. Got letter from Doreen. I had the afternoon off so I made up my mind to go up Table Mountain in the cable car. The weather was absolutely perfect and there wasn't a cloud to be seen in the sky. Freak conditions! I had to work until 2.00 but then one of the men and I rushed out, caught a taxi to the cable car halfway up the Mountain and generally marvelled at the view. The cable car takes about 20 people loaded and takes 6 minutes to reach the top. The car goes right to the top at one end of the Table. I couldn't wait to get there. The view when we actually arrived was fantastic. On the way up we gradually saw further and further. Table Mountain is almost flat on to the top but very rocky and rough. You can see in all directions for about 30 miles in yesterday's conditions. They say that on a particularly clear day it is possible to see for 100 miles! I can't describe the wonderful views, but I took lots of pictures. Came down again, had a sleep then dinner. Lovely day.

Tuesday 7th December 1965

Now another day has gone by and what a day it was. I shall never forget it. It started after I wrote the first part of this letter. Then I went for breakfast and came back to 3 letters, 2 from you and one from Ken Faulkner. I was so glad that you liked the tape - I thought it would be a rather splendid surprise! Hooray!

It was rather amusing to read the first letter when Daddy said that I didn't seem to be telling you much about what was happening, then to read the second letter with your comments on the tape. Glad it went down well anyway. Talking of going down well: yesterday morning at 10.00 was the Lifeboat Drill We All Look Forward To. We went through the normal drill, then everyone on the starboard side (dockside) had to go to the port side and help crew the boats, which were all lowered. Then having got down to the water (oh yes, me included, plus passenger list, crew list, hat and small towel to sit on) they sent one boat round in turn to all the other boats to collect in all 147 people, the absolute total one lifeboat can take. Was it a squeeze. We had to clamber from one boat to another and I was rather scared but it wasn't too bad. Everyone was the same (all the women anyway) and we got back into our boats safely, after chugging round the harbour just to prove the point. Couldn't see a thing from the bottom of the boat, even standing up. The whole operation took 1½ hours. My legs felt like jelly afterwards, must have been reaction I suppose.

Then it was a great rush, as someone had hired a car to take us down to Cape Point. The sky was fairly clear, and the sun seemed to follow us all the way. We had picnic lunch boxes (very different from the Yugoslav holiday type, that I had with Marion) with: 2 rolls filled with meat, 2 tomatoes, 2 pieces of cold chicken, an apple, an Outspan orange, a pear, an enormous piece of cheese and 2 serviettes. Needless to say, I couldn't eat it all. Set off from Cape Town at 12.15 and headed south. Stopped for lunch on an absolutely deserted beach called Llandudno Beach. Just sea, surf, sand, sound, sun, seaweed and bottles of Coca-Cola that we couldn't open because we had no opener. Most frustrating.

Further on we went round mountain passes and suddenly saw some baboons. They were sitting at the side of the road, among the eucalyptus trees. Just had to stop and photograph them. Got stuck in the sand, and one baboon just sat on a post and stared as we got unstuck. Very bad manners, I told him, so he went away.

14

Then on rapidly to the Cape of Good Hope Nature Reserve which covers all the Cape Point land. (I think this is going to be one of those letters which will take 2 aerogrammes again, so on we go.) The road winds and twists for about 5 miles, and then suddenly you can see the Cape Point itself. Just before you get there is the Cape of Good Hope itself. I have actually seen it. It was beautiful and the water around it was truly emerald green.

We left the car at the bottom of the last part of the ascent and climbed up to the very top of the Point (100 steps at the end). Absolutely exhausted by this time but managed to take in the views and take lots of pictures. There was a lovely view right across False Bay, a distance of about 10 miles I believe. We finally left at about 5.30 and headed north again. On the way back to the Reserve entrance we again met some baboons. There were about 20 of them (mums, dads and babies) all sitting in the road. One or two got out of the way and climbed a telegraph post, then slid down just for the fun of it. Others just sat and stared, others just sat and scratched, and one or two large ones just sat around and lorded it over the others.

We drove up to the end of their tails, sounded the hooter of the car and they finally decided to move. Got some good snaps of the ugly brutes. Then back along the east coast of the Cape Point seeing the other side of the land. Went through Simonstown, where I understand Ron Fenton is now, but didn't see him 'though I looked. On the outskirts of Cape Town (with a rather menacing sky over Table Mountain by this time) we got on to De Waal Drive, which is a very fine road. It is rather like a motor way, and we went past Cape Town University, the Rhodes Memorial and then suddenly, what do you think I saw in a mountainside field? No, I didn't. It was 2 zebras. Yellow and black striped. Then I was really happy, having seen some real African animals. It was a wonderful drive all the time; finally arrived back at the ship, grubby and tired at 7.00 p.m. Drink, wash and dinner, then out to the cinema to see "The Reward". Not bad.

Then another big treat - up to Signal Hill to look at the lights. It is a sight you have to see to believe. There are lights everywhere for as far as the eye can see, round the coast, inland, in the harbour (the "TRANSVAAL CASTLE" looked beautiful) up the mountainside and in the sky. So one way and another it was quite a day.

All for now. If I get a chance I will write again, if not, well this is the end of the First Chapter. Love, Ann.

UNION-CASTLE MAIL STEAMSHIP COMPANY, LIMITED.
DIAGRAM FOR USE OF BOATS' CREWS.

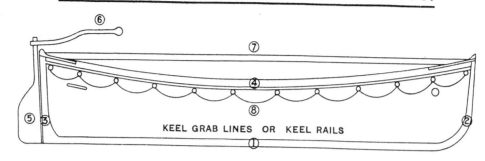

KEEL GRAB LINES OR KEEL RAILS

OAR
LOOM   SHAFT   BLADE

MAST
HEEL   MAIN HALLIARDS   RIGGING   JIB HALLIARDS   RIGGING   MAST-HEAD

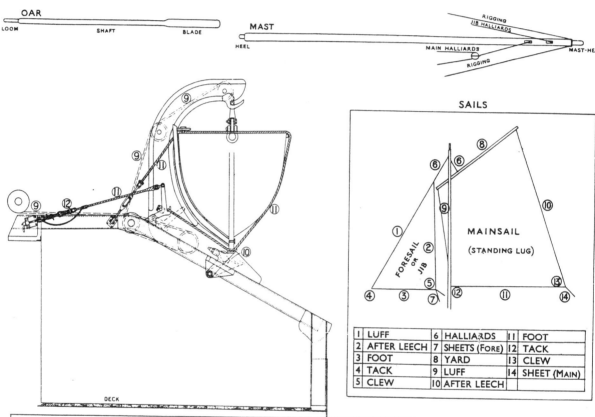

SAILS

FORESAIL OR JIB

MAINSAIL (STANDING LUG)

DECK

1	LUFF	6	HALLIARDS	11	FOOT
2	AFTER LEECH	7	SHEETS (FORE)	12	TACK
3	FOOT	8	YARD	13	CLEW
4	TACK	9	LUFF	14	SHEET (MAIN)
5	CLEW	10	AFTER LEECH		

1.	KEEL
2.	STEM
3.	STERNPOST
4.	GUNWALE
5.	RUDDER
6.	TILLER
7.	STRONGBACK
8.	GRAB LINES (ONLY FOR USE IN WATER)
9.	FALLS
10.	CHOCKS
11.	GRIPES
12.	SLIP-LINKS

TO LOWER BOAT.

NEVER LET GO ANYTHING UNTIL ORDERED TO DO SO BY OFFICER.

1. See Clutch out before commencing operation for lowering.
2. Let go centre support.
3. Let go Slip-links (12) and see that they are clear.
4. Lift lowering handle on winch and lower boat to embarkation deck. Griping tackles should then be passed out from each end of the boat.
5. When boat's complement is complete, ease off griping tackles, lift lowering handle on winch and keep it lifted until boat is in water.
6. Skates not to be touched without orders from Coxswain.

Athlone Castle
Bloemfontein Castle
Braemar Castle
Capetown Castle
Dunnottar Castle
Durban Castle
Edinburgh Castle
Kenya Castle
Pendennis Castle
Pretoria Castle
Rhodesia Castle
Stirling Castle
Warwick Castle
Winchester Castle

P.T.O.

EQUIPMENT FOR LIFEBOATS.

Single banked complement of oars, two spare oars.

Fine Weather Gear.

14-feet oars and 1 15-feet Steering Oar, blade of which is to be painted white and placed blade aft.
1 Set and half crutches.
1 Boat Hook.
Mast and Sail Equipment complete.
Rudder and Tiller.
2 Plugs for each Plughole, securely attached with Lanyards or Chains.
1 Efficient Compass, Binnacle Lamp to burn for 12 hours.
2 Axes with Lanyards attached.   1 at each end of boat.
Grablines outside of boat (not to be used at Boat Stations), also Keel Grab Lines or Keel Rails.
Locker for stowage of small items.

Bad Weather Gear.

Sea Anchor, not less than 2 feet 3 inches in diameter for 22–30 feet Boat and Hawser 3-inch Manilla, 20 Fathoms, with Tripping Line attached not less than 22 Fathoms in length of 2-inch Manilla Rope.
2 Painters not less than 20 Fathoms in length of 3-inch Manilla Rope (one a slip painter).
1 Gallon of Vegetable or Animal Oil, also if possible one spare gallon lamp oil.
1 Oil Bag for distributing Oil on the water in Rough Weather.
2 Galvanised Buckets to hold 2 gallons with Lanyard attached.
1 Bailer, not less than 8 inches in diameter, with Lanyard attached.
1 Manual Pump.
2 Light buoyant Heaving Lines.

Provisions.

1 lb. Barley Sugar for each person the boat is certified to carry, to be stowed in Air-Tight Tanks.
1 lb. Biscuits for each person the boat is certified to carry, to be stowed in Air-Tight Tanks.
1 lb. Condensed Milk for each person the boat is certified to carry, to be stowed in Air-Tight Tanks.
6 Pints Water for each person the boat is certified to carry, stowed in not less than Two Breakers (112 ozs. = 6 Pints).
At least 1 Dipper with Lanyards attached.
3 Drinking Cups, 1 graduated in ½ ozs., 1 and 2 ozs.).
1 Jack-Knife, fitted with tin opener.
1 First-Aid Outfit.

Lights and Signals.

1 Hurricane Lamp trimmed to burn for 12 hours, with Lanyard attached.
2 Boxes Self-Igniting Matches in Air-Tight Container.
2 Buoyant Smoke Signals.
6 Red Hand Flares.
1 Electric Torch (suitable for Morse Signalling) and 2 spare bulbs.
2 Parachute Distress Rockets.
1 Heliograph.

Crossing The Line – The author as a South Sea Maiden

Captain R.M. Wright, flanked by former Captains Jack Trayner and T.H. Whatley,
off Jamestown, St Helena

18

Extract from the Log of R.M.M.V. "Capetown Castle"

Captain R. M. Wright   Voyage 165

From Southampton to Cape Town, via Madeira, Ascension I., St. Helena

Date	Distance Run	Latitude Longitude	Temperature at noon Air	Sea	REMARKS
January 12		At Southampton	38°	42°	1300: departure Southampton Slight sea, low swell. Overcast and clear. Wind NE 4-5
13	389	45°40'N 07°42'W	48°	54°	Overcast, rough sea. Vessel pitching, rolling. Wind ESE 8 0056: rounded Ushant and entered Bay of Biscay. 2106: rounded C. Villano and left Bay of Biscay.
14	446	39°04'N 12°20'W	60°	60°	Slight sea. Cloudy and clear. Wind SW 3 2250: passed Company's vessel R.M.S. "Windsor Castle"
15	438	32°40'N 16°39'W	65°	64°	Slight sea. Partly cloudy, fine and clear. Wind WSW 2 1400: arrived Madeira 1830: departed Madeira
16	327	27°22'N 17°07'W	68°	68°	Calm sea. Few clouds and clear. Wind Lt. Var. 0840: passed between Islands of Tenerife and Gomera 1030: Divine Service conducted by Master
17	450	19°54'N 17°42'W	63°	65°	Slight sea. Partly cloudy, fine and clear. Wind NE 3 Captain's Cocktail Party. Dancing
18	437	12°37'N 17°35'W	74°	69°	Moderate sea. Partly cloudy and clear. Wind N 3 1720: Passed R.M.S. Southampton Castle.
19	436	05°27'N 16°23'W	82°	84°	Calm sea. Partly cloudy and clear. Wind N 1 Crossing the Line Ceremony.
20	404	01°13'S 15°09'W	81°	81°	Slight sea. Partly cloudy and clear. Wind S 2 0748: vessel crossed the Equator in Longitude 15°30'W. 'Capetown Castle' Derby Meeting
21	355	07°02'S 14°25'W	73°	78°	Moderate sea. Cloudy and clear. Wind SE 3 1600: arrived Ascension I. 20.22: departed Ascension I.
22	322	10°56'S 11°06'W	78°	77°	Moderate sea. Cloudy and clear. Wind SE 2 Children's Fancy Dress Parade and Tea Party.
23	429	15°50'S 05°47'W	75°	74°	Slight sea. Cloudy and clear. Wind ESE 2 1300: arrived St. Helena. 1030: Divine Service conducted by Master
24	200	17°54'S 03°08'W	74°	74°	0100: departed St. Helena Moderate swell. Cloudy, occ. rain. Wind ESE 4 Fancy Dress Parade and Gala Dance
25	427	22°28'S 02°39'E	74°	74°	Moderate sea, low swell. Cloudy and clear. Wind S 3 Children's Fair
26	409	26°41'S 08°31'E	72°	70°	Moderate sea, low swell. Cloudy and clear. Wind SE 4
27	401	30°48S' 14°30'E	69°	68°	Rough sea, mod. swell. Overcast & clear. Wind SSE 5-6 Prizegiving and Farewell Dance.
28	273	At Cape Town			0600: estimated time of arrival at Table Bay. 0070: E.T.A. Alongside Berth.

TOTAL DISTANCE : Southampton to Cape Town 6,143 miles

General Average Speed : 17.59 knots

Extract from the Log of R.M.M.V. "Capetown Castle"

Captain R. M. Wright   Voyage 165

From Cape Town to Southampton, via St. Helena, Ascension I., Madeira

Date	Distance Run	Latitude Longitude	Temperature at noon Air	Sea	REMARKS
January 29		At Cape Town	94°	70°	1220 : departure Cape Town Slight sea. Cloudless and clear. Wind SE 1
30	449	29°16S' 11°16'E	70°	67°	Moderate sea & swell. Overcast & clear. Vessel rolling Wind SSE 5. 1030 : Divine Service conducted by Master
31	453	24°34S' 05°00'E	75°	74°	Moderate/rough sea. Moderate swell. Cloudy and clear Vessel rolling. Wind SE 5
Feb. 1	431	19°54'S 00°52'E	76°	76°	1030 : passed Company's vessel M.V. "Tintagel Castle" Mod. sea & swell. Overcast and clear. Wind SE 4 Captain's Cocktail Party. Dancing
2	370	15°54'S 05°38'W	79°	74°	0940 : arrived St. Helena. Slight sea, mod. swell. Partly cloudy & clear. Wind SE 2
3	65	15°12'S 06°32'W	78°	76°	0830 : departed St. Helena Mod. sea & swell. Overcast, rain showers. Wind SE 3
4	436	10°12'S 11°55'W	79°	78°	Slight sea, mod. swell. Partly cloudy & clear. Wind SE 2
5	204	07°54'S 14°26'W	80°	79°	Slight sea. mod. swell. Partly cloudy & clear. Wind E 2 0130 : arrived Ascension I. 12.00 : departed Ascension I.
6	463	00°21'S 15°56'W	83°	80°	Slight sea. Partly cloudy and clear. Wind SSE 1 1030 : Divine Service conducted by the Master. 1308 : vessel crossed the Equator in Longitude 16°00'W.
7	455	07°10'N 16°57'W	83°	84°	Rippled sea, low swell. Overcast and clear. Wind N'ly 1 Crossing the Line Ceremony.
8	443	14°31'N 17°50'W	76°	72°	Slight sea, low. Cloudless and clear. Wind NE 2 1315 : Passed C. Vert distance 16 miles.
9	437	21°48'N 17°45'W	69°	65°	0843 : Passed C. Blanco, distance 42 miles. Slight sea, low swell. Cloudless and clear. Wind NE 3 1700 : Exhibition of Paintings in Lounge Balcony by Mr. A Schonk.
10	447	29°13'N 17°00'W	67°	68°	0814 : passed between Islands of Tenerife and Gomera Slight sea, mod. swell. Cloudless & clear. Wind NE 2 Midnight : arrived Madeira
11	322	34°08'N 15°33'W	64°	64°	0530 : departed Madeira. Slight sea, mod. N'ly swell Partly cloudy, clear. V/l rolling, pitching Wind WSW 2
12	440	40°40'N 11°22'W	54°	59°	Very rough sea, heavy swell. Partly cloudy and clear. V/l rolling, pitching Shipping light spray Wind WNW 8
13	407	46°40'N 07°03'W	51°	53°	Mod. sea, heavy swell. Cloudy & clear. Wind WSW 3 1030 : Divine Service conducted by Master 1920 : Rounded Ushant Is. entered English Channel
14	325	At Southampton			0530 Estimated time of arrival at Pilot Station 0730 : E.T.A. Alongside Berth.

TOTAL DISTANCE : Cape Town to Southampton 6,147 miles
General Average Speed : 18.16 knots

R.M.M.V. "CAPETOWN CASTLE"
CAPTAIN R. M. WRIGHT
VOYAGE 165
LEAVING SOUTHAMPTON 12TH JANUARY 1966

Friday 14th January 1966
off Madeira

Dear Family

What a crate this is! It is really a tale of woe all the time, but there have been some lighter moments. I cannot say that I am well and happy, as usual, because I am not, but I am certainly not beyond hope.

As I told you on the phone, the ship was freezing cold and I had about 8 layers of bedding on. There was no hot water also. Then we had Boat Drill in the freezing cold, and my feet must have got chilblains because they started to tingle, and then they swelled up and I started to limp. Must have looked quite a sight, shivering and limping along! My cold was very bad too. However we sailed on time, and the work continued. They are short of stewards, so we had to make our own beds and call ourselves in the morning. Yesterday they turned the heat on and it was absolutely stifling. So today they turned the ventilation on. But yesterday was not my day. I was sick again in the morning and couldn't get up at all. I tried several times during the day but had to rush back to the horizontal again. So I spent the whole day and night in bed. The other new Purserette (Maureen Fisher) was exactly the same.

We felt a bit better this morning, and managed a walk. They forgot to tell us about the change of clocks so we got up an hour too early! We had arranged to meet for breakfast and wondered where everyone else was. Then we found out! I felt better during the day but I still don't feel 100%. Still, tomorrow we get to Madeira and it should be warmer and calmer I hope. My cabin is okay but there are hundreds of creaks, and shudders. They say if they stop, then we panic! Although this is full of complaints I am fairly happy (mentally anyway) as the people are very nice and we all get on well. I should be better in a day or two so you can just put this down to "Bay Fever". I believe it is quite common. Nothing much else to report. Oh yes, the water keeps flooding in some of the passenger cabins, with fresh reports coming in of more taps leaking and overflowing every hour! Quite a bed of roses. Still, we can all laugh at it. From your long-suffering daughter/sister,
Ann xx

Wednesday 19th January 1966
At sea - tomorrow we cross Equator

Dear Family

What a crate still. But I love it. I am having a marvellous time. But to continue where I left off after the last moan at Madeira. At least, the moan before we reached Madeira. When I wrote that note to you it was 10 p.m. and I was feeling most peculiar. The day after I felt much better (and so did Maureen, the new Purserette) and the weather improved and we reached Madeira at 2.00 p.m. It was beautiful and we actually got an hour off and rushed into the town. I bought some Malmsey to bring home, but at the time of writing I cannot guarantee that it will see the Williams household. Never mind, there is always the return voyage. We left Madeira at 6.30 p.m. and it was dark and all the lights were on in the houses on the hills. It was quite beautiful.

We steadily improved in health and the sea behaved itself and became very calm. It has got steadily hotter and hotter and in fact it is now 8.30 p.m. on the Wednesday evening and I am absolutely glowing with the heat!

As you know, there is no air conditioning on the ship and it is extremely hot below decks. The Bureau is fairly cool, but today we have felt so hot that we have turned the big light off in here, and have simply got our individual light focused on our part of the desk and work by that. The large lights throw out quite an amount of heat, and it all counts!

There are so many things to mention I don't know where to begin and they are mostly odd thoughts. This morning we had the Crossing the Line ceremony. I thought I had seen most things, but this was quite something. We had custard pies, sausage meat, cocoa, the lot. I had a large trifle thrown straight into my face (and so did Maureen, as we were South Sea maidens) and I was absolutely smothered with meringue. It was hilarious. We had the "do" beside the deck swim pool which was quite deep, 5 to 6 feet, so I was a bit worried about being thrown in. It was a very near thing, but instead they threw huge buckets of cold water over me. I was one glorious mess. My hair had kipper, cocoa, sausage meat, meringue, water, greasepaint, and just plain dirt, all in it and so did the rest of me and my pink swimming costume and grass skirt. We really had a good time.

One funny side of it was that we are running short of water on the ship and today was the first day of rationing. Needless to say, the water was off when we had finished the "do" and we had visions of having to stay like that until 2.00 p.m. when the water was supposed to be on again. Fortunately somebody took pity on us all and turned the water on again, so I rushed back to my cabin and washed my hair (you should have seen the colour of the water!) and then had a shower. Then I went up to the hairdresser and had a quick hairdo (on the Company, of course) and then lunch. I had the afternoon off until 4 p.m. (sunbathing on the Monkey Island - great fun) so all in all I haven't done much work today.

The work in fact is going quite well. We have the two Bureaux and there are three of us in this Forward Bureau (it used to be the First Class one): Ian Fisher, the Assistant Purser and Cecilia, the Dutch purserette.

She and I take it in turns now it is hot to have the afternoon off, until 4.00 p.m. so we go and sunbathe. It's a lovely life. We have to do the News once every four days, so that is not too bad. I get up at 6.30 a.m. so that is quite good compared with the "TRANSVAAL CASTLE", and we do less copies too.

The Entertainments are going quite well, with the usual bingo, whist, beetle drives, dancing, quiz nights etc. The dancing in this hot weather is held on the dance deck - quite fun. Tonight the dance is to be on the Prom. deck, which in fact is the deck on the starboard side of the ship, so that should be lovely. They have even put coloured fairy lights up along the rails. Some wag suggested that they were the Equator lights (you know, like Blackpool lights and all that) and "don't forget to wait to feel the ship scrape over the Line".

What else, I have seen a flying fish, and the other day when I was on the Monkey Island at lunchtime I noticed something swimming along in the water. I shrieked out and everyone actually got to their feet to look. Someone said it was a whale, someone else said I was seeing things, and several others thought it was definitely something, but they didn't know what. It was left as being a whale, however, having discussed the matter it has been decided that it was only a porpoise or dolphin. The Bridge people (Bill, Peter or Ian) often broadcast when marine life is around but I never manage to be in the right place at the right time. Never mind.

Talking of broadcasting, though, the system is really quaint. There is a large black machine in a "band repeater room" on the Prom. Deck. It hums and grumbles and whirrs, and clicks, and you need the memory of an elephant to remember how to switch it all on to make a broadcast. Naturally, we make the minimum number of broadcasts. It's considered quite a feat if you manage to make a broadcast and it is heard where it should be.

Of course we get lots of complaints from the passengers who say they didn't know something or other, which had been broadcast previously, but yesterday we actually had someone come up and say she had heard something which we had not said <u>anything</u> about. It makes a change! I will close now and start a new letter in a day or two, to post at Ascension Island. Love, Ann.

Friday 21st January
Dear Family
We are now approaching Ascension Island, and are due there at 4.p.m. Two passengers landing there for Cable & Wireless are the parents of Graham Donald (2nd Purser on here). It is nearly lunchtime so I am taking 5 minutes off to type this. We are still quietly sweltering in the Bureau, but there is just a fraction more breeze today. We really have been very lucky, as we have most afternoons off and go and sunbathe up on the Monkey Island. Yesterday I got a very good layer, but unfortunately I must have been lying in an odd position because I have a semi-circle of white skin under my chin. It looks a bit odd, and I got teased, but I am really brown now.

Just odd items that crossed my mind: last night we had the "CAPETOWN CASTLE" Derby and it was quite amusing but not very well organised. The Derby is run by contestants having to cut along a length of ribbon with curved nail scissors! First one to cut to the end, wins. I wore my new pink hat. It felt marvellous and it won me lots of compliments. So well done, young Elaine, your ears should have been burning well and truly last night. We had a mad party afterwards in the Purser (Roy Funnel)'s cabin and naturally got to bed very late.

It's all very enjoyable. Life is very good. I know I had a good voyage on the TRANSVAAL CASTLE, but do you know, I think I am enjoying this voyage even more. It is certainly living up to its reputation of being a happy ship. By the way, today the water situation has changed yet again. It is now on from 6 a.m. to 10 p.m. It is all something to do with us having no permanent ballast, the viscosity of the oil, and the water tanks. All very confusing, and highly irritating to the passengers. I think I said we are filling in on the Mail run because of the delayed new ships. The Captain keeps making soothing broadcasts to the passengers, and this morning he even broadcast at breakfast and introduced himself as "That man again"!

Yesterday while we were on the Monkey Island we smelt burning. We all sniffed around and suddenly saw smoke rising from behind us. Apparently something in the Radio Room caught fire and went up in flames. It was quite a small fire and was soon under control and put out, but it gave us a few nasty moments. Apparently we can no longer provide passengers with a telephone service to Cape Town. Still, it will just give them something else to complain about.

I have just been for my bit of bronzing and it was pretty good. At 2.00 we sighted Ascension and it was 40 miles away. Hooray, we found it. The story is going round at the moment about the ship that was due at Ascension one day and was happily sailing along. They suddenly got a call on their equipment from Ascension saying, hey weren't you supposed to be calling here, you are 50 miles off course. I gather it is all a matter of luck whether you find the island at all!

We are getting closer now and will shortly anchor out in the bay. The island is only 8 miles across and is made of volcanic material. The water surrounding it is about 4 miles deep, so you can imagine how much island there must be under the water. There is a strong breeze blowing and it is a little cloudy. So this is Ascension. The US have an air base there and have an airmail service to the UK, via the States, so by the time you get this letter it will have gone to Ascension, America and then to England to you. Quite a well travelled aerogramme.

I will not be writing from St. Helena, as there's no mail of course, so next time it will be from Cape Town. Look after yourselves. I hope the weather is not too bad. I keep thinking about you all. Lots of love, Ann.

Friday 28th January 1966
Cape Town

Well, we made it! This morning we arrived at 6.00 and berthed at 7.00. Then I found a great bunch of letters for me. Lovely! Thank you all. Although we sail again tomorrow at noon, we had time off today: I was taken out to lunch and had a marvellous meal. We went to the Harbour Cafe, which sounds a bit off, but serves wonderful sea food. I had crayfish thermidor. Ask Elaine for details. Plus wine and coffee. Yummy, good job work wasn't too hard this afternoon. Had to be on duty from 2.30 again til 6.00.

Actually yesterday I managed to catch the "bug" that is going round here, among Officers and pax, which makes you feel sick and the Doc. says is colic. Couldn't face food yesterday anyway. Being so tired didn't help matters either. Had medicine and pills; today much better.

Hope you get 2 letters from Ascension - I now discover that the air service is not all it could be. Fingers crossed. I was lucky enough to get ashore at St. Helena and had a fascinating visit - lots of pictures and booklets to show you. We also carried passengers between the Islands - on deck. Mummy - I'm sorry you were ill - take care, and don't catch cold. It sounds as if "the shirker" is keeping the house warm for you. Sorry about the weather too. Here it is stinking hot, with bush fires sending smoke all round Table Mountain. It is wonderful to see it again. I get a great thrill seeing that place. What else. Yes, I have been swimming down in the pool. It was lovely. I must remember to weigh myself in the gym next time I go there.

Well, it is now 12.50 and I have had my night out. Wow, what a day it has been. Drinks here first, then changed into my black dress and went to dine at a large hotel. Shrimp cocktail, steak, Mateus Rose, coffee. Ride to Signal Hill to look at lights, then home and here I am. Now about the hairdryer: I cannot quite imagine what you mean about this £8.11.0. one, but if you think it's all right - fine, I'll have it. If you think it's worth paying that much - okay by me. As long as it will dry my hair quickly by a hood method (which seems best) that's fine. I'm glad my watch is back too, thank you.

Although I didn't feel good yesterday, today has been fine and I find it hard to believe we will be home in a couple of weeks   I'm looking forward to seeing you then. Have you fixed anything up about the Monday night, just supposing I get an hour off, or what? See you soon - you seem very far away at the moment. Lots of love, Ann xxx

R.M.S. TRANSVAAL CASTLE arriving at Cape Town (Photo Ian Shiffman)

S.S. REINA DEL MAR sailing from Cape Town (Photo Ian Shiffman)

M.V. CAPETOWN CASTLE sailing from Cape Town (Photo Ian Shiffman)

The author aboard CAPETOWN CASTLE off ASCENSION

Extract from the Log of R.M.M.V. "Capetown Castle"

Captain D. W. Sowden, R.D., R.N.R.   Voyage 166

From Cape Town to Southampton, via Walvis Bay and Madeira

Date	Distance Run	Latitude Longitude		Temperature at noon Air Sea		REMARKS
March 8		At Cape Town		68°	64°	1600: departure Cape Town Few clouds. Fine and clear. Wind SE 2
9	350	28°54'S	15°01'E	65°	63°	Rough sea, moderate swell. Vessel rolling. Partly cloudy and clear. Wind SSE 6
10	384	At Walvis Bay		64°	60°	1150: Arrived Walvis Bay. 1554: Departed Walvis Bay Moderate sea. Cloudy and clear. Wind SSE 3 Captain's Cocktail Party. Dancing
11	368	18°29'S	09°56'E	71°	70°	Vessel rolling easily to moderate SE'ly swell. Cloudy and clear. Wind SE 5
12	447	13°07'S	04°35E'	78°	78°	Vessel rolling slightly in moderate sea and swell. Cloudy -overcast and clear. Wind S'ly 2
13	418	08°00'S	00°12'W	83°	81°	Low/moderate swell. Cloudy and clear. Wind Var. 2 1030: Divine Service conducted by Master
14	422	02°53'S	05°02'W	84°	83°	Vessel rolling to low S'ly swell. Cloudy and clear. Wind S'ly 2
15	442	02°28'N	10°05'W	84°	84°	0110: vessel crossed Equator in D.R. Longitude 07°42'W Crossing the Line Ceremony. Low swell. Cloudy-overcast and clear. Wind Lt. Var.
16	397	07°22'N	14°29'W	84°	84°	Rippled sea. Negligible swell. Cloudy and clear Wind NW 2.
17	387	12°48'N	17°38'W	70°	66°	Moderate swell. Cloudy to overcast and hazy. Wind NNW 4
18	393	19°23'N	17°54'W	67°	68°	Rough sea, low swell. Partly cloudy and clear. Wind N'ly 5
19	395	25°57'N	17°21'W	68°	69°	Slight sea, low swell. Cloudy and clear. Wind NE 3
20	384	32°19'N	16°58'W	67°	66°	1030: Divine Service conducted by Master. Fine and clear. Wind N'ly 4. 1424: Arrived Funchal (Madeira) 1924: Dep. Funchal 2100: Passed Southbound R.M.S. Windsor Castle.
21	309	36°43'N	13°58'W	60°	61°	Moderate swell. Vessel pitching Partly cloudy and clear Wind NNE 4/5
22	407	42°47'N	10°09'W	55°	57°	Low swell. Mainly overcast & clear. Wind NNE 5/6 1300: vessel passed Cape Finisterre, entered Bay of Biscay
23	372	48°16'N	05°46'W	52°	52°	Low swell. Heavily overcast. Rain. Wind WNW 3/4 1345: rounded Island of Ushant, entered English Channel
24	220	At Southampton				0430: Estimated time of arrival at Pilot Station 0730: E.T.A. Alongside Berth.

TOTAL DISTANCE : Cape Town to Southampton 6,095 miles
General Average Speed : 17.00 knots

R.M.M.V. "CAPETOWN CASTLE"
CAPTAIN D. W. SOWDEN, R.D., R.N.R.
VOYAGE 166
LEAVING SOUTHAMPTON 15TH FEBRUARY 1966

A picture postcard from
Flushing, Holland
16th February 1966

We made it. Arrived 8.45 a.m., leaving 5.00 p.m. Very cold. 10 minute walk on Dutch soil, nothing to see but Docks. Saw windmill in distance! Bought wooden clog. Wish you were here, love, Ann x

At sea, 20th February.
Cher famille

What a night. We have been rolling and pitching ever since we left Flushing and the swell is tremendous. The sea hasn't been as rough as this for many years they say. I cannot type because the balance of the machine is put out by the rolling. The Bay was quite bearable, but since then it got very bad and last night, well it's hard to know where to begin.

I was a bit sick yesterday morning so took some tablets. I had one before going to bed last night but only managed to sleep fitfully. Most of the time I was rolling in my bunk, despite pillows under the edge of the mattress. I thought I had anchored most of my possessions securely, but still things jumped around. My booze is in the drawer under my wardrobe, standing upright. Everything else has been stowed into a drawer. Nevertheless 4 glasses fell off a shelf and smashed so there was glass everywhere. Then my basket of grapes tumbled and there were grapes added to the confusion. My rubbish bin kept sliding along the alleyway to the washbasin and back, and so on. The next door cabin is dreadful too, because Glenda had wine, beer cans and glasses in a top cupboard, which cannot shut or lock. All of these fell out at one time or another. Most of the time it is a steady tremendous roll, but occasionally an enormous wave comes and knocks everything for 6, and the ship shudders and throbs and we all hang on tight for our lives almost. I might mention that it is very tricky trying to put stockings on even whilst sitting down.

Anyway I woke this morning about 5.00 a.m. and couldn't get back to sleep: there was a continual noise of bottles tinkling in the drawer, apart from the sea, wind, and creaking of the ship. I staggered round to Maureen and four of us all sat on one bed feeling rather scared. Then the 4th Officer came to tell us that we would hove to for an hour or so, and head into the wind. So we did during breakfast. Lots of crockery has been broken and the furniture has been thrown around quite considerably. All in all we feel lucky to be in such a large ship - a smaller one wouldn't have survived. We can see the funny side of it sometimes, but it is rather scaring and certainly awe-inspiring.

We are going to be very late in Madeira, and there is even talk of us not being able to get the passengers off there. If we cannot then we may go to Las Palmas for oil and water, which we must have. It's all very much in the lap of the gods at the moment. Most of us are taking these tablets which make you dozey and dopey, but it is better to take them and stay upright I think.

Oh yes, Flushing. It was very very cold. I saw a windmill from the sundeck so I felt my visit was worthwhile. Apart from that there was nothing to see. Maureen and I had an hour off and walked along to the bus station, which had the nearest shop. That's where I bought my wooden clog, filled with sweets. Nice it is. Good chocolate they make there too!

We had Frog-Racing the other night in the Forward Lounge, and I was on the tote with 2 others. We sat behind a large table in the Forward Lounge, and had a fine old time trying to stop from sliding along the dais. Once we started to slide, the table, 2 chairs, us and Chris at the blackboard all shot away. Poor Chris even fell backwards off the dais (he didn't fall right over, of course). Quite amusing at that stage, but not now.

At the moment I am hanging on to my counter like grim death. It's quite fantastic. When we opened the Bureau door this morning the sight that greeted us was just like the wreck of the Hesperus. Everything was on the deck at one end, excluding typewriters, although they had slid along the counter quite a long distance. Sorry if this letter is a bit incoherent. It just can't be helped. We none of us feel right and it is just a matter of existing til the sea calms. I hope we manage to land the post in Madeira, never mind the passengers, so that you get this. I'm happy and quite all right, considering I'm hanging on with one hand, writing with the other, and balancing my feet around the base of the counter. One of life's little hazards and all that. Never mind, it can't last for ever, can it? ....Look after yourselves and take care. Love to everybody. Ann xxx

Saturday 26th February 1966

Dear Family
Well, this letter is what you might call hot from the press: in fact we passed the Equator some 50 minutes ago. I was prostrate on the Monkey Island at the time, eating cheese rolls and supping Dubonnet and lemonade. The temperature is huge, somewhere in the eighties and the humidity is dreadful. It hardly seems possible that only what five days ago we were being tossed around in that dreadful cold stormy weather.

To continue where I left off in my last letter from Madeira outskirts. In fact when I wrote I seem to remember that I was hanging on to my desk for dear life. In fact just after finishing those notes we heard that we had to go through a rather tricky manoeuvre to turn the ship round and go back into Madeira: the ship had to be turned almost right round because of the wind etc. and we were told to batten everything down and prepare for 5.00 p.m. turn around.

This threatened to be quite something, but in fact heaven seemed to be on our side, and the seas quietened down a little and the whole thing went off quite well, although we were still rolling around a lot. We reached the shelter of the island at 7.30 p.m. but it was still too rough (Force 6) to land anyone, so we just sailed slowly up and down one side of the island all night, rolling and pitching all the time. Things calmed down even more the next morning and the sun came out a bit too, so we finally got alongside at 8.00 a.m. Wow. We managed to sheer off two bollards on the quayside, which were fairly solid metal ones, but this excitement seemed quite ordinary compared with the sea on the previous days. I shall never forget it. The day before we got to Madeira we discovered that the sea was squalling at Force 12 several times during the day. How about that Daddy? We all feel like qualified sailors now.

It was a very grey day in Madeira. One thing I remember about it was an ancient man sliding up slyly to the counter and producing £100 in South African money which he wanted me to change into English. I did this, and he promptly produced a packet of Madeira embroidered handkerchiefs. Very nice too. He can call again.

Now for lots of oddments in the way of things to tell you. As I said, it is very hot (what an understatement) and I am on duty this afternoon in the Bureau so I decided to take time off and type you a note so that I keep you up to date before any more excitements come along. I am sure they will - it's that sort of voyage!

We left Madeira at noon on the Monday and things went back to being rough for many hours - everything in my cabin was stowed away for safety, just like the siege. That night we rolled quite a lot but the next morning (Tuesday) things improved and the sun came out and we gradually felt better, but terribly tired. Things rapidly got back to normal - work, sunshine, afternoons off, relaxing deck games, drinkies, pleasant dinners and a much happier relaxed atmosphere. It hardly seems possible that this was only 4/5 days ago.

The day before yesterday I saw two schools of porpoises for the first time. We were sunbathing on the Island just after lunch when the call went out and we saw about 40 of them jumping up and down in the wake of the ship. They were having great fun. Then in the same evening we saw some more, about 10 of them this time, obviously taking their evening exercise. Very graceful things. That night we went to the bioscope to see "Gideon of Scotland Yard" and were informed that the "TRANSVAAL CASTLE" was passing us so we rushed out on deck to look at the lights. She was at least 5 miles away but looked rather splendid all the time. I got a message the next day from our Radio Room saying that the Radio Officer over there sent his love to me. Wasn't that nice? The next day we passed the "PRETORIA CASTLE" but again she was just another ship on the horizon. Still, it was one of us.

Oh yes, we had a death on board. A man who was a diabetic died suddenly after lunch, so we had all that business again of making lists of his personal effects and making out all sorts of forms. I feel I am beginning to get used to it. Quite sad really: he was 62, had left England to go to S.A. to get married and had no relatives at all.

We are doing the Black and White Minstrels act again so we are having to practice again at lunchtime. Really, the day just isn't long enough to do everything. I usually get some cheese rolls organised now and take them up to the Island, with drinks and fruit and sweets. Lovely life. Oh yes, I had a pre-dinner party in my cabin the other day. Great fun - guess how many people got in? Fourteen altogether. I still don't know how, but somehow we managed it. What with no small quantity of wine at dinner, I got quite er, happy, that night. Don't remember much about it, except collapsing in giggles on my bunk, complaining that the light was too bright and insisting on wearing my sunglasses. Went to sleep after that. Oh well, it was fun. I have now got a map on my deckhead so I can study that from my bunk if I ever get a spare minute awake on my bunk.

I have used my hairdryer already and I have to report complete and utter success. It really is marvellous. Thank you very much for taking so much time and trouble over choosing it, it is really good. I had a plug put on it and last night when I washed my hair I even went into the next door cabin with the hood on and dryer in my hand to hear a particular Beatles record. It is certainly versatile. Maureen borrowed it the other day too and was delighted with it. It's so compact. I used it again this morning after the Crossing the Line ceremony, when needless to say I got my hair and self rather grubby. I have had my hair cut even shorter at the back Mummy, but the sides are still the same length. He refuses to cut them any shorter, and I think he is quite right. He cuts my hair beautifully when he does it. It seems so easy to manage. Another thing, my watch is going well, thank you. It is nice to have it with me again. And that ice bucket is marvellous. I get ice every day now and I really bless the day when that arrived. Just what the doctor ordered and all that.

And that table runner. I know you said you measured the dressing table top, but wasn't that a good fit. It looks jolly good and just finishes the top off. Thank you again. And my hairband has proved very successful. Earned lots of compliments too.

At the moment I am sitting at my typewriter, with my dress up round my thighs, my belt undone, my gold sandals hanging off, feet tucked up under my desk on a ledge, with one bright light focused on this letter. We have the big lights off in here when the temperature goes up, because they throw out quite a bit of heat in themselves, and everything helps. What with the high stools that we sit on, and the individual lights, I feel that I only need a quill pen at the moment to complete the picture. Touch of the Dickens and all that.

Well, it's now an hour later, and I have had a cup of coffee, some Polos, a rest and a chat to the Bell Boy, the Lift Boy and the Boots. All passes the time of day. I think I shall continue the tale of the voyage at a later date. Oh yes, one other thing, yesterday we were having a cool pre-lunch drink on the Verandah Cafe when it started to rain. And did it rain! It came down in torrents and the deck was awash in seconds. Quite amusing to see everyone flying around. They had planned a deck buffet lunch and of course this was cancelled, just 2 minutes before it was due to start. Such a shame.

Thursday 3rd March
Well, the later date has arrived and we have now left Walvis Bay behind and are heading for the Cape. Several more things have happened since the last movement report so here goes.

The day after the rain washed the deck buffet away the weather was perfect and a crowd of us made the effort and had lunch on deck. It was lovely. They have cold meats and salad and cheese and biscuits etc. The bits and pieces that go into the salads would make your mouths water, so I won't go into details. We all ate too much anyway. The weather was gorgeous again and afterwards we went sunbathing as usual and got another layer of the old bronzey. The next day again we had lunch on deck and this time it was much windier and this provided quite a lot of amusing incidents, such as plates of cardboard, complete with salad, flying past the deck railings, as someone happened to let go of their plate in a gust of wind. There was a big crowd of us all sitting around three tables pushed together, and it got quite tricky when the wind caught the coleslaw salad of the person at the head of the table and blew it down to the other end of the table. Then there were the knives and forks. We have special transparent plastic ones. Very effective, with good cutting edges, but rather brittle. It was nothing to hear the constant munching of starving Officers, followed by snap, snap, curse, as another fork snapped off at the neck. Still, it was all great fun and again we ate too much. Must tell you one comment that was made to me, after a particularly large lunch the other day: "I can see why they sent you to sea!"

What else, oh yes, we did the Black & White Minstrels again the other night and it was so successful this time. The audience were absolutely wonderful and were thrilled with the Show. We didn't feel quite so nervous this time and it all went quite smoothly. We made several boobs and had hysterics about them, and everyone had an hilarious time. Again, we were the cabaret act appearing at 11 p.m. After our act, we had the "CAPETOWN CASTLE" Hop and then a Conga which led down to the Dining Room and Egg and Bacon Supper at 12.00 midnight. The Purser, who was in the Minstrels as my partner, had us all sitting at his table and ordered 2 bottles of French champagne which we all did justice to. It was quite a night. Lovely!

Yesterday was just another day, with a sleep in the afternoon for an hour or so. Had a Beetle Drive in the evening. Then this morning we were woken at 6.25 a.m. because of arrival at Walvis Bay. It was my day for the News anyway so I had to do that. All in all I didn't surface onto the deck until after breakfast and then I could see the port. Did I say port?

It was a sight I could never have imagined. Parallel to the docks were railway lines (camel trains, you know) and then a few houses (shanty-town type) and then nothing but desert for as far as the eye could see. Sand dunes to each side of the town which apparently blow around and are almost here today and there tomorrow. That was the Kalahari Desert.

Everywhere there was the smell of fish and the fishing boats themselves were further along the quayside. Walvis Bay can boast of the following things: 1 church, 3 hotels, a population of 17,000, a thriving diamond industry and the fishing activities, and an airport.

The diamonds are just lying around, I was told, and they wouldn't let anyone ashore because of the security risks etc. They had great difficulty in holding me back. Just outside the town, and in the desert, is the airport. Apparently the airport runways are marked out with black oil drums and the planes land on the sand itself. Must be fun to be a pilot round here.

It must also be funny to be a sailor round here, because apparently the area is subject to volcanic goings-on and islands keep appearing just off the coast and then disappearing again. These islands are usually several hundred feet long and just as wide, and some have been known to appear one day and stay for a few months, and others to come at sunset one night, stay overnight and disappear suddenly during the following morning. They are all solid matter, and when soundings have been taken afterwards on the spot where these islands have been, the depth of water has always been exactly the same as before Strange, isn't it. The coast round here is known as the Skeleton Coast, just as another matter of interest. I don't know about you, but I like to know information about these places we visit, and I always like to see the charts up on the bridge which give lots of interesting snippets of information, apart from the odd things the Deck Officers tell us. They always know such peculiar things, like the fact that the air in Walvis Bay is so full of a certain substance (sorry, can't remember what, but something like a sulphate) because of the fishing activities and the sand, that the paintwork of some ships which was white on arrival there has changed to a brown colour at the end of two weeks sailing activities in the area.

And talking of sailing activities, apparently we caused quite a stir in the place - they haven't had such a large ship alongside the quay before. The people came out to stare at us all the few hours we were there, including two dogs. The best part of the morning of course was to get your letters. Although we arrived a day late in Madeira no-one got any post, and we were all very disappointed. So we were all very happy at getting post this morning. I had a letter from you both and one each from Marian Paget and Olive Preston. Did Olive tell you she is sailing on 8th June for Canada!

Mummy, how I laughed about you putting the wrong address on your first letter. I am looking forward to getting it in Cape Town anyway. That really made my morning! I'm glad the films are back and all right. I'm looking forward to seeing them. I did enjoy reading both your letters - it is nice to imagine you writing them and thinking about what to say. Everything is interesting, whatever it is. That's why I feel I can write such a lot to you - I feel I have seen so much of interest that I must try and share it with you. Did you get the card from Flushing I wonder? And my two letters from Madeira? Hope so. I reckon my letters from Madeira can go into the Williams family heirloom bag - exciting adventures and all that jazz.

Just to interrupt, I have just been given a box of chocolates, by one of the Boots boys, who came up to the counter and chatted for a while, then went away and returned with the chocs. I don't know what the occasion is.

Thank you for getting the premium back from Walker's for me. By now I suppose you will have started the Malmsey - cheers! I like Madeira wine. I like the sound of the projector stand - well done Mr. Williams. I suppose there must be lots of things that have happened since I last saw home.

I am looking forward to seeing it again, although I am satisfied just to see you two really. Well, I think that really is everything for the moment, so I will stop typing. And tea has just arrived too, so .... What a life - the Bell Boy has just put a hot cup of tea beside me and a pot of sugar. Sandwiches and cakes will follow.ι Wowee! I just daren't weigh myself.

By the way, I sent you a postcard from Walvis Bay, just to let you see the South West African stamps. The card is a Williams special as it is in fact the top part of one of our Dinner menus. It is a view of the famous jacaranda trees in the Parliamentary buildings grounds at Pretoria. Brilliant idea, I thought.

I will try and drop you a line from Cape Town after we arrive, on Saturday at 6.00 a.m. The current plan is to leave as scheduled so that we arrive in Southampton as arranged on 24th March. That means one day less in Cape Town at the moment which is a shame, but things may change. I hope. Be seeing you all. Take care of yourselves. Love, Ann xxxxxxx

Postcard from Walvis Bay, 3.3.66
Dear All
We got to South West Africa. It is chilly and oh, the smell of fish. All we can see is sand, a few railway tracks, sand dunes, one church, the Kalahari Desert, and we are told that there are diamonds all around, waiting to be found. No shore leave here. Everything fine.
Love, Ann xxxxxx
p.s. Thanks for letters this morning, x

Cape Town, 7.3.66
Dear Mummy, Daddy & Elaine (and Derek)

Thank you very much for the letters. It was lovely to hear from you again so soon. Things have been so hectic since we arrived here on Saturday that I have not had a chance to write to you even during working hours, because there are so many people embarking early. What I really want to tell you is that it appears I will be back next trip. That is the news of the day. This morning several others had letters saying they would be relieved next trip, and if we had not heard anything then we could assume we would be back. So there we are. We dock on the 24th, sail again on 29th. What time I will get at home is anyone's guess at the moment, but it should with luck be a day or two. We won't know anything definite for some time yet. We sail again tomorrow (Tuesday) at 4.00 .m. on schedule, so we have had a day less here.

But I have been very lucky and have had a wonderful time as usual - out into the country and vineyards (and mountains) on Saturday afternoon, dinner out in town in evening. Sunday I worked morning and afternoon, then out for a splendid meal p.m. at the Dutch Lanzerac Hotel near Stellenbosch, in the middle of the wine area. I will tell you more about these visits in greater detail in a later letter, as I'm now very tired, so I think I will move up to the other end of the bed and retire. Goodnight. Take care of yourselves. I miss you. Love, Ann xxxx

Walvis Bay, 10th March 1966
Dear Family

We are back in the smell again and I have just got a letter from you. It was lovely, thank you. I could imagine you all adding your little bit. I'm glad the Malmsey passed the test - I thought it would. Look after it. And I hope you enjoyed the "do" at Windsor. As far as I know we will dock on the 24th at 7.00 a.m. as usual. So you have had your hair rinsed Mummy. Well! Well! I'm looking forward to seeing it.

So you've got Spring weather have you. The sun is shining here but the wind is quite cool. I suppose it is up in the 60's but that seems quite cool. The sky is so blue, though, and the sand looks very golden. Remember I told you about the smell last time, well I was wrong about what caused it. I must pass on correct information - it is because of the volcanic substances and particles in the atmosphere here.

I went ashore just now, for all of 5 minutes. Walked down the gangway, along the length of the ship, and back again and up the other gangway. They let us ashore today, I don't know why. Oh yes, as soon as we got alongside, guess what, a local Brass Band turned out and played military-type music for 10 minutes, as a welcome. Very black men, 1 white conductor, and gleaming brass instruments. Quite touching. Again, the crowds gathered within seconds. These gentlemen then packed up, and came on board as passengers. Nice surprise! What else, I've been invited to stay with a dear old lady in Jersey for a few days when I can get time off. She lives with her husband, and is very sweet and quite a laugh. By the way, I would be glad if you could bring my films and viewer down on 24th please. Must go, sailing soon. Love to all, take care of yourselves. Love, Ann

P.S. What's this about getting married Elaine?

Ship Letter Telegram, Post Office Telegraphs - via Portishead Radio
GKGM/Capetown Castle
19th March 1966 to Williams family

Love and best wishes to you all from Ann looking forward to Thursday.

R.M.M.V. CAPETOWN CASTLE

King Neptune holding court

R.M.M.V. "CAPETOWN CASTLE"

CROSSING THE LINE CEREMONY

Opening of the Court

CLERK: Silence in Court! Silence in Court!
            Silence for his Most Oceanic Majesty King Neptune!

NEPTUNE: Silence, I say. Our time is short,
            Scarce time to hold our Solemn Court
            With due Solemnity.
            Where is the Ocean Clerk of Court?

CLERK: Here, Your Majesty.

NEPTUNE: Marshall the Court

CLERK: His Majesty the Royal Chief Ocean Justice (bows to King)
            Her Oceanic Majesty, Queen Aphrodite (bows to Queen with
            hand on breast)
            His Clerkship the Ocean Clerk of Court   (with appropriate
            His Bitterness the Royal Physician   gestures)
            His Sharpness the Royal Barber
            Their Executionerships the Royal Bears
            And the Flat-footed Constabulary.

NEPTUNE: The Court's in Session and Justice will be done.
            Oh, Clerk, prepare your briefs ore time shall run
            (to the Court) Forward Physician with Potions foul
            And Barber stand to lather jowl;
            Now, Bears, to bath and duck them well
            That purged they be of Landborne smell

            (Bears with a roar, dive into bath)

CLERK: Bring forth the first initiate.

HERALD: (To Policemen) Hoy! Bring up the first victim!
            (Policemen lead the first victim in front of the King).

CLERK: Put forward Mr.....................
            Mr..............., you are charged that you are lazy and
            indifferent. My Lud, no case has given us such regret
            and we bring it to your Most Gracious Majesty with dismay.
            This deplorable subject will have nothing to do with
            anything that requires effort or trouble. In short, he
            is described as being N.B.G. which is a condition for
            which there is no known cure.
            How say you, guilty or not guilty?
            GUILTY
            My Lord, would you be so gracious as to pass sentence in
            this poor misdirected landlubber.
            It is decided you shall have your bilges pumped dry, after
            which you shall have your heart removed by the doctor,
            after which our tonsorial artist will give you a shampoo
            and set, and you will be handed to our underpaid bears.

CLERK: Put up Miss/Mrs.............
            Miss/Mrs........... You are suspected of being drunk and
            disorderly and together with sundryfriends you did fling
            your arms around the necks of numerous, very indifferent,
            innocent and even totally inexperienced members of the
            Ship's Company thereby causing them great embarrassment with
            the result that they have confined themselves to their
            quarters as being their only defence. How plead you,
            guilty or not guilty?
            GUILTY
            You are sentenced to have your hair dyed by the Barber, to
            kiss the Surgeon, be given a dose of Sea Castor oil. All
            in order to suppress your enthusiasm, and finally to be
            thrown to the hungry bears.

CLERK: Put forward Mr.............
          Mr............. I must warn you that everything you say will
          be taken down, twisted and distorted out of all recognition
          and very definitely used as evidence against you. You are
          charged that you have insulted his Oceanic Majesty's hospi-
          tality by being seasick in the calmest of weather and that
          you attribute this to the lack of rations on board, whilst
          being the first in and last out of the Saloon. Guilty or
          not Guilty?
          GUILTY
          You are sentenced to be delivered to his Majesty's most heavy-
          handed Surgeon who will examine the contents of your stomach
          and then dose you with his most excellent soothing mixture.
          You will be shaved by the Barber and your moribund remains
          discarded to the hungry bears.

CLERK: Put forward Mrs/Miss..........
          Mrs/Miss............ You are hereby charged and found guilty
          of continuously conferring your attentions upon only one male
          member of the Ship's Company thereby denying your Majesty's
          most humble and deserving subjects the doubtful pleasure of
          your company. In consequence causing much gloom and despon-
          dency to spread to the detriment of subjects in your Majesty's
          domains.
          You are sentenced to a judicious application of Salted Kipper,
          your Crowning Glory attended to by the Royal Barber, after
          which you will be flung to the mercies of the Frustrated Bears.

CLERK: Put forward Mr.............
          Mr............. You are hereby charged that you have led many
          of his Majesty's loyal and impressionable Handmaidens up the
          garden path, and then escaped to this ship thereby avoiding
          until the convening of this Court the consequences of your
          philandering. How plead you, Guilty or not guilty?
          GUILTY
          You are ensentenced to kiss the Queen to atone for some of
          your greater evils, after which in order to keep the Surgeon
          you will have your largest tooth removed, and then thrown to
          the Bears.

CLERK   Put forward Miss................ for the case of Miss........
          versus all hands and the Cook. Miss.......... you are hereby
          accused of unpardonable and glaring exhibitionism by
          displaying yourself and your obvious attractions in a most
          undignified manner. Thereby causing much disturbance to all
          the males on board and a large majority of their wives. You
          have no option but to plead Guilty, and are hereby sentenced
          for the surgical removal of a leg or two. (Have it placed in
          my cabin). What is left is to be fixed up by the Barber and
          the remains, if any, are to be delivered to the Watery Bears.

FINALE

NEPTUNE: My Court must close. Form up the Court.

HERALD: Form up the Court.

          (Procession forms as on arrival except for the prisoners who
          have been released. Led by the Herald the procession moves
          off, the King and Queen graciously bowing and waving farewell to
          the assembled multitude.)

Southampton, Tangier, Cannes, Palma, Gibraltar, Lisbon and Southampton

Date	Miles	Latitude Longitude	Knots	Temperature Air	Sea	Weather and Remarks
April 6		Southampton		58		Mainly Overcast, fine and clear. Wind SWxS, force 2. 12.36 Gangway ashore. Vessel sails for Tangier
,, 7	399	45.54N 07.30W	17.35	58	54	Rough sea. Mainly O'cast, fine and clear. Wind W, force 6 01.08 I. de Ushant abeam to port. Vessel entered Bay of Biscay 23.50 Cabo Villano abeam to port. Vessel left Bay of Biscay. Clocks retarded 1 hour during the night.
,, 8	417	39.19N 09.50W	16.68	59	59	Rough sea. Overcast with continuous rain Wind SE, force 8 15.00 Mouth of River Tejo (Port of Lisbon) abeam to port.
,, 9	320	Tangier	16.50	67		Partly cloudy, fine and clear. Wind SW, force 2. 08.07 Gangway on board in Tangier.
,, 10	123	36.21N 03.25W	16.62	64	62	Slight sea. Partly cloudy, fine and clear. Wind WSW, force 3/4 10.30 Divine Service held in Cinema, Captain officiating. 03.58 Gangway ashore, vessel sails for Cannes. Clocks advanced 1 hr
,, 11	381	40.15N 02.41E	16.56	65	58	Slight sea. Cloudy, fine and clear. Wind WSW, force 2. 06.00 Island of Ibiza abeam to starboard, distance of 11 miles. 11.00 Island of Majorca abeam to starboard, distance of 20 miles.
,, 12	227	Cannes	14.81	64	57	Rippled sea. Cloudy, fine and clear Wind SE, force 2. 07.19 Dropped anchor at Cannes.
,, 13	110	42.10N 05.24E	16.33	56	57	Slight sea. Overcast with rain showers. Wind SE, force 2. 04.12 Anchor aweigh. Vessel sails for Palma.
,, 14	349	Palma	13.22	70		Cloudy, fine and clear. Wind SSW, force 2. 07.48 Gangway on board at Muelle de Poniente Berth, Palma.
,, 15	123	38.06N 00.47E	16.85	63	60	Slight sea. O'cast, fine, slight haze, good visibility. Wind SSW 3 04.05 Gangway ashore. Vessel sails for Gibraltar.
,, 16	328	Gibraltar	16.65	67		Slight/Moderate sea. Cloudy, fine and clear. Wind W, force 4 08.30 Vessel anchored at Gibraltar.
,, 17	251	37.55N 09.13W	13.87	61	62	Slight sea. Few clouds, fine and clear. Wind W, force 3. 10.30 Divine Service held in Cinema, Captain officiating. 17.45 Gangway aboard at Lisbon
,, 18	44	Lisbon	15.71	67		Cloudy, fine and clear. Wind SW, force 2.
,, 19	141	40.55N 09.37W	17.62	59	58	Slight sea. Few clouds, fine and clear. Wind WxS, force 3. 02.00 Gangway ashore. Vessel sails for Southampton. 20.00 Cabo Villano abeam to starboard. Vessel entered Bay of Biscay.
,, 20	408	47.08N 06.28W	17.00	52	51	Rough sea. Cloudy, fine and clear. Wind NWxW 7. 17.15 I. de Ushant abeam to starboard. Vessel left Bay of Biscay and entered English Channel.
,, 21	288	Southampton				04.30 E.T.A. Pilot. 07.00 Expected alongside.

Total Distance 3,909 nautical miles (4,501 land miles)   Average speed 16.08 knots   Passengers on board 959

S.S. "REINA DEL MAR"
CAPTAIN J. B. JAMES
VOYAGE 40
LEAVING SOUTHAMPTON 6TH APRIL 1966

Aerogramme marked PAQUEBOT
Good Friday, 8th April 1966 -

Dear Family

I am just having an after-lunch rest, so thought I would write, as we have to post these by 6 p.m. today. You were right about this ship sailing late, Daddy, we left Southampton at 1.00 in the end, as all the baggage had not been loaded by 12 noon.

The sea was fairly rough and in fact yesterday I was sick. I lasted until about 11.00 a.m. then retired with a tablet. Got up at 5.00 but still felt bad, so back to bed. Felt all right again this morning fortunately, but not quite up to much food. The sea is still quite rough, Force 8, although we will be passing Lisbon about 5 p.m. this afternoon. We dock at Tangier at 8 a.m. tomorrow. This morning we sold Moroccan stamps: we started at 9.00 a.m. and the queue disappeared at 11.00 a.m. Everyone wanted stamps. The passengers are mostly middle-aged, with some very young teenagers, and few in between these. Most of the older people seem to come from "up North". This evening is the Captain's Cocktail Party, which was postponed from last night due to the weather. Most of the passengers were also sick.

The rest of the Officers are very nice and the rest of the Bureau staff good fun to work with. The Purser on here got 'flu over the weekend, was confined to bed, and at the last minute Boffin (Mr Baker) sent another Purser down, so we have 2 Pursers on board (Keith Underwood and Tony Dyer) By the way, yesterday I got a "bon voyage" telegram from Brian Madeley (that friendly passenger from the CAPETOWN CASTLE). Wasn't that nice of him. It was re-directed from somewhere (in code) so didn't arrive til mid-afternoon. Nice thought.

I have just had my hair trimmed, so I will wash it after work and before the Party. Had to get 2 pin plug changed to 3 pin. Nothing much else to report, but I hope to write after Tangier, and from Cannes. Love, Ann.

Easter Monday, 8.15 p.m.
Dear Family

Again I am under the hairdryer in my little cabin, this time prior to a Masked Ball. I have had my dinner, plus pre-dinner drinks with some Engineers, so found time to wash my hair. There really is little opportunity for writing letters - we always seem to have something to do, and we always seem to be in port, or getting ready for the next one. It's quite a ship!

Tangier was fabulous. We all worked out what time off (day or evening) we preferred and planned accordingly. I chose daytime, because I wanted to see what I could. Left about 10.30 a.m. after 8.30 arrival. Two of the boys and me. Black Arabs on quayside tried to sell us all sorts of leather goods and jewellery but just caught taxi to Casbah. Wow! Very narrow, filthy, smelly, fascinating streets. Went first to Sultan's Palace (2000 years old) and saw ceramics, mosaics, marbles, weaving, pottery and black Arabs. Then into Casbah shops to barter. Great fun.

Had arranged to meet several others (including Robbie Rutt, Audrey Wakefield, Sheila McGregor etc.) in a restaurant on one side of town so made our way there for 1.00 p.m. We had a meal of onion soup (a meal in itself) ½ chicken and cheese sauce (literally half a chicken!) chips and salad, followed by creme caramel and then coffee. Plus wine of course. We all felt _very_ pleased with life after that. Walked back through Casbah, all way back to the ship. Needed the exercise really. I had to be on duty again at 5.00 p.m. so had very good day out considering. Closed Bureau at 10.00 p.m. then washing, then bed at midnight.

At sea yesterday, Easter Sunday, went to Communion a.m., and all of us girls were given a choc. Easter egg in an egg cup by one of the Purser/Catering men, kind Chris Dadson. Nice thought, especially as I had left my egg at home. I had a small party last night. Oh yes, saw the Sierra Nevada (snow-capped of course) from the ship at lunchtime yesterday; and island of Mallorca at lunch today. Sun hot so had barbecue lunch on deck, but far too many passengers around: 971, one death so far. Cannes 8.00 a.m. tomorrow. Looking forward to Palma also. Very happy now sea calm and sun shining, although expect to be in "blues" all the trip. Oh well. Wish you were here. Love, Ann xxxxxx

Wednesday 13th April 1966
Dear Family

This is the next episode of the cruise. Yesterday we spent anchored off Cannes, and was it a long day! The night before was the Masked Ball, and I wore a black mask, white lace doilies round the edge, and a red rose. Helped judge the passenger masks. We arrived at 8.00 a.m. yesterday and I worked till 9.00 a.m. Then Maggie Parry and I went off in the tender to the shore, free til 4.00 p.m. We met another Officer on the tender (Colin from the "CAPETOWN CASTLE") so we all went together. Cannes town is large, ancient part and very new hotel part. Mountains about 10 miles away all around. Lovely looking place. Visited old castle on hill overlooking town, walked near yacht-basin. There must have been many thousands of pounds worth of boats there. Fantastic luxury really. Then through market-type streets with lots of flowers, food and clothes shops. Bought French bread, cheese, tomatoes, rough wine (2/6d. a bottle!) and fruit flan, and took these to the Promenade beside beautiful sandy beaches. Gorged ourselves and reclined for several hours, just doing nothing. Lovely. The sun was out and very hot. Got my face done to a turn.

Oh yes, on getting to the Customs hall from the launch we were given a free gift. Beautifully packaged in a tiny plastic pot and fancy gold and white box, guess what it was? Anti-wrinkle cream! Also given a free carnation buttonhole. Back to work at 4.00 p.m. selling stamps and nothing much else, til 10 p.m.

Today was at sea and we were very busy selling stamps and changing French and Spanish currency. There is always a queue and you work at top speed all the time. We don't get afternoons off, at sea. I am also on the News tomorrow, so one way and another it should be a long day. Oh well, it's great fun. Hope to get ashore tomorrow in Palma.

Thanks for the letter yesterday too. It was lovely to hear from you. Also had one from Dorothy Edge. Suppose I ought to go to sleep now - very precious commodity! Love, Ann xx

Gibraltar, 16th April 1966
Dear Family

Here we are, anchored off near the Rock. There's nothing much to see, and it's rather windy and chilly. We arrived at 9.00 a.m. and leave at 5.00 p.m. Quite reasonable.

Unfortunately there is no shore leave here, ever. Too near England and too much cheap booze. It's now 10.45 a.m. and most of the passengers have gone ashore, so I am writing to you in between mouthfuls of coffee and toast.

Yesterday we were at sea, after leaving at 4.00 a.m. from Palma. We had a very good time there. Again, I had time off during the day and so four of us left the ship at noon to go out for lunch. I was so tired that I slept from 10 til noon, before going out. We went to a super bodega to eat. It was a large stone cellar, with huge wooden tables and benches, and bottles of wine (and dust) everywhere, and garlics and other odd things. All very clean and interesting. Had tomato soup, and enormous mixed grill, then creme caramel. Had continuous Bacardi and coke to drink, lovely yum. Staggered out to a taxi and went to C'an Pastilla, which is where Marion and I stayed. Patsy used to be Head Rep. for one of the big travel agencies using the island so we went to one of "her" hotels, the Hotel Embat. Great joy all round when she walked in, and we had drinks on the house. More Bacardi and coke.

I went then for a short "pilgrimage" round the corner to the Hotel Trianon. It looked just the same, and the beaches still look good. Had to be back by 4.00, on duty from then until 11.30 p.m. so I was very tired then, and fell straight into bed. Had 3 interruptions with tipsy staff coming in to tell me they had had wonderful evenings, then invite to a party which I couldn't refuse. So I didn't get much sleep, oh well. Enjoyed the party. Tonight we have a birthday party with a rumour of champagne cocktails. Should be quite a "do" - 56 Officers invited! Hey ho! This cruising is certainly very strenuous. See you all soon.
Love, Ann

" S.A. ORANJE "

(28,705 TONS)

Captain J. P. SMYTHE, D.S.C., R.D., R.N.R.

From SOUTHAMPTON to CAPE TOWN via LAS PALMAS.

VOYAGE 118　　　　　　　　　　　　　　**April 29th to May 11th, 1966**

Date	Distance Run	Speed	Lat. | Long.	Average Temperature Air	Average Temperature Sea	REMARKS
29.4.66	—	—	At Southampton	55°	51°	13.00 *Vessel Departed Southampton. 29 First Class and 322 Tourist Class Passengers aboard. Light variable winds. Rippled sea, low low swell. 23.45 Rounded Ushant Island, entered Bay of Biscay.*
30.4.66	480	21·92	44° 23' N 08° 52' W	60°	58°	*E'ly wind, force 5. Mod. sea and swell. Cloudless and clear.* 15.20 *Rounded Cape Villano, left Bay of Biscay.* 19.25 *Psd. Northbound Mail Vessel " Southampton Castle."*
1.5.66	533	22·21	35° 58' N 12° 34' W	66°	61°	*N.N.E. wind, force 4. Moderate sea and swell. Cloudless and clear.*
2.5.66	494	20·67	At Las Palmas	73°	68°	*N'ly wind, force 3. Slight sea, mod. swell. Cloudy and clear.* 12.54 *Arrived Las Palmas.* 17.00 *Departed Las Palmas. 20 First Class and 301 Tourist Class Passengers on board.*
3.5.66	408	22·05	21° 44' N 17° 36' W	70°	67°	07.00 *Crossed Tropic of Cancer. N.E. wind, force 4. Mod. sea and swell. Cloudy with slight haze.*
4.5.66	543	22·63	12° 43' N 17° 36' W	75°	74°	06.30 *Passed Northbound Mail Vessel " Edinburgh Castle."* 06.38 *Rounded Cape Verde, (most W'ly point of Africa.) N'ly wind, force 4. Moderate sea and swell. Cloudy with slight haze.* 15.00 *Set course direct for Table Bay.*
5.5.66	550	22·07	05° 08' N 12° 41' W	86°	85°	*Light variable wind. Rippled sea, slight swell. Cloudy and clear. Entered the Doldrums.*
6.5.66	546	22·92	02° 09' S 07° 15' W	82°	84°	04.57 *Vessel Crossed Equator in D.R. Longitude 08° 47' W. S.E. wind, force 4. Moderate sea and swell. Cloudy, occas. rain squalls.*
7.5.66	530	22·08	09° 14' S 01° 59' W	79°	80°	09.50 *Passed Cargo Vessel " Clan Maclaren." S.E. wind, force 4. Mod. sea, and swell. Cloudy and clear.* 17.53 *Passed Northbound Mail Vessel " S.A. Vaal."*
8.5.66	536	22·33	16° 18' S 03° 35' E	73°	76°	*S.E. wind, force 4. Moderate sea and swell. Cloudy, fine and clear.*
9.5.66	505	21·96	23° 04' S 08° 52' E	69°	72°	*S.E. wind, force 4. Moderate sea and swell. Cloudy, fine and clear.* 13.20 *Crossed the Tropic of Capricorn.*
10.5.66	490	21·30	29° 36' S 14° 18' E	65°	65°	*S.E. wind, force 6. Rough sea, moderate swell. Cloudy and clear.* 13.00 *Orange River abeam to Port.*
11.5.66	334	18·56	At Cape Town.			06.00 *Estimated time of arrival at Table Bay.*

Total Distance : Southampton (Nab Tower) to Cape Town (Table Bay) 5,949 miles.

Average Speed : 21·85 Knots.

" S.A. ORANJE "
(28,705 TONS)

Captain J. P. SMYTHE, D.S.C., R.D., R.N.R.

From CAPE TOWN to SOUTHAMPTON via LAS PALMAS.

VOYAGE 118   **May 25th to June 6th, 1966**

Date	Distance Run	Speed	Lat. | Long.	Air	Sea	REMARKS
25.5.66	—	—	At Cape Town	58°	60°	16.00 *Vessel Departed Cape Town.* 57 *First Class and* 471 *Tourist Class Passengers aboard.* *Light airs. Cloudy and clear.*
26.5.66	446	21·97	28° 25' S 12° 36' E	67°	64°	*S.S.E. wind, force* 6. *Rough sea, heavy S'ly swell.* *Cloudy and clear.*
27.5.66	551	22·04	21° 10' S 06° 25' E	69°	70°	04.00 *Crossed Tropic of Capricorn. S.E. wind, force* 3. *Slight sea, moderate S.W'ly swell.* *Cloudy and clear.*
28.5.66	539	22·46	14° 08' S 00° 35' E	74°	75°	*S.E. wind, force* 3. *Slight sea, low swell.* *Cloudy, fine and clear.*
29.5.66	541	22·54	06° 46' S 04° 41' W	84°	83°	*S.S.E. wind, force* 4. *Moderate sea, low S'ly swell.* *Cloudy, fine and clear.*
30.5.66	543	22·63	00° 39' N 09° 50' W	84°	83°	09.55 *Vessel Crossed Equator in D.R. Longitude* 09° 22' W. *S.S.E. wind, force* 3. *Slight sea, low swell.* *Few clouds, fine and clear.*
31.5.66	541	22·54	08° 09' N 14° 50' W	84°	85°	*Light variable wind. Rippled sea, low swell Few clouds, fine and clear.* 16.45 *Passed Northbound Cargo Vessel " Clan Sutherland."*
1.6.66	534	22·25	16° 12' N 17° 43' W	75°	74°	08.00 *Rounded Cape Verde, (most W'ly point of Africa.) N. wind force* 6. *Rough sea, moderate swell. Few clouds and clear.* 14.54 *Passed Southound Cargo Vessel " Clan Macdougall."*
2.6.66	531	22·13	24° 51' N 16° 29' W	72°	72°	08.00 *Crossed Tropic of Cancer. Light variable wind. Rippled sea, moderate N'ly swell. Few clouds with horizon haze.* 22.30 *Arrived Las Palmas.*
3.6.66	403	22·28	31° 12' N 14° 14' W	71°	71°	02.00 *Departed Las Palmas.* 85 *First Class and* 481 *Tourist Class Passengers aboard. Light variable winds, Rippled sea, low swell. Few clouds and clear.*
4.6.66	532	22·17	39° 36' N 10° 46' W	70°	68°	*S.S.W. wind, force* 2. *Slight sea, low swell. Few clouds and clear.* 22.00 *Rounded Cape Villano, entered Bay of Biscay.*
5.6.66	516	22·43	47° 24' N 06° 03' W	61°	60°	*S.W. wind, force* 4. *Moderate sea and swell. Overcast and clear with occasional showers.* 15.25 *Rounded Ushant Island, entered the English Channel.*
6.6.66	289	18·65	At Southampton.			07.00 *Estimated time of arrival at berth Southampton.*

Total Distance :   Cape Town (Table Bay) to Southampton (Nab Tower) 5,966 miles.

Average Speed : 22·07 Knots.

M. S. "S. A. ORANJE"
CAPTAIN J. P. SMYTHE, D.S.C., R.D., R.N.R.
VOYAGE 118
LEAVING SOUTHAMPTON ON 29th APRIL 1966

Monday 2nd May 1966 8.30 a.m.
Dear Family

I am sitting in my cabin, waiting for breakfast toast and lime marmalade to arrive. This ship is so organised. I have a large airy cabin, get up at 8.00 to have a shower, then breakfast arrives. There is a certain old steward (Ernie) on here who is prepared to do the News, every morning, for a price, so we Clerks don't have to get up early. And the room service is excellent. We had our first sunbathe yesterday afternoon on the First Class Sundeck. There are just 29 First Class pax., 4 of whom get off today. So we go First Class instead. The Tourist end is completely separate and the facilities are just as good.

I work in the Tourist Bureau, doing counter work, and try to do some paperwork. It all seems very different to every other ship I have been on. The other person here is the 2nd Purser (Bede Cooper) and he is excellent at his job and I like and enjoy working with him. I hope this does not all sound a bit disjointed. I am now in the Bureau waiting to open it. There is nothing much to report. Usual pre-sailing visit to The Red Lion, Southampton, then 1 p.m. sailing. The weather in the Bay was so calm, and the Channel was like glass. Today is Las Palmas at 1.p.m. for 3 - 4 hours, so we will be selling lots of stamps. Then 9 days at sea to Cape Town. Nice voyage I reckon. The other Purserette, Angie Palmer, is very nice and we get on well together, and with the Nursing Sister, Chris. Richards. We are in whites today, so you can tell how warm it is. Last night we had a Quiz, which was hilarious. Thursday we have a Buccaneers Ball, pirates and all that, and we just dance and drink rum punch etc. Lovely ship, no complaints so far. Glad the weather is so good for you too. Take care of yourselves. Love, Ann

Cape Town 11.5.66
Dear Family

Although I dated this on the 9th, I didn't get round to writing anything more, but now we are in Cape Town, I am on duty in the Bureau and there is no-one around, so here goes. Thank you for the letter this morning. It was certainly full of news. I got intrigued by several things: so Elaine is planning on the 11th June for the wedding. I'm glad I will be home. Where will the wedding be? And how is Nanna, and did you settle anything with the family I wonder. I like the sound of John's "do" as well. About my shoes in Slough, please could you ask them to hold on to them for me, when you go in about your shoes (if you do)? Ta. And please could you book me an appointment with the dentist for the day after I get home, i.e. 7th June. Perhaps just before or after lunch.

I was glad to hear that the CAPETOWN CASTLE brought some Tristan da Cunha people home this week, on holiday. Do you remember that when I was at grammar school one of my Geography projects was to research Tristan da Cunha? Sheila Marr and I spent a lot of time finding out about the island, that no-one had even heard of, and we were fascinated and so admired the people there.

My Las Palmas letter took enough days getting home, didn't it. I remember that was my first port of call, and my first letter home to you, after joining the Merchant Navy, took only two days. Way back in November, cor. I wish I knew what you are doing to change the house. Don't tell me though.

I am looking forward to seeing the cine films of "my" ships. Strangely enough, we passed the "VAAL" the other night just before sunset, and it brought back lots of memories to several of us on here. We were about a mile or two apart, which was quite near for Union-Castle drivers. All very friendly - enormous ocean, no land for miles, two large ships, lights, hooters sounding and whistles blowing, and us all lined up along the Prom. deck to watch. (First Class end of course!). It is so odd to be on a two-class ship, but it is quite pleasant at the moment as there were only 21 First Class passengers and after leaving our Tourist Bureau in the evening we really felt we were getting away from it all for a while when we went back home (we all call our cabins "home") to our accommodation. Very pleasant. The catch-phrase on here is connected with car-owning. We talk about taking the Mini to work today, parking problems, ignition trouble when you arrive late somewhere. And during an entertainment when someone is called for a message for a baby crying, Bede always says "so-and so's parking meter has expired".

This has been a very enjoyable voyage, and I am very happy as usual. One of the passengers is able to tell fortunes, and one night she held a séance. I attended and it was rather amusing. We sat in a darkened room with our hands resting on the table, and concentrated. Mrs Hatter (mad as) asked her spirit friends to prove their presence to us (the open-minded ones) by manifesting themselves to us by raising the table. So we concentrated very hard for ages and ages. Then we had to sing a hymn or two to let them know we were there. Then she asked 'them' to knock once if they were there, and the table knocked. So after establishing this contact we went on to other things, like making the table rise. All this had started at 10.30 at night so we were still concentrating and hoping for action at 11.30. Suddenly the table began to rise and Mrs Hatter got very excited. She asked for it to be raised even more (it was only a fraction up at one corner) and kept muttering and praying and thanking 'them' for doing this. The table began to rise all along one side and fell back with a thump, then got up again and stayed up for several minutes. She got very excited and thanked them for doing this for her. Unfortunately it wasn't 'them' that were doing it - it was the Purser Catering who had managed to get his knee under the table and raise it up. It was all rather a disappointment, because most of us were quite prepared to believe in something if it happened. But it was very amusing all the same.

Mrs. Hatter didn't know anything about Geoff. doing this, and doesn't to this day, and sincerely believes her power is the same as ever. How we kept straight faces I shall never know. We were a bit annoyed with Geoff. at the time for interfering, but he only said that we would all have been there all night if we had waited for a real manifestation.

She has since read my palm and informed me that I shall marry a man on this ship, have 2 girls and 1 boy, and I must make sure I choose the right man. She is so serious about it all too. Some of the men bet on a horse called 'Grandma' running at Brighton yesterday (Mrs. H. lives at Hove) and of course it won.

What else to tell you. The heat crossing the Equator was tremendous as usual and we couldn't sleep very well. The Neptune ceremony went well. As usual I was a mermaid and wore a splendid tail, made by the kids in the nursery. Some of the older boys (8 or 9 years old) seemed to form a fan club and they used to visit me, give me sweets, write odd notes, ask for autographs, and one even asked for my address! It was very amusing. We play deck games and I have bought a white towelling shirt. Looks good.

The other night we had a First Class Banquet. Horseshoe-shaped table, free wine, civilian clothes for us, and dancing all night afterwards. Excellent evening. Marvellous males on this ship. We have lots of impromptu parties which are hilarious. One Purser/Catering plays the accordion very well so we dance a lot after Entertainments.

Today I have the morning off and went into the town. Bought an ashtray, had coffee and cake with two of the Bandsmen I met by chance, they bought me some flowers, and came back for lunch. Work since then, til 9.00 p.m. I'm now extremely tired. Life is very good and I'm certainly happy on here. Love, Ann

p.s. I must buy a long evening dress!

Durban, Tuesday 17th May
Dear Family

I have half an hour before I go off duty, and no passengers or work at the moment, so I am shirking and writing to you all. Thank you for the letter yesterday Daddy - it was very interesting news, all of it. It's funny how you say that nothing happens at home, but to me it seems that lots of things are happening. I am looking forward to seeing the photos, especially of the car and the CAPETOWN. We heard about the Flushing incident shortly after it happened (it's funny how good the grapevine is) and I was very upset, as one or two people said that was the end of her. We did not expect her to be pulled off the sandbank, and thought she would just sit and rot and be a wreck. But then we heard that she had finally been pulled off and was safe. There were pictures (actually just one picture) in the Cape Town paper that evening. It must have been a very nasty experience.

I have a feeling that I didn't mention that in Las Palmas, although we were working, the Spanish dancers came on board and performed up on the Dance Deck, just above the Bureau. Bede Cooper said I could go and watch them as I hadn't seen them before so I rushed up there. They had gorgeous costumes on, the music was super and the dancing was wonderful to watch. They came round after their half hour performance and asked if anyone wanted to buy an EP record of their dance music so I bought one. It is very good, and a nice souvenir.

Cape Town was nice as usual. I had the morning off after we arrived and just went into town to look around. I met up with some of the Band so we went for coffee and cakes and they bought me some flowers. Just dawdled around and then back for lunch. Worked for rest of the day and evening, and we sailed next day.

Then Port Elizabeth and my day off. Went to see Haig and Dimple dolphin in the afternoon with new tricks, and in the evening went in a party to a new restaurant on the 7th floor of a new hotel. Good dinner and dancing.

Have to rush back to change now, as we are going out for the day. Big crowd in big car going on big drive to the Drakensberg Mountains and possibly Ladysmith (Boer War). Should be a wonderful day. Sorry I had to stop typing letter, but I will write again tomorrow. Just wanted to let you know I am still in the land of the living and certainly enjoying myself. We have a large car, and picnic lunch, so today should be fun: 5 men and me! Must catch the post to you, so cheerio for now. Take care of yourselves - I wish you could all be here too.

Lots of love, Ann

Durban, 18th May 1966
Dear family

Thanks for the letter first of all, and fancy the "WINDSOR CASTLE" getting to England many days late (2½ days - author's note) - the breakdown must have been worse than anticipated. And the "CAPETOWN CASTLE " went aground at Flushing, 10 tugs to shift her, and all on TV, whatever next. We don't always hear about these things.

Anyway, we had such a wonderful day yesterday. It was absolutely fabulous. After hastily scribbling that note to you, we all gathered in Bede's cabin and took off in the Zephyr. I think we left just before 11.45. First we went to Pietermaritzburg, along fast motor ways, between the hills. Stopped for Pepsi/beer in hotel there, then on for few more miles to a placed called World's View. We drove up a hill and came out on top on to a track used by the Boers (the Voortrekkers) in the 1800's. It was very narrow and strewn with boulders, as they say, but it was a lovely view from the top.

This was the first view of the plains and coastal region that the trekkers had when they came from inland in their wooden wagons. It must have been very rough going for them in those days. We had our picnic lunch up there on top of the hill, and took some pictures. Then on to Howick Falls. Tiny town of Howick, on a hill, with falls of about 100 feet, cascading down to bottom of canyon riverbed. Very impressive, again. Then along fast roads to Mooirivier, passing place called Rosetta on the way. Then we really took to the hills. We turned off the main road and went on to this dirt road, heading straight for the Drakensberg Mountains which we could see in the distance. It was such an hilarious journey. We felt as if we were on safari. We had this large primrose-coloured Zephyr 6 stirring up the dust as we did about 40 m.p.h. along the fairly wide track round hills, through a Bantu tribe reservation where they live in Kraals on the hillside. It was quite green around, but got more and more rocky. We climbed steadily all the way, stopping once or twice to take quick pictures. We didn't see another car all the way (40 miles) and the only traffic we met was Bantus on bicycles, and cows being driven back to the Bantu kraals. This was about 5.00 o'clock by this time, so we were in a rush to get to Giant's Camp Castle. The track simply went to this Camp and then stopped. The last few miles was a Game Reservation stretching over a large area of the Drakensberg Mountains and this covered part of Natal and the start of Basutoland.

In the Game Park we saw some springboks and some odd looking things called Elands. Apart from that it was mountains, craggy peaks, sunlight on the tops, fresh air and absolute peace. Then we arrived at the Camp and it was so green and lush, and so peaceful. People come there for a few days peace and quiet and live in little huts with solid walls and thatched roofs, looking after themselves like campers. We saw the peaks known as the King and Queen and the Giant's Castle.

Then back along the dirt road as the sun was setting behind the mountains. It was soon dark and we began to see the odd lights in the hills as the Bantu people lit their fires and lamps outside their kraals. We didn't see any cows on the way back fortunately, or Bantus on bikes. We reckoned that if one had come along and seen us they might have thought it was the very devil himself, with a primrose car, lights, dust being stirred up and 4 noisy men and 1 noisy girl inside.

We stopped in the middle of nowhere for a sandwich left over from lunch and some beer and Pepsi. All in all it was a very amusing drive. The boys took turns in driving and we got back to Durban finally at 9.00 o'clock. Back to the ship for a quick wash and change and then Bede and I went out for a meal in a lovely peaceful restaurant in the City. It had been a very exhausting day and all we wanted was to slow down and think about the day. Then finally back to drinks with the Deck crowd and I couldn't keep awake any longer so went to bed. Slept very soundly.

44

Don't think I mentioned that yesterday morning we had Boat Drill at 7.00 a.m. This was someone's mad idea, and very unpopular. So it was a long day, and we did 304 miles altogether. But we all agreed we wouldn't have missed it for anything.

Now to fill in the gap for East London. Two of us had the day off so we went first to the Museum. Do you remember the Coelacanth that was caught in 1938 and caused a sensation because they had been extinct for 50 million years? No? Ignorant lot. Well, it was caught off that part of the coast, and is now preserved in E.L. Museum. They are very proud of it, and I feel pleased to think I have seen it. They also have a stuffed dodo. (I know - so what). Then we went for lunch at an hotel nearby then back to the ship for a quick kip before sailing. Very satisfactory day. I am working for the next two days in port, but have two days off in Cape Town on way home so that should be nice.

By the way, I had a card from Ken Faulkner in Amsterdam, with no details. What is happening please? About the strike, we have heard rumours that if it is not called off by 6th June we may go to Rotterdam, or get long leave, or anchor out in Isle of Wight water. You can take your pick of the rumours! Hope everything is settled soon, and that it doesn't affect you in any way.
Ann

Cape Town
24th May (Tuesday)
Dear family

Just to let you know I am still in the land of the living. I am rather concerned about how you are affected by the Strike and the proposed National Emergency. It is rather worrying. It's certainly just about all we talk about down here at the moment, except for the big fight. Wasn't it a shame about Henry Cooper's eye again?

Thanks for the letter here, it was very welcome. We have had fairly rough weather downcoast actually. We could not leave East London because of high winds, so left 12 hours late. So we got to P.E. late, and left even later, and finally got to Cape Town on Sunday at 5.00 p.m. just before the fog and rain set in. And it has fogged and rained every since! Haven't seen the Mountain yet. Been out for dinner, shopping etc. Bought print of Table Bay and Mountain in P.E. and frame for it today. Very expensive picture frame (wood frame, glass, nails) from O.K. Bazaars. Cost me 4/6d.! Not bad eh?

I have just come home from a party and I am sitting up in bed to write this. I have a slight cold and cannot breathe properly. And we had another 7.00 a.m. Lifeboat Drill this morning too. I went back to bed and sleep afterwards.

Must stop now. I'm looking forward to getting home again, although I'm very happy on here. If the strike is still on, we will be docking and going on long leave. Hey ho. See you soon (fingers crossed).   Love, Ann.

Thursday 2nd June 1966
Near Las Palmas

Dear Mummy and Daddy

Just thought some miracle might happen and you get this on Saturday or Monday. Nothing much to report, but I just felt like writing. Whit Sunday got up early and went to Communion taken by Archdeacon of Cape Town. Nice.

Weather very hot and lovely for sunbathing. Tan going on well, sleeping difficult in heat. I slept in the air-conditioned men's hospital one night.

Oh yes. Tuesday was Republic Day and we celebrated it in the evening with a special Dance. The Purser Mr Connelly had arranged for three of us girls to wear hired costumes - long dresses, aprons, lace collars (and bonnets which we refused to wear). Real Voortrekker costume. Three men dressed up too, as partners. Dance Deck all decorated, barbecue food at 11 p.m., band under "Covered Wagon" stage, and lights, balloons and murals. Super evening. Great fun in long dress.

Have been concerned about my weight recently so now attending gym. daily after work. The masseur is quite prepared to assist in spot-reducing, so hey ho!

Just came back from dinner. We are due at Las Palmas in half an hour, so must finish this as mail closes then. I'm looking forward to seeing you on Monday, very much. Hope to be home as soon as possible. My cold has gone, and I feel fine.

All our Port forms I've been preparing for the end of this Voyage are dated 6.6.66. Something to remember in years to come.

Take care. Hope wedding arrangements going well. Love to all. See you.   Ann

S.A. ORANJE

31st May 1966 Voortrekker Night – The author and Bill Fleetwood

This should have been Voyage 119 on the S A ORANJE but because of the Seamen's Strike the Voyage did not take place.

All our port forms for arrival in Southampton had been dated 6.6.66, a memorable date that always sticks in my mind.

During the Strike we Purserettes had to use some of our leave so I enjoyed my sister's wedding on 11th June 1966 and spending time with my family and friends. Then we had to work in one of the London offices of Union-Castle and I found myself going up to London daily for a couple of weeks, doing secretarial work etc. at Cayzer House, in St. Mary Axe, and Greenly House, in Creechurch Lane, London, for Mr McIver and Mr Bedford amongst others. We had quite a social time there as we Purserettes were previously just names - girls with a very glamorous job but unknown to the office staff. We had time to talk with Mr A. M. H. Baker, the Superintendent Purser, (known affectionately as Boffin), and kind Mr Peter Hall, who looked after the Purser/Catering sea staff movements from Head Office, as well as other staff, like Cyril and Freda Remfry, who all helped to ensure the smooth running of the Fleet.

We also found time to see the Tower of London, Tower Bridge, the local Street Markets and coffee bars.

I have photographs of Maureen Fisher and me by the Tower of London (and yes, we usually wore a hat and gloves!)

Ann
July 1999

David Haynes, second from left, and future husband of Ann Williams (third left) with Alan Beech, Jim Innis, and Ron Crook. S.A. Oranje September 23rd 1966

" S.A. ORANJE "

Captain J. P. SMYTHE, D.S.C., R.D., R.N.R.

From SOUTHAMPTON to CAPE TOWN via LAS PALMAS.

VOYAGE 120   **August 5th to August 17th, 1966**

Date	Distance Run	Speed	Lat. | Long.	Average Temperature Air	Sea	REMARKS
5.8.66	—	—	At Southampton	62°	- °	13.00 *Vessel Departed Southampton. 74 First Class and 494 Tourist Class Passengers aboard. W.S.W. wind, force 5. Cloudy and clear. Rain showers.*
6.8.66	465	21·14	44° 33' N 08° 36' W	66°	66°	00.15 *Rounded Ushant Island, entered Bay of Biscay. S.W. wind, force 5 - 6. Moderate to rough sea, moderate swell. Partly cloudy.* 16.38 *Passed Cape Finisterre, left Bay of Biscay.*
7.8.66	533	22·21	33° 11' N 12° 21' W	72°	70°	*W'ly wind, force 3. Slight sea, low swell. Overcast with scattered showers*
8.8.66	510	22·47	At Las Palmas	74°	71°	11.54 *Arrived Las Palmas. N.N.W. wind, force 4 - 5. Cloudy, fine and clear. 16.24 Departed Las Palmas. 58 First Class and 466 Tourist Class Passengers aboard.*
9.8.66	395	20·90	21° 57' N 17° 45' W	69°	71°	*N.E. wind, force 4. Moderate sea, low swell. Cloudy and clear.*
10.8.66	537	22·38	13° 00' N 17° 39' W	83°	84°	07.18 *Rounded Cape Verde, (most W'ly point of Africa.) 11.15 Passed Coy's vessel " King George." N. W'ly wind, force 1 - 2. Rippled sea, low swell. Cloudy and clear. 21.00 Passed Coy's vessel " Clan Ranald."*
11.8.66	541	22·54	05° 08' N 13° 31' W	79°	81°	*S'ly wind, force 4. Moderate sea and swell Overcast and clear.*
12.8.66	557	23·21	02° 28' S 08° 13' W	74°	73°	05.45 *Vessel Crossed Equator in D.R. Longitude 09° 35' W. S.S.E. wind, force 3. Slight sea, low swell. Cloudy and clear.*
13.8.66	535	22·29	09° 32' S 02° 57' W	66°	75°	*S.E. wind, force 5 - 6. Rough sea, heavy swell. Overcast with rain showers.*
14.8.66	529	22·04	16° 24' S 02° 41' E	65°	67°	*S.E. wind, force 5. Rough sea, heavy swell. Cloudy and clear.*
15.8.66	501	21·78	22° 56' S 08° 11' E	62°	65°	*S.E. wind, force 6. Rough sea, heavy swell. Overcast and clear.*
16.8.66	493	21·43	29° 15' S 14° 00' E	59°	62°	*S.S.E. wind, force 6. Rough sea, heavy swell. Overcast and clear.*
17.8.66	360	20·57	At Cape Town.			07.00 *Estimated time of arrival at berth in Cape Town.*

Total Distance : Southampton (Needles) to Cape Town (Table Bay) 5,956 miles.

Average Speed : 21·98 Knots.

———•—•———

" S.A. ORANJE "

Captain J. P. SMYTHE, D.S.C., R.D., R.N.R.

From CAPE TOWN to SOUTHAMPTON via LAS PALMAS.

VOYAGE 120   **August 31st to September 12th, 1966**

Date	Distance Run	Speed	Lat. | Long.	Average Temperature Air	Sea	REMARKS
31.8.66	—	—	At Cape Town	62°	- °	16.00 *Vessel Departed Cape Town. 47 First Class and 402 Tourist Class Passengers aboard. S.E. wind, force 4. Cloudy and clear.*
1.9.66	456	22·35	28° 14′ S 12° 33′ E	64°	62°	*S.E. wind, force 4. Moderate sea, low swell. Few clouds, fine and clear.*
2.9.66	564	22·56	20° 53′ S 06° 08′ E	65°	65°	*S.E. wind, force 4. Moderate sea and swell. Overcast and clear.*
3.9.66	547	22·79	13° 43′ S 00° 15′ E	67°	68°	*S.E. wind, force 4. Moderate sea and swell. Overcast and clear.*
4.9.66	542	22·58	06° 22′ S 05° 03′ W	77°	75°	*S.E. wind, force 2. Slight sea, low swell. Few clouds, fine and clear.*
5.9.66	540	22·50	01° 03′ N 10° 08′ W	78°	78°	08.48 *Vessel Crossed Equator in D.R. Longitude 09° 30′ W. S.S.W. wind, force 3. Slight sea, low swell. Few clouds, fine and clear.*
6.9.66	534	22·25	08° 26′ N 15° 05′ W	76°	81°	*W'ly wind, force 4. Moderate sea, low swell Cloudy, with occasional rain squalls.*
7.9.66	533	22·21	16° 35′ N 17° 42′ W	84°	84°	07.00 *Passed Company's "S.A. Vaal."* 07.05 *Rounded Cape Verde, (most W'ly point of Africa.) E.N.E. wind, force 3. Slight sea, low swell. Cloudy, fine and clear.*
8.9.66	535	22·29	25° 20′ N 16° 28′ W	75°	71°	*N.N.E. wind, force 5. Moderate sea and swell. Overcast and hazy.* 21.30 *Arrived Las Palmas.*
9.9.66	388	21·32	31° 26′ N 14° 07′ W	74°	74°	01.30 *Departed Las Palmas. 94 First Class and 434 Tourist Class Passengers aboard. N. wind, force 5. Rough sea, moderate swell. Cloudy with horizon haze.*
10.9.66	528	22·00	39° 46′ N 10° 38′ W	70°	70°	*N. wind, force 3. Slight sea, low swell. Cloudy, fine and clear.* 21.45 *Passed Cape Villano, entered Bay of Biscay.*
11.9.66	514	22·35	47° 35′ N 06° 08′ W	65°	66°	*N.E. wind, force 3. Moderate sea and swell. Cloudy, overcast and hazy.* 15.10 *Rounded Ushant Island, entered English Channel.*
12.9.66	283	18·26	At Southampton.			07.00 *Estimated time of arrival at berth in Southampton.*

Total Distance :   Cape Town (Table Bay) to Southampton (Nab Tower) 5,964 miles.

Average Speed : 22·00 Knots.

M. S. "S. A. ORANJE"
CAPTAIN J. P. SMYTHE, D.S.C., R.D., R.N.R.
VOYAGE 120
LEAVING SOUTHAMPTON 5th AUGUST 1966

Port Elizabeth
Saturday 20th August

Dear Mummy and Daddy

I thought I would take a chance and write to you at the Camping Site at Ostia. If you get there you might well look at the letter rack. If not, well ………

Hope you are enjoying yourselves so far, and the journey was all right.

I got your letter in Cape Town thank you. Funny about the weight of the petticoat though but best not to send it of course. I shall just have to remember to bring it back next time.

Life has been extremely hectic on here, and the party rate is quite something, with "snifters", and Biblical-type invites as usual. Two ex-seafarers (Reg. Kelso and David Macmillan) are doing a Company project this voyage so there's even more social life! The 2nd Purser this time is Peter Bazlinton, we work well together, and the voyage down here has seemed extremely short.

East London, Sunday 21st.

Off again. I was on duty yesterday and didn't manage to finish this letter. This morning I went for a walk, washed my hair and now feel ready for lunch. Sherry by my side. The weather has been very chilly. We had <u>one</u> day's sunbathing, the day we crossed the Equator. It has rained and blown, Cape Town was wet and chilly and the sea has been rough all round the coast. Couldn't sleep the night after Cape Town!

Nothing much to report. Life is very enjoyable, we have lots of impromptu parties and the latest craze in music is Petula Clark's LP - "Strangers in the Night". Also on there is "Monday, Monday" which we play to ourselves for arrival Southampton! I have bought it, and so have 2 others. Every good party-giver has a copy! I haven't worn my long dress yet, but we expect to have a dinner/dance homeward bound. Hope so!

Oh yes, I have had my hair cut very, very short. I just couldn't stand it at the 'in between' stage and as usual the male hairdresser from Steiners is excellent. I said I wanted my hair cut and his eyes gleamed. It looks rather good I think.

East London
25.8.66
There just isn't time. I give up.

P.E.   26.8.66
This letter is doomed, I shall just finish it and post it home. Thanks for sending me the letter and photos the other day. They aren't too bad, are they.

I was going to send this to Italy but you say you expected to be there on the Sunday, so this will go to the UK for your return home . If you got to Sorrento in 4/5 days that's pretty good. Lucky you. I want to go there too! Not doing too badly myself of course.

Day off in Durban, and went to the Valley of 1000 Hills. Fabulous drive, just mountains, blue sky, peace and few Zulus in kraals. Back to nature and all that. Nice passenger gave me flowers at Cape Town, wasn't that nice! Will write again before leaving coast. Love, Ann.

Cape Town, Monday 29th August
Dear Family

Hope you had a good holiday. Got your sailing letter from Dover, yesterday. Thanks. Didn't expect to hear from you again this trip, so it was a lovely surprise. I have had a full day on duty today, and now cannot leave the ship tonight so I have just washed my hair and I'm sitting up in bed writing this with the tape playing organ music in my left ear. Tomorrow we have 7.00 a.m. Boat Drill so an early night will be useful. I have all day and evening off tomorrow, from 10.00 a.m. so am looking forward to it.

Really can't remember what I have already told you, so may repeat myself in this letter. Sorry. Should have told you about nice people who bought me daffodils in Cape Town up-coast. Dear old lady left ship at CT, then sent me bunch of proteas (long-lasting cactus-type flowers) next day. She then rang up and chatted and suggested coming to see her next time I was here. Nice of her. I seem to remember I mentioned the day out in Durban. While in Durban I bought a dress to wear in the evenings. Nice 'useful' dress, suitable for day or evening. Black with coloured bodice, no sleeves or neck. Bought a picture in Las Palmas. Spanish Las Palmas scene. So original an oil painting, it was still wet! How about that. Thought it was hilarious. Hardboard frame too. On voyage from Cape Town saw wreck of the "Seafarer". Remember her? She somehow managed to run aground on rocks near Sea Point. Broken into 3 parts, all quite visible. Captain made a boob they say. Went for car ride yesterday and went to see wreck at close quarters from promenade, quite a sight. Also went right along road around Table Mountain halfway up, from Cable-car station. Lots of cloud on top, almost rolling down on to us. Lots of waterfalls, nice. Good view from end.

Remember the ship "Joanna" carrying oil for Rhodesia? She came into Durban Harbour the day we left, but I didn't see her. Last week we picked up several people in P.E. downcoast. I was working at the counter about 7. p.m. before sailing at 8 p.m, looked up, and said "Mr Collett". It was an Engineer I remember from I.C.I. Paints Division at Slough. He is always seconded to foreign parts to design paint factories. I last saw him 1 year ago at Slough. Didn't know he was over here. His son is coming with us from P.E. to U.K, Farnham Common. How about that!

Our Engineers had a party last night. Pictures to show you! Mummy, please could you buy me some more Pretty Polly sheer stockings, usual size and colour. Daddy, please could you look into availability/price of Phillips portable, battery, record-player? One with a lid-speaker, I think about £18. Thanks again. See you soon. Love, Ann.

" S.A. ORANJE "

Captain J. P. SMYTHE, D.S.C., R.D., R.N.R.

From CAPE TOWN to SOUTHAMPTON via LAS PALMAS.

VOYAGE 121   **October 19th to October 31st, 1966**

Date	Distance Run	Speed	Lat. | Long.	Average Temperature Air	Sea	REMARKS
19.10.66	—	—	At Cape Town	69°	- °	16.00 *Vessel Departed Cape Town. 22 First Class and 283 Tourist Class Passengers aboard. Light airs. Few clouds, fine and clear.*
20.10.66	457	22·29	28° 25' S 12° 18' E	67°	63°	*S. W. wind, force 4. Moderate sea, low swell. Partly cloudy and clear.*
21.10.66	568	22·72	20° 55' S 05° 58' E	69°	65°	*S.E. wind, force 5. Rough sea, low swell. Mainly overcast and clear.*
22.10.66	546	22·75	13° 40' S 00° 14' E	69°	69°	*E.S.E. wind, force 3. Slight sea, low swell. Overcast and clear.*
23.10.66	545	22·71	06° 11' S 04° 58' W	77°	75°	*Light variable winds. Slight sea, low swell. Cloudy and clear.*
24.10.66	548	22·83	01° 18' N 10° 11' W	81°	80°	08.12 *Vessel Crossed Equator in D.R. Longitude 09° 26' W. S.S.W. wind, force 2 - 3. Slight sea, low swell. Cloudy and clear.*
25.10.66	540	22·50	08° 37' N 15° 25' W	82°	84°	*Light variable winds, Slight sea, low swell Cloudy and clear.*
26.10.66	535	22·29	16° 47' N 17° 40' W	85°	83°	06.30 *Rounded Cape Verde, (most W'ly point of Africa.)* 09.12 *Passed Company's "S.A. Vaal." N.N.E. wind, force 3. Slight sea, low swell. Cloudless and clear.*
27.10.66	542	22·58	25° 37' N 16° 14' W	72°	73°	01.00 *Passed Company's vessel "Capetown Castle." N.N.E. wind, force 3. Slight sea, moderate swell. Few clouds, fine and clear.* 21.30 *Arrived Las Palmas.*
28.10.66	380	21·47	31° 37' N 14° 09' W	71°	73°	02.00 *Departed Las Palmas. 62 First Class and 302 Tourist Class Passengers aboard. E.N.E. wind, force 3. Slight sea, moderate swell. Cloudy, fine and clear.*
29.10.66	516	21·50	39° 49' N 11° 01' W	61°	66°	*N.E. wind, force 6. Rough sea, heavy swell. Cloudy and clear.* 21.30 *Passed Cape Finisterre, entered Bay of Biscay.*
30.10.66	524	21·83	47° 40' N 06° 10' W	54°	59°	*N. wind, force 4. Moderate sea and swell. Cloudy and clear.* 14.30 *Passed Ushant Island, entered English Channel.*
31.10.66	270	18·00	At Southampton.			07.00 *Estimated time of arrival at berth, Southampton.*

Total Distance : Cape Town (Table Bay) to Southampton (Nab Tower) 5,971 miles.

Average Speed : 22·04 Knots.

M. S. "S. A. ORANJE"
CAPTAIN J. P. SMYTHE, D.S.C., R.D., R.N.R.
VOYAGE 121
LEAVING SOUTHAMPTON 23RD SEPTEMBER 1966

Cape Town, Thursday 6th October.
Dear Family

I'm ill in bed at the moment, with some bug or another. Started the night before last by being violently sick all night, despite tablets, and so yesterday I was sent to bed. And I'm still here. I've had tablets, injection, care and attentions, and am now at the stage of feeling very fragile but better than yesterday. My head feels very heavy and objects to being moved far. But my temperature is down more this morning apparently. Off work again today but may be back tomorrow. Still gobbling tablets anyway.

Thought you might like the enclosed picture, taken last Friday. We were on our way to the Crossing the Line Ceremony and one of the First Class passengers took it and gave it to me at lunch time. Too bad it's all fuzzy, but it's better than nothing.

Good voyage to date but very busy. Famous passengers included Basil D'Oliveira and Rumsey of Test Cricket fame and Lightfoot and Newman of County Cricket fame. Heard of them? Very nice people.

Had dinner-dance (long dress) last Saturday night - excellent evening. Can't think of anything more at the moment. Thanks for your letter yesterday. The record player is fine and gets used frequently. I expect I shall think of lots more later on. Take care, love, Ann.

Durban 10th October.
Dear family

Just wanted to reassure you that I am still around. Had a nasty bug for several days, which was when I wrote to you from Cape Town, from my sick bed. And I was very very sick I might tell you. Ugh.

I am now back in circulation again thank goodness, so please don't worry. I hope my Cape Town letter didn't worry you too much. Quite honestly I don't know what I said, because I don't remember much about the last few days. It started Tues. night by being very sick all night. Had lots of pills etc. then injection. Got up for arrival Cape Town and sent back to bed with large temperature. Sick during day, then that stopped. Then a round of pills, sleep, temperature taking, and no food or liquid. Just couldn't face anything. Then Friday allowed up for a short while, and then Saturday in Bureau for an hour or two, then sleep etc. Sunday short walk off the ship, and today Durban feeling much, much better.

Thanks for the letters anyway. Sorry this is scrappy. Had first night ashore tonight, so now its rather late. Working tomorrow so will tell you more then I hope in longer letter. This should stop you worrying I hope. Dr. Roger and Sister Phil have been marvellous, especially Phil. See you soon. Love, Ann.

East London, Thursday 13th October.
Dear Mummy and Daddy

I really do believe I have got a chance to sit down and type a lengthy note to you. I'm sure you might think it's about time too. Round the Coast I have one big typing job and that is now finished, so I can do more or less what I like to pass the time on duty in the Bureau, including work.

First of all I wonder how the wedding went. Your various comments were quite amusing, completely different. And I did think of you with your 1st October party. It sounded good. I thought about you all (with envy). And so Brian is leaving Rank Xerox is he. Thank you for giving him his films back. I'm glad you enjoyed the Nederberg Rose wine and that ciné films are down in price. I think I shall have to get some film next time home. Must check up about that. Good for Elaine getting that job. She must feel very pleased with life again. I nearly fell off my chair when I read that you and "the workman" are going to do the back room before I get home. Cor.

Now for news about the voyage. The big event was being ill last week. It was very nasty indeed but now I feel extremely well, though just a little tired after a 6.30 start this morning with arrival here. Last night for the first time I went to the pictures and saw the last hour of "That Darn Cat" with Hayley Mills, quite funny, good slapstick at times.

What else. Odd items now. The night after leaving Cape Town up coast we had an unusual atmospheric occurrence. It is called a Berg wind, which comes off the mountains round that part of the coast. It was about ten minutes to midnight, fairly warm with the temperature in the sixties. Ten minutes later the temperature had gone up 20 degrees F. The poor Extra 2nd on the Bridge, Jim Inniss, said later that he thought No. 1 Hold was on fire, the heat felt so tremendous. We were about 30 miles away from the coast at the time, so it must have been quite a powerful hot wind that came over us. I know I suddenly got very hot in my little pit and threw most things off. That was the explanation the next day. Quite interesting I thought.

Oh yes, I was still in the out of action stage that night. And while I was ill I was sent a big notice to put up, beautifully drawn in black and gold which said "Get well soon Ann!". Very nice. I have on my inside cabin door a notice which says "Bang" with lots of explosion noise lines coming away from it. This arose because the same scribe crept to the Bureau one day, put his finger to his lips and said "shush", and handed me this roll of paper. I unrolled it and it said "Bang". I thought it was very funny.

Just took time off from this letter to go and do something rather exciting. I have just been to blow the Ship's Whistle. They test it before we leave each port, together with various other whistles and equipment and the 2nd Officer, David Haynes, rang up to ask jokingly if I wanted to come up to the Bridge and blow the whistle. I did and did. That surprised them. Something different anyway. Made a break from the Bureau.

Where was I. Oh yes. I have been moaning all voyage about not going up the East Coast, and joking about turning left at Durban when we leave. People started teasing the Deck officers about it and it became quite a thing for a while. Then I made a Charter in verse about please can we turn left at Durban. We all signed it, sealed it with a Queen's head from a sixpence and put a pink ribbon on it and presented it to the 2nd and Extra 2nd Officers. They were rather tickled with it and even tried to go into print themselves with a reply. Unfortunately they forgot to turn left when we left Durban. I shall send you a copy of the Charter from PE or Cape Town. The Captain's wife is travelling this trip. She goes in for floating-type clothes, and has now been christened 'batman' because she appeared on the Bridge one day in a wind wearing a black cloak, which of course billowed out behind her.

This morning someone came back from the local bus tour (the only tour) and was carrying all sorts of bits and pieces. He came and dropped one in front of me and do you know what it was. Of course you don't. It was a large and beautiful pineapple. All for me. I was very grateful. We will all be eating that this evening.

Durban was interesting this time. I had Monday off but it was a Public Holiday and everything was closed. I went with one of the other Bureau bods and we went on the Go Karts in the morning. My first ride in a go kart and it was great fun. Went for lunch at a big hotel, very pleasant, then visited the Oceanarium with big beautiful fish and sharks. Went out in the evening for dinner and dancing.

Must go now as the ship is about to sail very very shortly. See you soon. Love, Ann.

Port Elizabeth, Friday 14th October
Dear Family

Yesterday I wrote to you at East London and mentioned the charter I sent up to the drivers, about turning left at Durban. I said I would send you a copy of it and here it is. I think it might amuse you. I'm rather proud of it. One or two things you should understand before reading it: David and Jim are the 2nd and Extra 2nd Mates respectively, and are not particularly tall. They are always teased about it. (One night while I was ill in bed Nursing Sister Phil. threw open the door and ushered in Davey and Jim by saying "I've brought the diddy people to see you".)

And the explanation of Bang Bang Roy, is that Roy is the 4th Mate and drew the Bang notice I told you about. He is also rather fond of his beer, and had an extremely high wine account that particular week.

Again I am in the burrow on duty but I'm not too worried because I have time to write my letters and catch up on odd jobs. People drop by and chat and it's all quite fun. At least it means that I get virtually two days off in Cape Town next week. Oh yes, Barry Thomas (the 2nd Purser here) and I have been invited to lunch with two of our VIP passengers, on Sunday. They are the Venerable Archdeacon and Mrs. Van der Byl. He is the Archdeacon of Cape Town, and they travelled with us before. Very pleasant and friendly. So for the first time I shall be going to a Cape Town home. Looking forward to it. By the way, I hope you didn't think yesterday's letter was too abrupt at the end. It was simply minutes before the gang plank was being removed and I had to rush it.

Just a final line to say that this morning we all feel very fragile. We stayed here overnight for the first time and therefore were in port with the "WINDSOR CASTLE". I went out last night for a meal and dancing (acquired some chopsticks somehow) and came back with the crowd to find parties all over the ship. All great fun, but utterly shattering. Everyone, but everyone, is like this. It may improve as the day goes on. We hope so. We sail this morning at 11.45 a.m. (Saturday) and arrive in Cape Town tomorrow at about 10. a.m. Much saner time of arrival we reckon. Must finish now - we sail in 40 minutes. Take care. Love, Ann.

Cape Town, Wed. 19th October
Dear M & D

Hooray, you have got my letters. By now they should be rolling in thick and fast. Thanks for the one here, it was very welcome. I was looking forward to hearing about cousin John's wedding, but I have many questions which will just have to wait. Sounded a very good do. So you've had fog have you. That is early this year, isn't it.

I have almost forgotten what happens when, with English weather these days. Out here at the moment the sun is blazing down, the sky is very blue and there are a few odd clouds around. It is very warm, and it is 9.50 a.m. on sailing day.

Since I last wrote in P.E. (is that right?) I've had a very enjoyable time. We got here on Sunday just after 10 a.m. The sailing time/arrival time was altered because of wool we had to collect in P.E. We got off at 12 noon and Barry and I then went off to the Van der Byls. They have a lovely house halfway up Klook Nek, with lovely views of the Bay, Mountains etc. Had drinks, then lunch - very filling and very good. They are charming people and great fun. We had a red wine with the meal and thoroughly enjoyed it. Mrs Van der Byl told me I must look on her home as my home, and I could just ring up and say I was on my way. Wasn't that sweet of her. I think I may well do that next time here. She said I could just come along, even if she wasn't there.

Got back to the ship about 3.00 p.m. and then went for a snooze on the Monkey Island. Gave a party in the evening which went quite well. Worked on Monday, very easy going. Played scrabble after coming off duty at 9.00 p.m.

Yesterday was absolutely super. The S.E. wind from Monday dropped, the sun blazed down and there wasn't a cloud to be seen. I rushed off at 10.00 a.m. to the town with 2 of the boys, and we pottered around. Bought a 45" record of "Lara's Theme" from Dr. Zhvago. Know it? It is very popular out here. Then back at 12.30 to meet the Staff Commander and Extra 2nd to go out to the beach. Went for lovely drive to a place called Miller's Point, round on False Bay. The sea was freezing cold so I didn't swim in the pool there, but just sunned myself amongst the huge boulders. It was beautiful white soft sand (tasted delicious with pots of hot curry) and I later walked around and collected shells, and got caught unawares by extra-large waves and got a bit damp. Got very sun-tanned and thoroughly happy. Left beach about 4.30 and went back to Cape Town another way, and had tea at Constantia Nek, in old timber Dutch house. Super day. Drinking evening. Goodnight.

Odd things: please could you fix a car for me for 31st October as usual at Southampton? I've ordered some oranges and will be bringing them. Daddy please could you order an LP record for me? It is by Catarina Valenti, and I want the one where she sings "The Breeze and I, Jealousy, Tonight we love, etc." All very good. Ta. Record make is Polydor. All for now. See you soon.

Love, Ann.

M.V. CAPETOWN CASTLE viewed through the Gateway of Jamestown, St Helena

S.A. ORANJE at Cape Town (Photo Ian Shiffman)

Dearest Diddy Dave and Jim
We want to go where you have bin.
Up the East Coast we should go,
Leaving Durban - please make it so.

And "Bang Bang Roy" must help you too,
If you can drag him from the brew.
Please manage it without a fuss.
But don't let Father know it's us.

We want to see the sights of Dar
Their fame has travelled near and far.
And Beira too, and old LM,
And other places north of them.

Just to do the thing in style,
We will call upon the Nile.
And round the Medi. we must go,
Not too fast and not too slow.

Then when we have tired of this,
We must see that place of bliss:
Off we go to Chittagong,
And other places near Hong Kong.

There's lots of things to cure the yawns,
Like chicken peri-peri, prawns,
Lagosta, too, I've often heard,
Can put men down without a word.

These are the things I mustn't miss,
So all your help I must enlist.
You wouldn't like me all bereft,
So please, at Durban, do turn left!

Ann Williams
October 1966

" S.A. ORANJE "

Captain J. P. SMYTHE, D.S.C., R.D., R.N.R.

From SOUTHAMPTON to CAPE TOWN via LAS PALMAS.

VOYAGE 122   **November 11th to November 23rd, 1966**

Date	Distance Run	Ave. Speed	Lat. | Long.	Temperature Air	Sea	REMARKS
11.11.66	—	—	At Southampton	48°	- °	13.00 *Vessel Departed Southampton.* 138 *First Class and 457 Tourist Class Passengers aboard. Light variable winds. Cloudy, with slight haze.*
12.11.66	442	21·05	44° 54' N 08° 23' W	57°	59°	00.30 *Ushant Island abeam, entered Bay of Biscay. S.E. wind, force 4. Moderate sea, low swell. Overcast, fine and clear.* 17.10 *Passed Cape Villano, left Bay of Biscay.*
13.11.66	512	21·33	36° 52' N 12° 02' W	65°	66°	*S. x W. wind, force 4. Moderate sea and swell. Cloudy to overcast and clear.*
14.11.66	539	22·46	28° 16' N 15° 20' W	74°	72°	*S.E. wind, force 4. Moderate sea, low swell. Cloudy, fine and clear.* 13.30 *Arrived Las Palmas.* 19.12 *Departed Las Palmas.* 127 *First Class and 454 Tourist Class Passengers aboard.*
15.11.66	378	21·85	22° 26' N 17° 42' W	74°	72°	*E. x N. wind, force 3. Slight sea, low swell. Mainly overcast and clear.*
16.11.66	542	22·58	13° 25' N 17° 45' W	85°	84°	07.00 *Passed " Edinburgh Castle."* 08.30 *Rounded Cape Verde, (most W'ly point of Africa.)* 11.35 *Passed "Capetown Castle." N.E. wind, force 4. Moderate sea, low swell. Cloudless fine and clear.*
17.11.66	544	22·67	05° 42' N 13° 15' W	80°	84°	*S.S.E. wind, force 2. Slight sea, low swell Cloudy to overcast with frequent rain squalls.*
18.11.66	530	22·08	01° 28' S 08° 08' W	79°	78°	07.00 *Vessel Crossed Equator in D.R. Longitude 09° 18' W. S.S.E. wind, force 4. Moderate sea, low swell. Cloudy, fine and clear.*
19.11.66	541	22·54	08° 38' S 02° 41' W	76°	75°	*S.E. x S. wind, force 4. Moderate sea, low swell. Cloudy, and clear.* 20.05 *Passed Company's vessel "S.A. Vaal."*
20.11.66	541	22·54	15° 40' S 03° 04' E	69°	70°	*S.E. wind, force 4. Moderate sea and swell. Cloudy to overcast and clear.*
21.11.66	516	22·43	22° 29' S 08° 36' E	67°	67°	*S.S.E. wind, force 5. Moderate to rough sea, low swell. Cloudy, fine and clear.*
22.11.66	510	22·17	29° 19' S 14° 11' E	66°	65°	*S.E. wind, force 6 - 7. Rough sea, moderate swell. Fine and clear.*
23.11.66	351	19·50	At Cape Town.			07.00 *Estimated time of arrival at berth, Cape Town.*

Total Distance : Southampton (Needles) to Cape Town (Table Bay) 5,946 miles.

Average Speed : 22·00 Knots.

" S.A. ORANJE "

Captain J. P. SMYTHE, D.S.C., R.D., R.N.R.

From CAPE TOWN to SOUTHAMPTON via LAS PALMAS.

VOYAGE 122   **December 7th to December 19th, 1966**

Date	Distance Run	Ave. Speed	Lat. | Long.	Temperature Air	Sea	REMARKS
7.12.66	—	—	At Cape Town	74°	- °	16.05 *Vessel Departed Cape Town.* 128 *First Class and 472 Tourist Class Passengers aboard.* N. W. *wind, force 2.* Cloudless *and clear.*
8.12.66	459	22·39	28° 14' S 12° 27' E	73°	69°	S.S.E. *wind, force 4.* Moderate *sea and swell.* Few clouds, fine *and clear.*
9.12.66	558	23·25	21° 04' S 05° 58' E	73°	70°	S.S.E. *wind, force 4.* Moderate *sea and swell.* Few clouds, fine *and clear.*
10.12.66	572	22·88	13° 29' S 00° 03' W	73°	73°	S.S.E. *wind, force 4.* Moderate *sea and swell.* Cloudy and *clear.*
11.12.66	547	22·79	05° 58' S 05° 15' W	80°	79°	S.S.E. *wind, force 2 - 3.* Slight sea, low swell. Cloudy and *clear.*
12.12.66	551	22·96	01° 31' N 10° 32' W	84°	83°	07.14 *Vessel Crossed Equator in D.R. Longitude 09° 26' W.* S. x E. *wind, force 4.* Moderate sea and swell. Cloudy, fine and clear.
13.12.66	541	22·54	08° 54' N 15° 41' W	85°	80°	E.N.E. *wind, force 4.* Moderate sea and swell. Cloudy with *frequent rain squalls.* Good visibility.
14.12.66	548	22·83	17° 31' N 17° 45' W	75°	77°	04.30 *Passed Cape Verde, (most W'ly point of Africa.)* 05.30 *Passed Company's vessel "S.A. Vaal."* N.E. *wind, force 3.* Slight sea, low swell. Cloudy and clear.
15.12.66	536	22·33	26° 10' N 16° 01' W	67°	69°	N.E. *wind, force 5.* Rough sea, low swell. Few clouds, fine and *clear.* 19.45 *Arrived Las Palmas.*
16.12.66	365	20·51	31° 58' N 14° 03' W	66°	68°	00.03 *Departed Las Palmas.* 117 *First Class and 466 Tourist Class Passengers aboard.* N. x E. *wind, force 3.* Moderate sea, low swell. Cloudy and clear. 15.58 *Passed "Clan Ross."*
17.12.66	514	21·42	40° 06' N 10° 44' W	56°	60°	E.N.E. *wind, force 5.* Rough sea, heavy swell. Few clouds, fine and *clear.* 18.30 *Passed "Pendennis Castle."* 21.09 *Passed Cape Villano, entered Bay of Biscay.*
18.1.266	523	21·79	48° 05' N 05° 57' W	53°	55°	W.N.W. *wind, force 4.* Moderate sea, heavy swell. Overcast and *clear.* 13.50 *Passed Ushant Island, entered English Channel.*
19.12.66	261	17·40	At Southampton.			07.00 *Estimated time of arrival at berth, Southampton.*

Total Distance : Cape Town (Table Bay) to Southampton (Nab Tower) 5,975 miles.

Average Speed : 22·10 Knots.

R.M.S. "S. A. ORANJE"
CAPTAIN J. P. SMYTHE, D.S.C., R.D., R.N.R.
VOYAGE 122
LEAVING SOUTHAMPTON 11TH NOVEMBER 1966

Dear Mummy and Daddy,

Here is the usual posting list, plus one extra. There is also one of the transparencies in the sellotaped packet. Please could you get a copy of it made in Boots please (just the usual small size) and send it to me? Ta. It will probably take about 10 days, so perhaps you could send it out to me in South Africa, possibly Cape Town downcoast. By the way, the Mailing List does not show that we are going to Durban - don't panic - we are! The lists are typed in London and sent down to the ship and obviously someone boobed this time.

What else to report. I have been doing things while trying to type this, so now I am back on a different machine. I will be working in the First Class Bureau this voyage, as I told you. Angie Palmer and I are doing this changeover and are not too happy about it. However, there is absolutely nothing I can do about it, so we are trying to make the best of it. Actually, it should be quite fun, but there seems to be more typing this end, and less passenger work. I imagine we will change again next time.

What else. Oh yes, Mummy there is a cheque enclosed for you. Please buy yourself a dress (how about a blue crimplene one) and anything else that you need (shoes) and anything for Christmas that you usually buy. Them's orders!

The carpet is super in the cabin and so is the table. I put my record player in the Bureau Safe so didn't get it out until last night. Now it looks splendid on the table and my cabin looks rather plush I reckon. Someone gave me a white furry Bambi yesterday and that has antlers of red leather. That perches on the end of my bed. Angie bought me a fancy pincushion which is a fluffy white poodle on a red cushion, so that sits around the place too. What with Brer Rabbit, the bonk gonk Elaine gave me ages ago, and the new crowd, my cabin is beginning to be known as the zoo. People keep asking what it is like to wake up in the morning and find all those faces staring at me. I haven't noticed them yet. Can't think of anything more to tell you at the moment. Must go, someone is going to post this for me. Be seeing you. Love, Ann.

14.11.66, Monday, very near Las Palmas

Dear Family
Just to let you know I'm still alive and kicking. We have lots of passengers and life is hectic. We arrive at L.P. in an hour and that means more panic. It has been cool until today, and the ship has been rolling badly, yesterday in particular. I was given another present, a record I like called "Guantanamera", in the Hit Parade at the moment. Very good tune. Life is fair in the First Class Bureau, but there seems to be too much typing - I don't care for that. Haven't done any sewing yet.

Saw a large American Aircraft Carrier yesterday afternoon, going from the Med. to back home. Don't know the name. No more real news - it's too rushed for me to think clearly. Today is Las Palmas then 2 Cocktail Parties this evening. Tomorrow we start the real voyage (sunsets at sea, green flash, world news, etc. etc.) Must go. Be seeing you. Love, Ann.

At sea, 22nd November 1966.

Dear Mummy and Daddy,
Here we are, the day before Cape Town again and time as usual has just flown by. I put a new ribbon in my typewriter this morning and now sit and type and admire the words. So I made time to write a note to you. We seem to be fairly prepared for Cape Town arrival tomorrow morning, and so I thought I would drop you a line now while there is a chance. As usual, as far as I know, I am off duty tomorrow morning at 10 o'clock until 2.00 o'clock, so I expect I will go shopping in Cape Town and just potter

To start with the oddments from last week first, on Sunday last I had to sell poppies outside the Dining room at breakfast time and again just before Church time, for the British Legion. All part of the job. Had to wear a large cardboard tray round my front, you know the sort I mean. Felt a bit odd - tin box rather heavy, and had a slight list. Ship also rolling slightly so must have looked a bit odd. The service itself was very enjoyable.

During the week, can't remember offhand which day, they had Aquatic Sports on the tourist deck pool and I went and watched that for a few minutes. Our young David Howden in this Bureau was running it. One of the things is a greasy (soapy) pole across the pool. Two people have to edge their way along it from opposite sides and then have a sort of pillow fight, with a pillow filled with two balloons, the whole lot very wet, and try and knock the other one off the pole. It is very amusing. Took several pictures. Got a bit damp myself. On Wednesday, I think it was, we passed my old CAPETOWN CASTLE at sea, on a beautiful day at 11.30 in the morning. This is the first time we have ever met at such a short distance at sea. Even then she didn't come all that near. But we could just distinguish dark blobs which were people on the decks. Made my day. In fact, I received a telegram from Maureen and Bill on the ship.

On Saturday last we had the usual southbound Dinner and Dance, most unexpectedly, and had rather a good time. Being the First Class bird, I had to help with the Fancy Head Dress Parade and organise people to stand in the right place at the right time. I wore my long dress and had my hair done and felt dishy. The same evening we passed the TRANSVAAL CASTLE, lights blazing, at 7.30 p.m. She also looked rather fine.

On Sunday, Cozette had another of her Cheese and Wine parties just before lunch. It was very very good and we all flaked out in the afternoon. Another successful party died.

Yesterday, Monday, was the Childrens Fair and I also went to see something of what was going on at this. The kids each have a table stall, with things like Guess the Weight of the Child, Guess how many Smarties in this Jar, How many Candles can you light with one Match, Where is the Stowaway hiding, Name the Doll, etc. ad infinitum.

One big attraction was a Fortune Teller. He was hidden under a large flag and I queued to take my turn having my fortune told. He asked for 6d. and then asked if I wanted my fortune read in the crystal ball in the front of him, or read in my palm. I asked for a palm reading. He told me that I would not like Cape Town, would emigrate to Australia, my husband would not settle there and would go alone to America. I mentioned that I was not married, but he just shrugged and said, oh, well I soon would be. So my husband would stay in the States, and I would then return to England, buy a shop and run it and live in a little cottage very happily. The fortune teller was all of 12 years old. I felt I had got my money's worth!

This afternoon a bit earlier on I met Albert. Albert Ross you know. Known to seafarers as Albatross. One decided to hang around the ship, and did so. I was informed (my contacts are efficient) and managed to hang out of a porthole.

This is just about all the news from the ship at the moment, which reminds me - I still try to go and listen to the 6 o'clock World News with that memorable signature tune. Life is jogging along fairly quietly this voyage in fact. The work in this Bureau has been fair and I have certainly not been rushed off my feet, although I have had to work rather late on a couple of evenings and miss Entertainments. The work in fact is rather dull, and I feel just like a machine. A typing machine, with no personality. It's such a change after last voyage, and not one that I welcome really. However, we all get on extremely well and have a lot of laughs. At the moment I am being teased and called the lesser-spotted Purserette bird, flying around the Bureau. 25 points if you can catch me!

Time for Boat Drill now, so must go and get my white cardigan on. We are still in whites and enjoying it. The weather has been super, very hot and humid of course, but bearable and today is very very blue, although a bit chilly after last week. Sense of excitement and anticipation throughout the ship today - it's a lovely feeling.

Brer Rabbit has made lots of friends. My sewing is not going along very fast, but then I didn't expect that it would. Abbe (Nevard) gave me a small handbag frame - wasn't that lucky. It is just the size I would have liked to buy. By the way, those chrysanthemums (is that spelt right?) are still alive in my cabin and look fair for a few more days.

Well, that was Boat Drill, and a few more of the Ross family were seen around, all rather small but nevertheless the Ross sort. This evening we have a passenger Cocktail Party at 6.45, which we must attend. Should be all right. Then we will probably all be attending the Tourist Dance later tonight. Should be good. The Band are usually in fine form. I still play in the Band occasionally (well, with me on one side of them) when they do cha-cha's. I play a wooden thing like a corn cob, with 3 holes in it. I scratch its ribbed surface with a little wooden stick. Nice noise.

It is now 6.15 and things are rather hectic. Just what you might expect, with such a peaceful afternoon. I must seal this letter now and then I won't have to worry about it tomorrow. Hope there's a letter for me tomorrow morning. Be seeing you. Love, Ann.

P.S. It is now 11.30 and I have had my evening, all rather pleasant. The Cocktail Party wasn't too bad, the Dance was pretty good. The Band (I love them all) played Annie Laurie, as they usually do when I get there. Isn't that sweet of them! Makes me laugh. Then went for a drink and chat with Angie and 2 Vicars. Great fun. Now very tired. Must sleep, 6.15 start tomorrow. Goodnight. Ann xxx

Port Elizabeth (at the moment)
27th November 1966
Dear Family

This is the next instalment of what is now a saga - everything is quite fantastic. Today is Sunday and we ought to be leaving East London. It is now 8.45 p.m. and I am sitting in the Bureau waiting for us to sail from P.E. It all started I suppose on Thursday. We sailed from Cape Town late. We were supposed to leave at 10.30 a.m. but eventually left at 12.30, because of cargo loading. It was a lovely voyage but as usual it rolled a great deal that night. Naturally we were due to arrive late at P.E. so they decided we must have a Newspaper. It was my turn to do the News so lucky old me had to get up just after six o'clock. Nasty. The sky looked all grey and overcast and after finishing I went back to bed.

When we got up, all ready for arrival and mail and all that, we were told that there was a high wind and we couldn't enter the Harbour. In fact the wind was blowing at 60/70 m.p.h. It was quite fantastic. It was raining a little, and the surf was blowing upwards and so was the rain.

Everywhere on deck (they tell me) was wet, salty and sandy. The wind howled through the ship and made odd noises in the Bureau Square. We tried to anchor but couldn't, so cruised up and down for ages at 1.5 m.p.h. We eventually got in at 5.45 that evening. We were so relieved. Of course we still had the same amount of cargo to off-load and load so here we stayed, and stayed and stayed. Last night a crowd of us went to Macy's, a lovely place in town, for a meal. Had today off (my East London time off) and sunbathed and slept. Tried Operation Egg, trying to cook an egg on a metal sheet by the heat of the sun, but not successful. Must be patient. Today the sailing time was set for 6 o'clock. It came and they carried on with the cargo. Then they said 7, then 8, and now it is 9 o'clock and they are finally at Action Stations. Thank goodness the weather is fine.

Tomorrow we call at East London, as arranged, and arrive in Durban a day late. We will leave Durban on time (fingers crossed) so will miss some leave I expect. Shame. End of saga for today.

28th November At Sea

This is the next page of the story. It is now Monday at 5.30 (closing time) and we have just left East London (well, an hour ago). It was a beautiful day weather wise, and we arrived on time at 7.00 a.m. I worked until 10, then we had Boat Drill, then I was off at 10.30 until 3 o'clock. Sunbathed this morning, and got quite pink. Tried Operation Egg. Partial success. Half the top of the yolk went hard (it only took about 2 hours) and then Davey Haynes dropped it. The whole lot fell splosh on the deck. Ruination! It was hilarious. Actually, although the sun was hot, there was quite a breeze and this didn't help the operation. So we will try again another day.

Today I felt inspired. One of our favourite Engineers, Don Hunt, is in the Hospital with suspected jaundice. I gather he is feeling rather sorry for himself, so I wrote one of my verses for him. I shall let you have a copy of that. I am beginning to make my name on the ship at last (but what a way to do it!).

Oh yes, on the way out of Cape Town Harbour, we got a bit worried when a tiny plane flew around us several times, just missing our funnel and masts. Nasty. Then going round Cape Point way, we passed another Safmarine vessel, rather large and white and splendid, and then noticed another large Navy-type plane circling around us both. Then someone enlightened us. Apparently a tiny East London trawler had been lost in the area and the aircraft were both searching for it. Sadly, they didn't appear to find anyone, and nothing more has been heard of any survivors.

At Durban, 29th November 1966
Dear family

Well, we made it to Durban early in fact. Wonders will never cease, cause apparently there was quite a gale last night at sea, and even now the Harbour waters are rather rough, and wind-whipped.

Thank you for the letter this morning, and for the photograph.

There is something I thought about recently and that is the car at home. Someone mentioned a company in Southampton that is prepared to hire cars out to us sea-types quite reasonably. Someone had a Mini for 9 days during his leave and paid £9 approximately. This was just a lump sum, not calculated on miles and petrol. This sounds a bargain. I think I shall make some serious enquiries about it, and if there are no catches I think it might be worth hiring such a car, especially as it would be for all the leave. What do you think?

I could always ring Godfrey Davis if I wanted to cancel their car. Still, I will not do anything yet, and please could you leave the G. Davis car booked for me? Ta.

Is the film that you got back the one of John's wedding? I suppose it is. Looking forward to seeing it.

I am on duty today in Durban, but off this evening. I shall be going out for a meal as far as I know. Should be good. I am now waiting for my lunch and feel rather hungry. We sail tomorrow at 5 p.m. It should be interesting to see whether we do. We are not very full up going down Coast, which is pleasant. Life is dull this morning and now I can't think of anything more to say. I shall be working down Coast most of the time, so maybe I will get something to write about then. See you soon. Bought that dress yet Mummy? Love, Ann.

Port Elizabeth, 2nd December 1966
Dear family

What a crazy world this is. It is 8.50 a.m. on a bright Outspan-type South African morning and here I am writing my Christmas cards, and I have just finished them. We arrived here at 7 a.m. and opened the shop then. Had breakfast at 7.30 and then back to sell the odd stamp and consult my list of people to send cards to. So I typed the envelopes and wrote the cards, and now that's that job done.

Yesterday my chore for the day was to stick all my postcards in a scrap book. I bought a children's crayon book in Woolworths in Hounslow if you remember Mummy, and now I have stuck all my postcards in it. The pages are quite thick and different colours, and the cards look rather good.

As you can tell, I am not busy these days. I had time off up coast, as I told you, and now I have to work. And hard work it is too. Getting paste all over my hands, deciding whether I want to keep this or that particular card, and deciding whether to send this or that person a Christmas card. All very exhausting. But at least I am getting my odd jobs done.

Now for news. Well, I had my evening out in Durban, after working most of the day. Went out for a meal and dancing at a rather super place decorated in a slightly Spanish, castle sort of style, known of course at the Castilian Room. Wednesday we actually sailed from Durban on time, at 5 o'clock. We nearly fell off our Bureau stools with the shock of it all. We are all horribly pessimistic about sailing from any port on time now. They say we will sail from here this evening at 7 o'clock, but I'm sure we won't. At East London yesterday we managed to leave an hour late. I suppose we will get to Cape Town eventually.

At Sea, 3rd contd.

Dear family,

This just another useless type note, because we are at sea between P.E. and Cape Town and I have nothing to do. My desk is clear and my odd jobs are all done (for the moment anyway) and so I thought I would just do another page for the Cape Town letter home.

We are cruising along the Coast at the moment, and it is just like a pleasure cruise. The sea is a lovely shade of aquamarine, the coast is sandy and hilly, with occasional signs of habitation, mountains in the background and a pale blue sky. It is rather warm and there are not many people around. The ship is quite empty in fact We are in whites and expect to be, still, until Las Palmas.

We left P.E. last night only 1 hour late, not too bad. We just <u>knew</u> we wouldn't manage to leave on time, and we didn't. Last night I had an evening off and managed to get to bed fairly early. Didn't have to get up early this morning, so got up at 8 and had a shower then breakfast. Work at 9 and then odd clearing up jobs. Now David Howden and I have decided to be very good and do a rather necessary large checking job.

What I wanted to mention was certain passengers we had on the way out. I cannot remember if I told you about our famous film star. She used to be known as Clare Trevor and she was in the original version of "Stagecoach" with John Wayne. She is married to an American film-producer (Mr Milt Bren) and they were going to Johannesburg to make a film. She was very nice and had some gorgeous clothes. I did some typing for her husband (letters to Bette Davis, Los Angeles, Mr & Mrs John Wayne, Rock Hudson, etc.). He was slightly insane, but quite amusing.

Another thing that happened only the other day. One of my coastal passengers was leaving the ship at his port, and came to return his key to the Bureau. He suddenly slipped 5/- into my hot little hand, said "Buy yourself a drink on me, my dear, you've got a lovely smile". Wasn't that nice of him! He had been quite pleasant during his short time on here (I had only seen him during Bureau hours anyway) but there he was, giving me a slight gratuity. Always welcome. That made my day.

That was in Durban so I treated myself not to a drink, but to something I have wanted for a long while. It is a ring, made of some sort of African silver metal, engraved with little African animals. It is a fairly wide band, with a gap in it, so that it can be adjusted. There are five animals engraved on it, so you can imagine how tiny and beautiful they are. I'm very pleased with it, and grateful to the man who gave me the money. End of story.

Basil D'Oliveira, the cricketer, came on board in East London, and drank with his mates on here, mainly from the Radio Office. He passed me in the Bureau and said "Hullo, how are you" - contact with fame! We read in the paper about him and his cricket teams - the Aussies are over here at the moment, and on our day upcoast in P.E. they were playing an Eastern Province team in P.E. All the keen cricketing Officers headed in the same direction that day. It's funny how big a part the Mailship plays in the life of this Coast. We take everyone everywhere, and always seem to make news, not just our ship, but all the Mailships.

Cape Town, Monday 5th December
Dear M and Da,

I'm sitting in the Bureau absolutely glowing after a super day in the sun on a beautiful beach in the middle of nowhere. The day started at 10 o'clock when four of us headed by car down towards the Cape peninsula. The weather started out cloudy but soon cleared and the sun blazed down on us. We took the coastal route and came first to Hout Bay where there is quite an important fishing and canning industry. Bought some snoekies and drove a bit further on and up mountain road and then walked onto promontory and ate fish and took pictures and just rested. It's very energy-consuming just sitting in a car on a hot day!

Then we went further south and headed for Buffles Bay. It was absolutely gorgeous. Fine white sand, green sea, a little creamy surf, and mountains behind us. When we arrived the local fishermen were just finishing loading their catch onto a local lorry to take away and sell presumably. The little boats (well, three of them) were drawn up on the sand, and the men were taking fish out of the nets in the boats, hitting the fish on the head and putting them into wicker baskets. The baskets then went on the lorry. The nets were spread out to dry and that was that for the day. Away they went and we were the only people left in the world.

Had a large picnic lunch and then strolled and rested for the rest of the afternoon. Lots of marine life, including live and dead anemones. Got some lovely shells. We left there just before 4, and went a bit further down the road, inside the Nature Reserve. Guess what we saw on the roadside? Some zebra, just wandering about grazing stripily. Yes, real live zebra, in their natural habitat, as they say, with a baby one nearby. Couldn't believe my eyes. As you can imagine, that made my day right at the start.

So we went down right to the Cape Point and climbed the 100 steps to the top of the point, and stood puffing for some time. The view was quite wonderful. It was fairly hazy and we couldn't see across False Bay, but we could see quite well, all the way up the Cape Peninsula back to Table Mountain. It was beautiful.

I had to be back on duty at 6 so we had a great rush back here, and I managed to change in 2 minutes. Now I am sitting here absolutely on fire, to tell the truth. I am longing for a shower and to sit down and rest, because the sand feels everywhere about me. But wasn't it worth it. It was a beautiful day.

Actually I had most of yesterday off too, so I feel rather lucky. (It's not that I have more time off than anyone else - I just have most of mine in Cape Town downcoast. I call that clever planning!) Yesterday one of the bods in here had time off also and so we organised picnic lunch and went to town. First we caught the bus from the Dockside to the local Bus Station. We went halfway round the world, it seemed, and finally arrived in a part of town I'd never seen before. We walked along Adderley Street and into the Botanical Gardens, which were in full flower. There were lots of hydrangeas and other large colourful flowers in large beds, and large green lawns, which we could not walk on. There were rose beds as well, but not like England. The gardens are huge and extend up the side of the start of the Mountain for a very long way. We walked all the way up, stopping for lunch beside a rose bed, with pigeons walking around, and wandering along paths to super white-painted buildings which are museums and art galleries and churches. Then we walked out of the gardens and through Parliament Square.

At the bottom of the town again we decided to go to Cape Town Castle. Yes, there really is one. It is a pentagonal shaped place, which is now just outer walls with five towers. One is called Oranje Tower and we walked up to the top and looked over the walls. Canons poke out at intervals and grassy slopes lead up the side of the walls outside. These are a mass of colour now. One flower bed says "1866" which is when the Castle was built by Simon van der Stel, Governor of the Cape at the time, to protect the city from invaders. It is now a barracks although visitors are allowed inside part of the buildings. Across the centre is a building of rooms now housing pictures, art treasures etc. and on the outside is a balcony where old Simon and Co. used to make their speeches to the people and all that. All very impressive, with white walls, brown Dutch-style frontings and gold knobs on the balcony edges. Green lawns in front just complete the picture. Very peaceful.

After sitting on the grass on top of the Oranje tower and waiting for David Howden to have a 10 minute snooze and wake up, I discovered the grass was full of ants, so we decided to come home and get some tea. Our dogs were barking something 'orrible, and we simply wanted to get a drink and rest. So back to the ship and into the Cafe on the corner of the quay. It is an odd place, they sell everything in the way of food and drink if you want an odd snack, and this is where we order our fruit. So we had a Coca-Cola, then came onto the ship and had some tea. Then I went to bed until dinnertime, and then there was a riotous party. It started off with Christmas carols, progressed to Welsh hymn-singing at the Albert Hall, then to Black and White Minstrel songs and then David Padmore started playing tunes on his accordion. He plays very well indeed so that gets everyone singing. It was a very good, hoarse-making, party, in the Nursing Sister's cabin. Bed rather late.

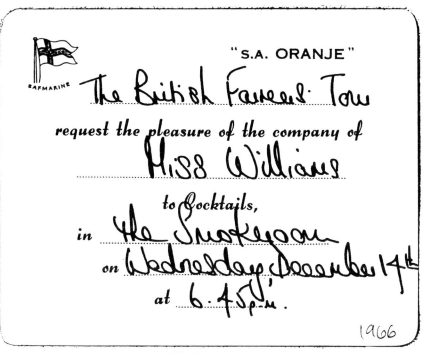

"S.A. ORANJE"

The British Farewell Tour

request the pleasure of the company of

Miss Williams

to Cocktails,

in the Smokeroom

on Wednesday, December 14th

at 6.45 p.m.

1966

The Invitation

S.A. ORANJE

The Party

I really think this must be all I have time for, or can think of.

Oh yes, yesterday morning, guess what happened with arrival here. It was foggy. The hooter started about 4.30 a.m. and we parked outside the Harbour and just waited for it to clear. So much for our 7 a.m. alongside arrival. I got up to see what was happening and then went back to bed. It was all quite civilised in the end. I got 4 letters, and was the envy of everyone in the Bureau. Thank you for the two from you. I hoped you had got something from me.

Well, that's just about it for this letter. I can see that it is nearly time to finish, so I will finish this off and say see you at Christmas. Hooray for a shower and a little drink and a rest.

Be seeing you. Take care, especially in all that nasty weather you seem to be having. Take brandy - pretend (like me) that you are a St. Bernard. Love, Ann xxx

At sea, 14 December
Dear Family

Just thought that I would type a note to tell you about the odd things that have happened on the way home, so far. And there have been several.

It started with the First Class cocktail party after Cape Town. We have a tour group of people on board who are British Farmers from the West Country travelling out with us to Cape Town, quick flip round South Africa, visiting farms etc. and home again with us, so they invited us to a Cocktail Party. Then there were the 2 Tourist Class Cocktail Parties. Saw a man with glasses that I recognised and went to talk to him. He said he had travelled with us before, in May. He had a strange job - he was a chicken sexer and had his own company. Wealthy man. I felt a bit embarrassed and didn't like to ask him too much about it. (Could just imagine him tossing a chick from one hand to another and guessing its sex.). He offered me a job Mummy if I left the sea, but I think there was more to his offer than that.

Then there was the Dinner and Dance First Class on Saturday evening last. This was earlier in the voyage than usual, but "they" decided to hold it then. Wore my long dress, had my hair done, and did my usual First Class job of assisting with the Fancy Head Dress Parade after dinner. 3 men dressed up as the Magnificent Men in their Flying Machines (the film is being shown tonight) and had paper windmills on their heads. I was so impressed with the windmills, that 2 of the men gave me theirs. I have one in my cabin on the bulkhead, and one in the Bureau attached to a moving light - it blows happily in the air from the punkah. Little things please little minds. (Laughter line: someone asked me for a suggestion for a costume head dress. I suggested she wore her normal clothes, and walked all to one side, leaning over sideways, if you see what I mean. I said she could be a Passenger List.) End of joke.

There was a tremendous party after the dinner dance and 3.30 a.m. found several of us sitting in the Purser's cabin singing the 23rd Psalm, and trying to get the descant right. It was Church the next day, so we had to try.

By the way we have a stowaway on board. He got on in Cape Town and turned up 24 hours later. He was wearing all his winter woollies while everyone else was in whites, and looked a bit odd, so they tell me. Talk about history repeating itself - this happened on the TRANSVAAL on my first voyage, remember?

Also there is a woman on board who is expecting a baby in the extremely near future. Phil. reckons it will arrive Las Palmas night. Should be quite interesting. It's against all the rules, having her on board in that condition, but she seems to have got round the Consul, in Cape Town, and so our medical staff were given wrong information.

Crossing the Line went off very well on Monday, but in the afternoon the weather distinguished itself. We had a tropical rainstorm to end all rainstorms. There was thunder, lightning, rain, foghorn, wet, noise, floods, me and Phil on the Sundeck in our swimming costumes getting soaked just for the hell of it, and a man running round the Sundeck chasing a bar of soap, with which he was washing himself while the rain was torrenting down on us all. The soap kept slipping out of his hand and sliding away, so he had to chase it. I believe he caught it.

This morning - guess what I did. I went to see the Gold, in the Bullion Room. Yes, I actually did. Father (Captain Smythe) always goes down there every morning at 9.30 a.m. and this morning I plucked up courage and asked him if I could come with him, and the Purser. He didn't know what to say at first, then smiled and said "Nosey, all right, come along then!" So off we went, single file, Master at Arms, Father, one small Purserette and Purser. Down to the depths of the ship and lots of unlocking of doors, clanking, cool air, and suddenly the last door swung open and there it was: lots of blocks of gold (they said) in wooden boxes, with steel bands. Two nuggets in one box, each box worth £5,000. Total gold in boxes in Bullion Room at present - £9,700,000. I touched it. Father said if I could carry one I could have it (I wonder if he meant it?) - and I tried and of course I couldn't lift it. So that was my big excitement of the day. My favourite Deck Officer told me later he had "smoothed the way" with Captain Smythe by mentioning how I would love to see the gold!

Actually, this afternoon I went with Cozette and the Staff Commander ("Lofty" Lofts) to judge the kids Fancy Dress. It was fun - it always is and the kids always look sweet. We get a free bar of chocolate out of it, and a lot of amusement.

Yesterday was Boat Drill at 4.30 and after that we saw dozens and dozens of porpoises, all having the time of their lives. We have never seen so many.

Well, that was yesterday. I saw the film last night and had a big laugh. We will be in Las Palmas at 8 this evening, leaving at midnight, fingers crossed. Blues tonight, and the rest of the time. Shame, but it is suddenly much cooler. Soon be home, then winter and Christmas. I'm looking forward to seeing you although you may see me before you get this letter. Love, Ann.

OPERATION EGG

OPERATION PARTICIPANTS:

Mr David Haynes
Miss Abbe Nevard
Miss Ann Williams

OPERATION:

1.   Mr. Haynes will survey the weather
at 0930 on 25.11.66 (Operation Day).

2.   Mr. Haynes will report weather conditions
to Miss Nevard and Miss Williams.

3.   If Mr. Haynes considers weather conditions
satisfactory, he will place clean metal sheet
on Sundeck in place suitable for successful
operation.

4.   If weather satisfactory (i.e. hot, dry and not
too windy) Operations Party to meet on
Sundeck at 12.30.

5.   If weather conditions not considered
satisfactory, Operation postponed.

6.   At 12.30 party to meet on Sundeck.

7.   Miss Williams to produce three Operation
subjects and place individually on metal sheet.

8.   Operation to be surveyed by all other party members.

9.   Events to be closely studied by all party
members, and recorded for posterity by
Miss Williams.

10.   Operation Egg to be judged a success or
not a success.

D O N

This is just a note for Don,
Who from our midst has "upped and gone".
"He's engineered a change" they said,
"You'll find him in a hospital bed."

I asked our Phil. about the fellow,
And she said "Well, he's rather yellow!
He also talks of things he's seen,
Today it was a submarine*."

"He talks about a lifeboat class,
Somehow he doesn't think he'll pass**.
Although he wanted to be C.L.***
I told him he must just get well."

You lucky man, you'll get a rest,
Attention of the very best.
Old Rog. and Phil. are quite a team,
You'll think you're living in a dream.

Don't worry any more, C.D.****,
Just think how well you're going to be.
With love from all of us to you,
We hope you'll soon be good as new.

With luv from Ann, 28.11.66

*   Don goes mad over the Beatles song "Yellow Submarine"
**   He was taking his Lifeboat Certificate this voyage.
***   C.L. stands for Certificated Lifeboatman
**** C.D. stands for chrome dome - Don is bald on top, curly
      round the edges, known to all as C.D.

" S.A. ORANJE "

Captain J. P. SMYTHE, D.S.C., R.D., R.N.R.

From SOUTHAMPTON to CAPE TOWN via LAS PALMAS.

VOYAGE 123   **December 30th, 1966 to January 11th, 1967**

Date	Distance Run	Ave. Speed	Lat. | Long.	Temperature Air	Sea	REMARKS
30.12.66	—	—	At Southampton	50°	- °	13.00 *Vessel Departed Southampton.* 142 *First Class and* 464 *Tourist Class Passengers aboard. W'ly wind, force 2. Cloudy with moderate visibility.* 24.00 *Rounded Ushant Island, entered Bay of Biscay.*
31.12.66	449	21·28	44° 55' N 08° 32' W	56°	56°	*S. W'ly wind, force 5. Moderate sea and swell. Cloudy and clear.* 15.30 *Passed Cape Villano, left Bay of Biscay.*
1.1.67	541	22·54	36° 26' N 12° 23' W	59°	62°	*W.S.W. wind, force 1-2. Rippled sea, low S.W'ly swell. Fine and clear.*
2.1.67	520	22·13	At Las Palmas	66°	67°	*E. x N. wind, force 2. Slight sea, low swell. Few clouds and clear,* 13.24 *Arrived at berth, Las Palmas.* 17.00 *Departed Las Palmas.* 148 *First Class and* 473 *Tourist Class Passengers aboard.*
3.1.67	408	22·05	21° 44' N 17° 45' W	68°	66°	*E'ly wind, force 3. Slight sea, low N.E'ly swell. Overcast and dull.*
4.1.67	542	22·58	12° 44' N 17° 30' W	76°	74°	05.35 *Passed R.M.S. "Edinburgh Castle."* 06.30 *Passed Cape Verde, (most W'ly point of Africa.) N.E'ly wind, force 3. Slight sea, low swell. Cloudy and clear.*
5.1.67	547	22·79	05° 09' N 12° 50' W	84°	85°	*Light airs Rippled sea, low swell. Slight haze, good visibility.*
6.1.67	536	22·33	01° 55' S 07° 24' W	81°	80°	05.17 *Vessel Crossed Equator in D.R. Longitude 08° 55' W. S.E'ly wind, force 3. Slight sea, low S.W'ly swell. Cloudy and clear.*
7.1.67	528	22·00	08° 57' S 02° 08' W	78°	78°	*S.E'ly wind, force 3. Slight sea, low swell. Cloudy and clear.*
8.1.67	535	22·29	16° 05' S 03° 18' E	74°	74°	*S.E'ly wind, force 3-4. Moderate sea, low S.E'ly swell. Overcast and clear.*
9.1.67	508	22·09	22° 57' S 08° 32' E	71°	71°	*S.E. wind, force 4. Moderate sea, low S'ly swell. Overcast and clear.*
10.1.67	492	21·39	29° 29' S 14° 01' E	67°	68°	*S.E. wind, force 5. Moderate sea, heavy swell. Overcast and clear.*
11.1.67	349	19·94	At Cape Town.			06.00 *Estimated time of arrival at Cape Town.*

Total Distance: Southampton (Needles) to Cape Town (Table Bay) 5,955 miles.

Average Speed : 21·97 Knots.

" S.A. ORANJE "

Captain J. P. SMYTHE, D.S.C., R.D., R.N.R.

From CAPE TOWN to SOUTHAMPTON via LAS PALMAS.

VOYAGE 123   **January 25th to February 6th, 1967**

Date	Distance Run	Ave. Speed	Lat. | Long.	Temperature Air	Sea	REMARKS
25.1.67	—	—	At Cape Town	67°	-°	16.17 *Vessel Departed Cape Town. 65 First Class and 290 Tourist Class Passengers aboard. S. W. wind, force 2. Few clouds, fine and clear.* 22.15 *Passed " Capetown Castle."*
26.1.67	448	21·86	28° 24' S 12° 34' E	70°	74°	*S. W'ly wind, force 3. Slight sea, low S. W'ly swell. Cloudy and clear.*
27.1.67	580	23·20	20° 52' S 05° 56' E	76°	74°	*S. E'ly wind, force 4 - 5. Moderate sea, low swell. Cloudy, fine and clear.*
28.1.67	530	22·08	13° 50' S 00° 25' E	77°	75°	*S. E'ly wind, force 2 - 3. Slight sea, low swell. Cloudy and clear.*
29.1.67	535	22·39	06° 34' S 04° 49' W	80°	80°	*S. E'ly wind, force 1. Slight sea, low swell. Cloudy, fine and clear.*
30.1.67	546	22·75	00° 51' N 09° 55' W	80°	81°	09.17 *Vessel Crossed Equator in D.R. Longitude 09° 22' W. S. x E. wind, force 3. Slight sea, low swell. Overcast and clear.*
31.1.67	520	21·25	08° 04' N 14° 50' W	83°	79°	*N. W'ly wind, force 1. Rippled sea, low swell. Cloudy, fine and clear.*
1.2.67	530	22·08	16° 00' N 17° 49' W	71°	64°	08.30 *Passed Cape Verde, (most W'ly point of Africa.)* 08.45 *Passed Company's vessel " S.A. Vaal." N'ly wind, force 3 - 4. Slight sea, low swell. Cloudy, fine and clear.*
2.2.67	529	22·04	24° 42' N 16° 43' W	64°	65°	*N.E'ly wind, force 3 - 4. Moderate sea, low N.E'ly swell. Cloudy fine and clear.* 23.45 *Arrived Las Palmas.*
3.2.67	364	20·85	30° 29' N 14' 36' W	65°	64°	04.13 *Departed Las Palmas. 76 First Class and 295 Tourist Class Passengers aboard. N. x E. wind, force 4 - 5. Moderate sea and swell. Cloudy, fine and clear.*
4.2.67	530	22·08	38° 58' N 11° 36' W	60°	57°	*W'ly wind, force 4. Moderate sea and swell. Few clouds, fine and clear.*
5.2.67	525	21·88	47° 00' N 06° 54' W	50°	55°	01.00 *Passed Cape Villano, entered Bay of Biscay. W'ly wind, force 3 - 4. Moderate sea and swell. Cloudy, fine and clear.* 17.20 *Passed Ushant Island, entered English Channel.*
6.2.67	329	19·94	At Southampton.			08.00 *Estimated time of arrival at berth, Southampton.*

Total Distance :   Cape Town (Table Bay) to Southampton (Nab Tower) 5,969 miles.

Average Speed : 21·95 Knots.

M.S. "S. A. ORANJE"
VOYAGE 123
CAPTAIN J. P. SMYTHE, D.S.C., R.D., R.N.R.
LEAVING SOUTHAMPTON 30TH DECEMBER 1966

Las Palmas, 2nd January 1967
Dear family

It's the night before Las Palmas, so here goes with odd news. There isn't much, and there certainly isn't much time. Life is extremely hectic, specially in the Tourist Class Bureau. The new 2nd Purser John McFadyen is very nice and we get on well. Mr Connelly is still Purser, another pleasant man. We are full up with people. The ship has been rolling rather a lot too, and lots of passengers have been ill. Last night was a New Year's Eve Dance both ends, and tame it all was. I was going to bed early, but had to help with Father Time and Miss 1967. Went to bed straight after. I don't feel too well, as I have a cold. The ship is hot and stuffy, so I feel a bit sorry for myself. It should be better in a day or two.

Hope your New Year's Eve "do" was good. I was thinking of you frequently during the night. And did you enjoy yourselves on Friday night? Nothing more for now, so goodnight.
X
a.m. no time to write. Take care, love Ann.

Monday 9th, at sea.
Dear family

Something rather touching and nice has just happened to me, so I thought I would tell you about it.

First of all, I'm well, although my cold seems to be coming and going rather frequently. It was fine in the heat, as I expected, but now it is much cooler (we're still in whites) and I have the sneezes and sniffles. Ugh. However, the voyage is progressing extremely well. We have one or two new people on here, all very good company. Las Palmas was very hot as usual, and I sold millions of Spanish stamps from 4.30 p.m. on Sunday til 6 p.m. and then all day Monday until we sailed. Then it was Cocktail Parties Tourist Class, then the voyage had really started. The passengers on here are marvellous and I really feel at home down the 'slum' end. Must be my upbringing!

The time has flown past and it is hard to believe that we get to Cape Town the day after tomorrow. Today at 5 p.m. we had the Prize giving, done by Father, aided by the Sports Committee, and us 2 from the Bureau. We dished out the prizes, and the Chairman of the Committee got up to say thank you to Father, and then suddenly said thank you to John and Ann and 'I have a little present for each of them, here you are - thank you for all your hard work'. We were both absolutely flabbergasted and rather confused. It was so sweet of them and quite unnecessary. However, it is very pleasant when someone does say thanks. I know it's all part of the job, but .... Guess what my gift was. You won't. It was Miss Dior Perfume atomiser! It must have cost a bomb, but it is my favourite perfume and I'm very grateful.

Nothing much else to report - the weather has been fine - what I've seen of it - and the Crossing the Line do went off well, even with a few very large and heavy drops of rain in the middle of it, from the only 2 clouds in the sky. I managed to get a little sun on two afternoons, but work has been a bit hectic.

Opened the Bureau one day and found a small wigwam handed in for lost property. Someone took a picture of me peeping out of the entrance! I took a picture of John holding a handful of money.

Today was much more organised, and tomorrow should be a bit nasty. Still, then it is Cape Town, and letters. I wanted a letter on Sunday and of course I couldn't have one. Had to be patient. Only one more day then news. More tomorrow.

Well, this tomorrow has come. It is Tuesday afternoon - I feel it is the lull before the storm. The ship and sea is fairly calm - but we are bobbing about a bit. I forgot to tell you that the other day I saw some whales blowing. I had taken one of my Bridge visiting parties up to the Bridge and suddenly there was a shout, and we all rushed to look at the whales blowing. I also saw a very large fish jumping out of the water, that the Chief Officer thought might well be a swordfish. He didn't know, and nor did I, but we decided it might be one!

Then on Saturday I think it was, they had the annual Rocket Firing practice. I was asked to attend after showing great interest (they hadn't much option) so at 4.15 I went up to the Bridge. The X/2nd showed a rocket, the holder and line attached, and fired one off. It fell into the sea, at some distance from the ship. Then he asked the Cadet to fire one also. Unfortunately the rocket exploded in the canister when he fired it and cut his chin and body rather a bit. Poor chap was stunned and had to be rushed to the Doctor, given a sedative and put to bed, all deaf and cut up.

It made an extremely loud bang, and there was clouds of grey smoke all around us. I was standing safely in the wheelhouse all the time, except for the actual demonstration loading, and then when all this smoke and bang appeared, and a large flashing object hurtled towards us, we all ran to the other side of the Bridge. Nasty, very nasty. It hit the deck, burning a large hole; the Security man appeared with a fire extinguisher; bits of paint, 20 years thick, flew off the wing of the Bridge paintwork where the metal can hit it, and people flew everywhere else, out of the way. The lucky thing about it, if anything, was that the rocket did not hit the wing of the Bridge, but exploded in the air - it could have come straight back at that short distance and killed several people who had to be near at the time. Father was sheltering near me at the time (until I ran) and he was most upset. It was all very unpleasant. We all kept our distance when they next sent up two flares. That was the end of fireworks for that day and the year!

Cape Town
Well, here we are again, and thank you for the letter this morning. It was very welcome. I wonder if it has snowed by now - poor you if it has. It is 10 o'clock in the morning and seems to be fine outside - haven't seen it since 6.15! I hope Elaine is better now. Thanks for taking the gift to Marian, and the money to Doreen. Haven't heard from either of them yet. It is so quiet and everyone has gone ashore, passenger-wise. I am off after lunch and shall rush down the gangway, then back for duty this evening. I'll write again soon. Take care. love, Ann.

Saturday 14th January, Port Elizabeth
Dear family

Thank you for the letter yesterday - I was one of the few lucky people to get one. Ta.

Just to bring you up to date with the latest happenings, you might like to know about us leaving Cape Town etc. We were in the harbour with the PENDENNIS and the REINA DEL MAR.

The REINA was due to sail on Wednesday at 2 o'clock, but did not leave until 5 o'clock. Then there was a rather high wind, which blew rather a lot, despite the tugs helping her out of the Harbour, and she swung round, straight towards the quayside on one side of the harbour. We were all gazing fascinated from our Prom. Deck, as she got nearer and nearer the quay.

The anchors were hurled down, the engine went into reverse, obviously in a great big hurry, and she went on and on and on. Then suddenly when people started running quickly away from the quayside, she seemed to stop, the anchors dragged but she finally did stop, and the little tugs threw themselves through the water to rush to her side to push her away. We were informed later that she had been 20 feet away in fact at the front end and 50 feet at the blunt end. All rather dramatic anyway. The ship seems to have a jinx on it.

It took us an hour to get out of the harbour when we sailed on Thursday at 10.30 a.m. because of the manoeuvres necessary to counteract the wind, but at least we did it. We rolled all the way round the coast to Port Elizabeth, and heaved into our berth just after 9 o'clock yesterday morning. It was my day off and did I enjoy it. I left the Bureau at about 10.30, changed and went to sunbathe up top, after having my elevenses of beef tea. Took my yellow dress sewing up there and even managed to do some of it. I have put the sleeves in now and part of the zip. Should be wearable one of these days I suppose. Then we had another Thirst Aid party on the Sun deck - Davey doing his reviving act with the brandy, ice and ginger. Lovely, then I went to bed, until just after 4. Such luxury. Got up, showered, washed my hair, nattered to Abbe, and got dressed ready to go out. Then we had a lovely piece of news. Our present Chief Officer is being transferred at Durban to be Master of a cargo ship, so all our Deck people are being up-graded. That means that Davey will now be Chief Officer on the way home. We are all very pleased about it. He is thrilled to bits, and rather surprised about it all.

Then we went out to the Marine Hotel nearby. It is about 5 miles along the coast and the restaurant is the Skyroof, 7 floors up in the sky. It had super food and a dance floor and good band, and I got slightly merry and had a super time. Got back extremely late and feel like death warmed up at this moment. And it's quite warm.

Something funny happened there. We had a table for 2 by the window and a bottle of Reisling. At one point we went to dance and then came back to the table. Just after we sat down the man at the table next to us got up, went to the ice bucket with our bottle in it and proceeded to pour himself a glassful! We were all put out. The waiter rushed over (like a guardian angel) and told the man that it was not his wine, and we continued to watch with interest. The waiter took the bottle away from him, and put the remainder back in the ice bucket. Then this large, loud-spoken man, had the cheek to turn round to us, and in a leering confiding manner, jokingly told of how he had in front of him a glass of someone's wine.

He roared with laughter, and I spluttered to myself. Davey let him finish then said, yes I know, it's <u>our</u> wine. The look on the man's face was a picture! You can imagine it. He recovered himself, gave another roar of laughter and turned his back hastily. Then it was our turn to laugh, 'cause we thought it was hilarious. However, some time later, he sent a half bottle of wine to our table in apology! The whole scene was classic, I thought. I haven't laughed so much for a long time.

Are you better now, Mummy? The brandy certainly seemed to do something to you writing my letter. Quite funny - I can just imagine you saying everything. You seem a long way away at the moment though, both of you. Wish you could be here - it's nice and warm, and the sun is shining and the sky is blue. Just what you could both do with. It's all a bit unfair.

Well, my cold seems to have gone (I reckon it must have been drowned) and I am getting rather a pleasant coating of sunshine. Don't seem to be able to eat much these days, but never mind. Life is as pleasant as usual, even with the prospect of Tombola this evening. Never mind, soon be Durban and then Cape Town, and time off again. And I'm off tomorrow in East London (how exciting!) so I can catch up on sleep then, I hope.

See you soon, take care of yourselves. Love, Ann.

East London, Sunday 15th

Hullo there. I reckon I'm doing very well for letters these days. Thank you for the letter this morning - a real letter too. I always expect aerogrammes (they're cheaper) so I don't usually look for a plain envelope.

I wonder what you are going to do about your holiday. I think you will have to be firm about the sunshine by the sound of it. You can't just endure something second-best because Aunty Doris wants something else. It's your holiday too! End of preaching. I liked the pun about being in the pink, or brown, your humour is quite good Mummy.

By now I suppose you will have got the ciné camera back, working properly. And I hope the car is all right.

It is only 9.15 and I'm yawning happily whilst typing this. I'm off duty at 10 and then the Chief Engineer, Ron Crook, is taking me on an Engine Room visit. That should be interesting. I suppose I had better do some work now - I'll tell you more later.

Later.
Well, I've had my engine room visit and now it is getting very late and I haven't time to write much before the ship sails from here. The engine room was very hot, and the fridge-plant was very cold. I have just been given a lychee (is that how they are spelt) and it tasted quite interesting. Have you ever eaten one, Daddy?

This morning I sunbathed until lunchtime, then went to my little bed. I've just got up (3 o'clock) and we sail at 4 o'clock.

Must post this here, then more in Durban. It's Davey's birthday on Tuesday so several of us are going out to celebrate. Should be fun. Tell you more another time. Take care. Love, Ann.

Durban Wed. 18th
Dear family

Can't remember for sure where I got to with the news. I think I must start with arrival Durban. Thank you for the letter there, it was full of bits and pieces. About my letter from the income tax bods, please will you open it and if it happens to be my rebate, please could you send it to the bank, as they are expecting it. If it isn't, never mind. Ta.

On Monday I had the day off, and very good it was too. I went to the Indian Market in the morning and bought myself a bracelet. Do you remember me mentioning that I wanted to buy a topaz bracelet to match my ring? I have been looking for a long time, and now have one. It is rolled gold with small topaz stones between links. Very dainty and attractive I think. I'm very pleased with it.

Had to barter with a man but got it for a <u>very</u> reasonable price, considering. I'm wearing it at the moment. Then I went pottering around the main shopping centre on my own, having gone with David Howden to the Indian Market.

Got back after lunch, so then went to sleep. Woke up at 4 o'clock because I was expecting a visitor. Guess who it was. Again, you can't, so I'll tell you. It was Tony Edwards, from the CAPETOWN CASTLE last year, last seen in London during the strike, now Chief Steward/Assistant Purser on the KINPURNIE CASTLE, currently loading in Durban!

He had rung me up in the morning and asked if he could come over and see me and the rest of the crowd. So he came for tea. Caught up on all sorts of gossip. He also invited me out to lunch yesterday, so he picked me up at 12.30 (I was on duty all day until 5.30) and we went to one of the restaurants right on the beachside. It was a super hot day and lovely to be away from the ship. Got back about 2 and decided to keep the Bureau closed for a little longer. This is the first time we have had to open the Tourist Bureau in Durban and it is a one-man band. So if I decide to close it, it stays closed, if I'm on duty. I rested until 3 then came back and somehow managed to exist until 5.30. It is so hot and humid it's almost unbearable. One feels rather irritable. Phil. has just looked in and sends her love. I am gobbling my salt tablets but I still feel very 'ot and 'orrible.

However, where did I get to. Finished work then washed hair and had cup of coffee with Abbe and Cozette. Dried hair and admired Angie's suntan and had more interruptions with people popping in and out of cabin. Somehow managed to shower and have 5 minutes rest on bed, then big discussions with Phil. about what to wear for our big evening out.

As it was Davey's birthday we had arranged to go out (me, him, Phil. and Phil. - all very confusing as both called 'Phil'.) and we went to the Edward Hotel which is a splendid hotel on the beach front. Dinner and dancing was the order of the day. It was great fun and we all enjoyed it. Then a midnight stroll along the beach (how romantic can you get) with the Indian Ocean waves pounding on the shore, feeling very hot. Back to ship and drinks, then late to bed. Lovely birthday I thought. First day of Davey being Chief Officer too.

Another thing while I remember it. I have written a letter to Woolston Garage Ltd., of 170 Portsmouth Road, Southampton, booking a car for 6th/15th February at those lovely cheap rates I told you about. I have thought about this quite carefully, and decided to try it this time home. I have asked them to confirm the booking to me at Las Palmas, so I hope they will.

I have written to Mrs Van der Byl and said I would ring her when we dock in Cape Town on Sunday, because I would like to go and see her on the Sunday. Hope she says I can go then.

Oh yes, I swapped some of my unfortunate Christmas smelly presents in Boots in Southampton before we sailed. I bought a record with the money - an LP (cheap of course) of Strauss waltzes and polkas. It's got things like the Tritch Tratch polka on it and so on - lovely and stirring.

Well it's sailing day Durban and I must work, I'll write again in a day or two. Take care of yourselves, and I hope the weather stays fair. Love, Ann.

Cape Town, Monday, 23rd January 1967
Dear family,

Thank you for the lovely letter yesterday morning. I was very amused by it all, especially the way Mummy was cut off in mid-sentence.

I know I haven't written since Durban but really nothing happened at East London or P.E. to warrant any note at all. I was on duty all the time and did nothing much except write letters and read my book.

One thing though, after leaving P.E. on Friday evening. The sky was beautifully clear on the landside, but stormy on the sea side, and about an hour after we left it was still light but on the sea-side there was a beautiful rainbow. It was very wide, and looked lovely. Then on Saturday we had our one coastal day at sea and it was rather bumpy, and I didn't feel too good.

I was up at 6 o'clock yesterday (Sunday) and the view from my porthole was super: the 12 Apostles, Table Mountain and the sea, in three slightly different shades of purple and silver and grey. The mist was down you see and blended the sky, mountains and sea together. Lovely. Then we got the Pilot and the Mail and there was my letter. Ta. I always like the Cape Town letter because by that time you have heard from me and you know how it goes.

Davey says thank you for the best wishes about being Chief Officer. He is very pleased about it of course, though rather worried about the job - he has all the responsibility of the cargo loading. He looks rather weighed down with it all these days, especially with all the extra gold braid!

Anyway, I was off duty at 10 yesterday so I telephoned the Van der Byls. I was immediately invited to spend the day with them, and the Archdeacon would pick me up at 11.45. So I had a big rush to finish the hem of my new yellow dress and press it in time to wear. But at long last you will be pleased to know that my yellow dress is wearable!

Sir collected me and we set off up the Mountain, passing on the way a very large white Italian cruise ship on her maiden voyage, dressed overall, just berthing in the harbour, named Eugenio C. Very large and luxurious, by the look of it.

Then it was sherry time at the Rectory and I met a lady staying there for the weekend. Her name was Miss Cowdray, and guess what, she is a great friend of Matty Read, ex-Personnel Officer at I.C.I. Paints Division in Slough, remember me speaking of her? Talk about a coincidence. Miss Read retired from I.C.I. last year, as you may remember me saying, and set off round the world to see her relations and friends abroad. She stayed with Miss Cowdray in Cape Town. How about that!

We had lunch and then I was offered a bed for the afternoon. You wouldn't have wanted me to refuse their hospitality, I thought, so what else could I say but thank you and retire for the afternoon. They told me I was family, and the family always slept on a Sunday afternoon. I slept for 2 hours and woke up just after 4, having been told that 4.30 was tea time. We had tea and paste sandwiches from the family silver in the drawing room, talking most of the time. They are such nice people and good company in a fairly sedate sort of way. He says rather un-Archdeacon things sometimes which are highly amusing.

After tea the Archdeacon went to do some work and so did Miss Cowdray so Mrs Van der Byl and I nattered for a while. Then I had my orders to do the flowers. Sir had picked lots from the garden so I had to stand large bunches first in hot water then in cold. That passed the time until Sir went to Church and we started to prepare supper. Mrs Van der Byl wanted a certain sort of biscuit and we had our orders to find them. We were sent to the biscuit tins and then I knew I was really family. She had 17 biscuit tins! I nearly fell over the dog laughing about it! One of the young Deacons came back to supper with Sir and we had an enjoyable time, then coffee and then Sir said he would run me back to the ship.

So we went back down Adderley Street and all the Christmas lights were still up and on and looked rather fine. Then went along the harbour to look closer at the Italian liner, lights all ablaze, then home and bed.

Today I am working right through until 9 this evening, then it's a party to celebrate the passing of the Lifeboat Certificates by the Nursing Sister and the 4th Radio Officer. Champagne and all that.

I'm off tomorrow and am planning to go with David Howden to Kirstenbosch in the morning. They are huge Botanical Gardens round the side of the Mountain and are quite fabulous so they say. I mean to find out, so I will tell you more about them in a day or two. I must finish now and think about some lunch - it's ages since breakfast. See you soon. Take care. Love, Ann.

Cape Town, Wednesday 25th January
Dear Mummy and Daddy

Well, I'm at the scribe machine again, so here goes with the latest saga of life at sea.

I told you on Monday about my day out on Sunday. For the rest of Monday I worked pretty hard, doing all the odd jobs that need doing before we leave, so that I don't have a big rush today. After 6 o'clock I read my book and felt very tired and depressed - it's a long day when you're rather bored. Then at 9 o'clock I went to a party, that I think I told you about, to celebrate CL Certificates for Phil. and Jim. The party was well away, with champagne and brandy and everything else, and I enjoyed myself. Didn't stay too long, washed my hair and changed, and then went back. Very amusing evening.

Then yesterday arrived at last. I was off at 10 and had organised a picnic lunch. At 10.30 David Howden, Phil. and I left here and went to Kirstenbosch, which are the national Botanical Gardens, and are vast. They extend for about 25 acres, and one of the boundaries is the side of the Mountain. It was green and hot and blue sky and flowers, and streams and tiny waterfalls and tiny bridges and a ford with tadpoles and tiddlers. Very very peaceful and very satisfying. Just the side of Table Mountain up above, and a view across the Bay and Cape Flats on the other side, through the trees.

It was laid out fairly tidily but in a fairly haphazard way, if you know what I mean, so that you weren't aware that you were in a formal garden. The smell was lovely too, in various parts, all hot English summer-type smells, and a tiny plane droning in the heavens some miles away. Can't describe it more adequately but I'm sure you know what I mean.

Well, I've just been for my beef tea, and very good it was too.

We left there about 12 noon (Kirstenbosch I mean) and set off back to town. Then we went to the Cableway and Phil. the Legs and I went up the Mountain. David had to take his car back and had to be at work again at 1.30. It was rather chilly going up and at the top we met a cloud. It was curling just round the cablehouse at the top and was rather cold and damp. We walked along the Table top and found a sheltered boulder on the edge and sat and had our picnic. It was lovely and the view was very clear. We were just on a level with the top of the Hottentot-Hollands Mountains which were visible in the distance and we felt very much on top of the world. Gradually more clouds hurled themselves off the top of the Mountain and curled round Signal Hill and down into the city. It was alternatively damp and sunny, but I got a bit suntanned on my legs. After the picnic we went to the Swiss-type chalet near the cablehouse and had a super cup of coffee, watching nothing out of the windows, because nothing could be seen.

We caught the 1.30 cablecar down and we were in the cold damp cloud a lot of the way. Then we were back in the sunshine, although I noticed that the cablecar carried bags of ballast on the way down as some sort of weight against the wind, which was quite strong. Then we caught the special mini-bus down to the main road again, and an ordinary service bus down to the city centre. Then we pottered round the shops for a while, and I very nearly spent big money.

I almost bought a false hairpiece. Ooooh, I was so nearly tempted. Yes, I was tempted, but I resisted. They were in a sale and a woman demonstrated how it would look on me, she matched the colour beautifully and tried a couple of styles. It felt strange to have long hair again and rather nice. However, the price was high.

The first piece I tried on was £14 and the second shorter piece was £10. I gave it back, very regretfully. If it had been about £3 I would have bought it, but not £10. Cor! So you very nearly had a hairy daughter again.

We got back about 3.45 I suppose and went and had a drink and then some coffee. Then I retired to my little bed and woke up in time for dinner. Had a drink then dinner. After dinner lots of us went down aft to watch the liner EUGENIO C sail for Durban and the rest of the world. It seemed to take an age to get her out of her berth and turned and headed out into the Bay. She looked rather splendid, especially as it was just after sunset and the light faded in the sky, the first star came out and the ship's lights winked. She finally left the harbour and we all stared and the tugs hooted. She gave three enormously long hoots (trust the Eye-tyes!) and set off into the darkness. That was that.

Then all the thirsty souls standing around me followed me back home and we drank brandy, ginger and ice, and ate peanuts (they all said thank you Mrs. Williams) and cracked walnuts all over the floor for an hour or two and talked. Everyone left just after ten, yawning their heads off, so I got to bed quite early.

This morning I feel almost indecently well-slept, and keep yawning my head off. I think maybe I must do some work and get my mind on the right tracks. We sail at 4 and it can't come soon enough. Oh to be at sea in the sunshine again. See you in a week and a bit. Take care. Love, Ann.

At sea, day before Las Palmas, 1.2.67
Dear family,

This is just for the records as usual. I just wanted to boast about your very clever daughter. Guess what I did last night? I won the Officers Frog Race! You know that one of our Entertainments is Frog Racing (and the betting on it) with six wooden frogs on individual strings. A team of people sit on chairs, pull the strings and the wooden frogs bump along the floor, and first past the line wins. We always finish with an Officers race, with a big laugh at them all. John called me in to the Race (glamour and all that) and I sat in place number 4. Then suddenly he produced tea towels and we were all blindfolded. Somehow I managed to win the Race. It was a question of being slow but sure. Aren't I clever. My head was so large after that, that I could hardly get through my cabin door!

Sunday, day before arrival Southampton
Well, I didn't seem to finish this letter to be able to post it at Las Palmas, so I shall add a bit more now and post it from Southampton tomorrow from the ship.

We have had an extremely hot trip home, the humidity was terrible. Still, it has changed rapidly and it is now rather parky outside. We are in the Bay and it is a pleasant bright morning, blue sky and clouds - it might snow at any moment!

I went to Church this morning, as usual, and specially because Davey read the Lesson. The Staff Commander took the Service, as usual at the end of voyage, and the Chief Officer then reads the Lesson. He did it very well, although yesterday we were concerned that he would not be able to see over the lectern. But he could. He was very nervous about reading the Lesson, but we all arranged not to look at him. It must be very nerve-wracking for anyone taking a service, to see all us Officers in the front row.

I have just been given a box of Contrast chocolates for doing the Shopman's typing, and so John and I are munching away at them. They are going rather quickly. It's John's birthday today, and he is merry, well and truly. Someone said it looked as if we were about to be married when we staggered back to the Bureau after lunch. You may care to know that we were not.

It is now much later, John has a headache, I feel rather weary, we are rather busy, and people are asking for 6d. pieces out of boredom. I must close the Postbox and post this. See you tomorrow. Love, Ann.

S.A.ORANJE

Frog Racing

Extract From The Ship's Deck Log

R.M.S. Edinburgh Castle
COMMODORE W. S. BYLES, R.D.

SOUTHAMPTON TO CAPETOWN via LAS PALMAS

VOYAGE 122   March 10 to March 22, 1967

Date	Distance Run	Speed	Latitude-Longitude	Wind force	Temperature at Noon Air Sea	Itinerary
10-3-67				SW6	51° 50°	1300 Departure Southampton. 77 First Class and 381 Tourist Class Passengers on board Vessel pitching to heavy SW'ly swell. Cloudy and clear
11-3-67	470	21·30	45°22N 08°06W	W6	53° 53°	0100 Vessel rounded Ushant and entered Bay of Biscay 1900 passed Cape Finisterre and left Bay of Biscay 1918 passed Company's N'bound vessel Pendennis Castle Pitching and rolling heavily, shipping seas. Overcast, rain
12-3-67	542	22·58	36°50N 12°05W	NNE4	61° 59°	1030 Divine Service in First Class Lounge, Commodore officiated. Moderate W'ly swell. Cloudy and clear 1715 passed Company's N'bound vessel Rothesay Castle
13-3-67	539	22·49	Las Palmas		69° 65°	1424 arrived Las Palmas. 1836 departed Las Palmas 68 First Class and 374 Tourist Class Passengers on board
14-3-67	384	22·13	22°18N 17°32W	NNW3	67° 65°	Low NW'ly swell. Cloudy, moderate visibility
15-3-67	550	22·92	13°15N 17°40W	NE3	69° 68°	0800 passed Cape Verde, Dakar, the most westerly point of Africa. Vessel rolling easily. Moderate visibility 2300 Passed Company's N'bound vessel Rotherwick Castle
16-3-67	552	23·00	05°22N 13°11W	N1	84° 83°	Low swell. Cloudy with heavy rain
17-3-67	532	22·17	01°48S 08°00W	S2	84° 82°	0604 Vessel crossed Equator in DR Longitude 09°07W Low swell. Cloudy and clear
18-3-67	525	21·88	09°02S 03°14W	SE3	82° 82°	Low SSE'ly swell. Cloudy with frequent rain
19-3-67	528	22·00	16°13S 02°05E	SE5	75° 75°	1030 Divine Service in First Class Lounge, Commodore officiated. Moderate swell, pitching easily. Cloudy and clear
20-3-67	500	21·74	22°58S 07°15E	SE5	70° 70°	Vessel pitching to moderate SEly swell. Cloudy and clear
21-3-67	499	21·69	29°07S 13°27E	SE5	68° 69°	Vessel pitching to moderate swell. Fine and clear
22-3-67	381					0700 Estimated Time of Arrival Cape Town (S.A.S.T.)

DISTANCE 6,002 Miles   ...   **AVERAGE SPEED 21·12 Knots**

Extract From The Ship's Deck Log

R.M.S. Edinburgh Castle
COMMODORE W. S. BYLES, R.D.

CAPETOWN TO SOUTHAMPTON via LAS PALMAS

VOYAGE 122   April 5, 1967, to April 17, 1967

Date	Distance Run	Speed	Latitude-Longitude	Wind Force	Temperature at Noon Air Sea	Itinerary
5-4-67			At Capetown		77°	1606 Departed Capetown Low swell. Fine and clear 149 First Class and 449 Tourist Class Passengers on board
6-4-67	444	22·09	28°22S 12°43E	SSE3	77° 68°	Low SW'ly swell, vessel rolling easily. Cloudy and clear
7-4-67	571	22·84	21°10S 05°54E	SSE4	79° 71°	Vessel pitching to moderate swell. Cloudy and clear
8-4-67	557	23·21	13°34S 00°21E	ESE4	74° 76°	Low swell. Overcast with occasional rain
9-4-67	531	22·13	06°33S 05°05W	SE3	91° 83°	1030 Divine Service in First Class Lounge. Commodore officiated. Low following swell. Cloudy and clear
10-4-67	542	22·58	00°39N 10°30W	Light Airs	85° 83°	0952 Vessel crossed the Equator in DR Longitude 10°03W Low SSE'ly swell. Cloudy with heavy rain showers
11-4-67	527	21·96	08°00N 15°18W	WNW3	80° 80°	Low swell. Fine and clear
12-4-67	537	22·38	16°23N 17°43W	NNE6	69° 70°	0644 Passed Company's S'bound Mail Vessel S.A. Oranje 0733 passed Cape Verde, most westerly point of Africa Cloudy, slight haze
13-4-67	541	22·54	25°13N 16°21W	NE4	69° 65°	2300 Arrived Las Palmas Fine and clear
14-4-67	338	20·74	30°32N 14°29W	NxW4	64° 66°	0342 Departed Las Palmas 147 First Class and 462 Tourist Class Passengers on board Vessel pitching to moderate swell. Cloudy with showers
15-4-67	535	22·29	39°02N 11°04W	NNE3	61° 59°	2300 Passed Cape Finisterre and entered Bay of Biscay Low swell. Fine and clear
16-4-67	511	22·22	46°54N 06°49W	NE6	56° 53°	1030 Divine Service in First Class Lounge, Staff Commander officiated. Pitching to heavy swell. Moderate visibility 1730 Vessel rounded Ushant, left the Bay of Biscay and entered the English Channel
17-4-67	363		Southampton			0700 Estimated Time Of Arrival at Southampton Docks

DISTANCE 5,997 MILES   - -   AVERAGE SPEED 22·28 KNOTS

R.M.S. "EDINBURGH CASTLE"
VOYAGE 122
COMMODORE W. S. BYLES R.D.
LEAVING SOUTHAMPTON 10TH MARCH 1967

Las Palmas, 13th March (Monday)
Dear Family

Just thought you would like to know that I am still in the land of the living. I think the word should really be "existing". The work is fine so far and I am certainly not overworked - John Ingram is making sure of that, quite apart from Ann Williams!

But it was so rough coming here. The ship rolled tremendously all the way and in fact I was sick on Saturday morning, although I worked all the time and didn't take to my bed. The First Class party was cancelled and held last night instead. Oh yes, I had my false hair piece put on properly on Saturday night and again last night and everyone said it looked super. I was very pleased with the way it was done. The hairdresser is excellent, again, and he is very interested in making it look as good on me as possible. All for free too. I had my own hair cut on Friday and that feels much better.

My cabin is large on here, even bigger than the one on the S. A. ORANJE but only just, and at the moment it doesn't look very lived in because everything has been stowed away for fear of damage during the rolling. Still today the sun is shining and I have had a letter from Davey in Port Elizabeth and I feel better. The atmosphere on here is not very amiable and that is not just comparison. I know I was very happy on the ORANJE, but the Bureau crowd on there were such nice people - the sort you like to know out of work. The only nice person as I said is John, and he is simply waiting to get to Cape Town to see his wife Judith and child again. The two of us moan away about the weather and how we are going to sign off in Cape Town. The thought had certainly crossed my mind - I thought of coming back on the WINDSOR from Cape Town. It was only a dream because I have no intention of leaving here, it's not that bad. But it is certainly different and certainly not so happy. I'm quite all right so don't worry.

My films of the ski-ing holiday are rather good I think and I will bring them home next time for you to see.

The Tourist Cocktail Parties are held tomorrow night on here which is a much more sensible idea. By the way, Mrs Haynes rang me up at about 10 o'clock on Sailing day to wish me "bon voyage".

That is just about all the news I can think of for now, so I shall post this as it is.
Take care, and see you soon.
Love Ann.

P.S. How about the stamps on this envelope? Are they all right.

20th March Monday at sea, posted at Cape Town
Dear family

I thought I had better start this note to you now, while there is a chance. I thought it was a Tuesday today, but apparently it is Monday. Never mind.

First of all, I am very happy on here. After Las Palmas the sun came out and the sea was calmer and we had a good ride to here. Today the sea is a bit bumpy and we are pitching a bit. There is just tomorrow to get through and then it is Cape Town and mail. There have been lots of parties and get-togethers on here. I gather that last voyage was unpleasant because there was a lot of ill-feeling amongst all the departments, caused particularly by one Purserette. I am all in favour of being friends with everyone and have had several parties to get to know other people. So all in all we all get on extremely well and I am suffering from my usual feeling of lack of sleep.

Last night those of us in our alleyway held a huge party, inviting just about all the Officers. There were six of us giving the party, and the alleyway is just the right size for a party. We decorated it with drawings, balloons and toys (Brer Rabbit was suspended from the deck head, upside down, because one chap insisted that is the right way up for the southern hemisphere), and we had a lot of coloured light bulbs. There was lots to drink and eat and music to listen to. Commodore Byles came and thoroughly enjoyed it, he said. All the top brass came and stayed and drank. We started at 7 and decided about 10.15 that maybe we should stop drinking and go to see the end of the film so we did. So that was our alleyway party. Everyone says it was a great success so that was good. We also lost an hour on the clocks last night which wasn't so good.

The night before that, Saturday, was dinner dance night to which we all still wear uniform. I had my hair done and felt fine. I was very excited though because I had a phone call from Davey on the ORANJE which we passed about 7.30 p.m. at a distance of about 10-15 miles. Last week I had received a telegram from Cozette on the ORANJE wishing me all the best etc. and I had sent her one back saying best wishes to everyone. Then on Thursday I got one from Davey saying he would ring me when we passed. I was very excited and pleased. So at 7 o'clock on Saturday evening I went up to take the telephone call. It was lovely to talk to him - he has asked for a trip off and has said he is coming to meet me in Southampton on 17th April. Isn't that lovely! I also spoke to him a little later on the VHF from the Bridge but the reception wasn't very good. I was having a party in my cabin at the time, pre-dinner dance, so you can imagine I was rushing in and out like a yo-yo a lot of the time, and feeling rather pleased with life.

I have started my sewing Mummy and it looks quite good. I am just finishing the green stitches on one traycloth. That is just about all the news for today.

Well, it is now Wednesday in Cape Town. Thanks for the letter this morning. I imagine that what I have written will answer a lot of Daddy's queries. I am not overworked by any means; I work only in the First Class Bureau; the previous 2 girls left, one because she wanted a change of job, and the other because she was expecting to get married and go to Canada soon.

I hope Mummy's cold is better now, it must have been fairly bad to stop her going to the meeting. I have written to arrange a Mini, but if Davey is meeting me and intends to give me a lift home, I will ask him to cancel it. Anyway, it is booked.

I had a package this morning which Davey left me - a long letter written round the coast, and also a sailor doll from the S. A. ORANJE. That was a nice surprise. Did I tell you that the 2 sailor dolls of the TRANSVAAL CASTLE and CAPETOWN CASTLE were stolen in Southampton from my cabin last leave? They were hanging on the bulkhead as usual, with pictures, and this time they disappeared. I informed the right people but of course there was nothing anyone could do. Actually, I judged the kids Fancy Dress the other day and was given an EDINBURGH CASTLE sailor doll so now I have two again. It is a lovely day here, they tell me, and I have the afternoon and evening off. I think I may go to the shops this afternoon and then take the sun. More news from next port. Take care. Love, Ann.

Port Elizabeth, Good Friday
Dear Mummy and Daddy,

Thank you very much for the letter again this morning. It certainly seemed to be full of news again. We didn't dock until 9 a.m. which was a much more sociable hour to get anywhere. It seems ages since we left Cape Town although it was only yesterday.

I worked in the morning in Cape Town but was off in the afternoon and evening. In the afternoon I went up on the Monkey Island and had a lovely sunbathe. Watched the WINDSOR CASTLE sail at 4 o'clock and waved to Derek (Mason). Then had a shower and did some sewing. I have finished one tray cloth, the easy one.

Then unexpectedly Vicky (Craig), the Hostess, had a visitor from the nearby Clan boat and asked if I would make a foursome up to go out in the evening. I said provisionally yes, and she asked the Chief Engineer on here to come with us. He is a super dancer and good company so we had a pleasant evening. We decided to go to the Sable Room, and I was thrilled about that. If you look at the pictures of Cape Town you will see that there is a skyscraper building fairly near the quayside, which has about 25 floors. It is the biggest one seen around this part of the world, except for Johannesburg. However, on the 22nd floor is this restaurant with dinner and dancing, looking out over the lights of the harbour and Mountain and city of Cape Town. It was super and the food was excellent. So that was an unexpected late night.

Yesterday morning, Thursday, I had a super surprise. We opened at 8.30 and just about 10 o'clock a boy came from a local florist. He handed me a spray of flowers and asked me to sign, which is quite normal, until I discovered they were for me. Guess what, Davey had arranged to send them to me. It was a long spray of a dozen red roses, with a blue bow, and all done up in cellophane. There was a little card with them, which Davey must have written just before they sailed. The final touch, as if it was needed, was the name of the florist: The Henry Williams Co. (Pty.) Ltd. How about that, Mr. Henry F. Williams?

I was so pleased with the flowers and they look superb in my ugly black vase. Everyone has admired them and I only hope they last a long time. They have very long stems so they should do.

Oh yes, while I think of it. Do you want me to bring you some brandy home this time, or would you like something else. And Mummy, could you let me know what Blue Grass item you would like this time please, I seem to remember you saying you would like the body lotion. Anyway, please could you both let me know what you would like. Ta.

I'm glad you sent an Easter card to Mrs Van der Byl. She rang me up on Wednesday and invited me to go and see her when we come downcoast, so I will. It's Good Friday here (and most other places, I know) and I had a hot hot cross bun for my breakfast today. It was nice.

It is very hot and sticky and it is also raining. I'm almost glad that I am working, or shall we simply say 'on duty'. John is also here and drinking lemon tea. He is working all round the coast so that he can be off in Cape Town all the time. Judith his wife and baby Simon came on board to collect him on Wednesday and then went off for the rest of the time there. Simon lay on the floor of one cabin and slowly revolved on his tummy and stared at each one of us in turn. He is rather sweet and obviously enjoys life.

Well, I have just been for some soggy tomato sandwiches and enjoyed them. We feed quite well on here, although the Chef is odd and is frequently seen wandering around the dining room in his dirty galley trousers, apron and chef's hat

I gather he takes violent dislikes to most people most of the time, and cannot even be excused because of his cooking. However, I am not starved.

Ernie is our Steward and makes sure we are all well fed and watered etc. He also does the News for us in the mornings and that is an absolute Godsend. He was on the ORANJE my first voyage there and did the News for us then, you may remember.

Suppose I must do a bit of Company typing for a change. More in a day or so, when there's more to report. Take care, see you soon. Just remembered something. Last night I met an old gentleman whose father started the shop called Edmonds (Slough, Hounslow etc.). The son has run it since his father's death and has just sold out, and that's why they are closing down. Small world isn't it. Love, Ann.

Durban 28th March
Dear Family

Happy Easter + 1. Thank you for the letter yesterday morning. Did you have a good weekend I wonder. Hope the weather was good for you anyway.

I had rather an unusual time. On Sunday we were at East London and the weather was not sunny, but it was quite hot and lovely. I had the day off, and Katy and I went to the beach. It was very damp but pleasant. Then we decided to go to the snack bar on the beach front and have our Easter Sunday lunch. I had a cup of coffee and an enormous chicken and salad roll. It was super. Isn't it strange the things you do sometimes. Then we came back to the ship (about 5 minutes walk) and sat on the Monkey Island for another short while, getting the ultra-violet rays, then I washed my hair and went to bed. Got up again at 4 and back at work at 4.30, sailing first at 5.30, then 6 p.m.

Yesterday we got to Durban at 9, which was a very nice time to arrive. I had the day off again. I worked frantically doing things for the Commodore until 11 o'clock and then rushed away to change. Some of us (Colin, Vicky, me, Katy and John Sparling) went off in a hired car to a beach about 35 miles away, called Chakis Rock. Apparently Chakis was the leader of a particular African tribe and they had an odd custom of selecting a victim, who went through some tribal ceremony and then got pushed over the cliff and died. The custom has now died out. It was a super beach and the water was thundering on the beach. We got there about noon I think and had a drink and quick lunch, of curry and rice. There was this one small hotel/restaurant and we sat outside on the stone seats/table looking out over the beach. Then off we went along the beach clutching all our bits and pieces. There weren't many people around and we walked along quite a way and then found a nice spot of sand (it's all super) and put the fishing rod in and claimed it as ours. The boys went in the sea and got thrown around in the surf and us girls just paddled and got pretty wet too. The sky was a cloudless blue and it was very hot. Sunbathing, walking and paddling, and a short walk back for drinks mid-afternoon.

Had a snooze about 4, made sandcastles and watched the tide come in and make a moat, then the sun suddenly got cooler and we started to pack up. Colin tried to fish but had absolutely no luck, but I was allowed to record his try on his cine camera. Then we set off back to town and stopped on Durban beach front at the go-karts. Had three rounds, while boys whizzed round many times. Katy and Vicky just sat and watched. It was dark by this time, as the sun sinks very very quickly, and so we drove in the dark with all the lights of the city sparkling around for many miles. Lovely.

OPERATION EGG aboard S.A. ORANJE December 1966

The author goes "Red Indian" in her wigwam aboard R.M.S. EDINBURGH CASTLE

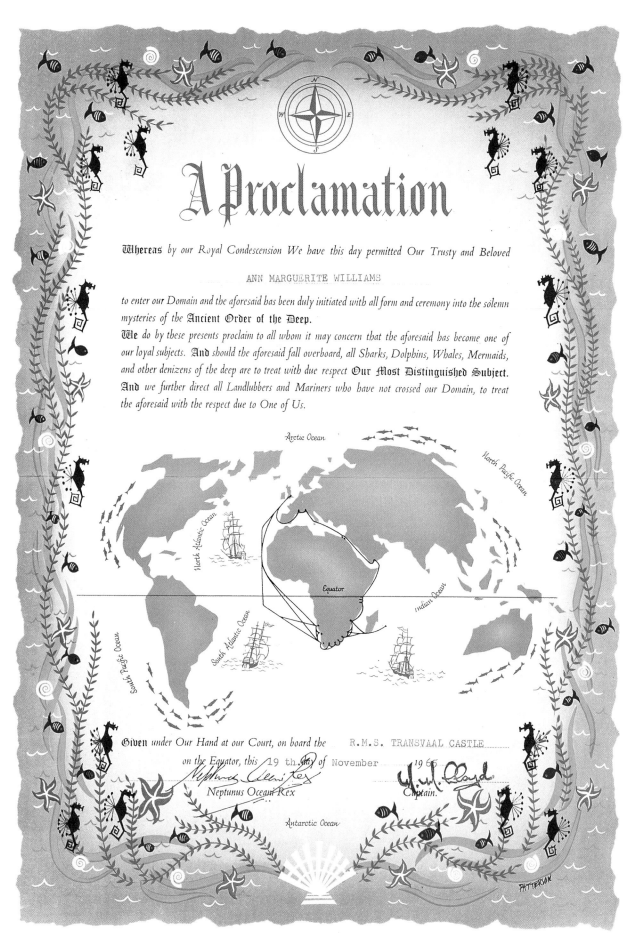

A Proclamation

Whereas by our Royal Condescension We have this day permitted Our Trusty and Beloved

ANN MARGUERITE WILLIAMS

to enter our Domain and the aforesaid has been duly initiated with all form and ceremony into the solemn mysteries of the **Ancient Order of the Deep.**

We do by these presents proclaim to all whom it may concern that the aforesaid has become one of our loyal subjects. **And** should the aforesaid fall overboard, all Sharks, Dolphins, Whales, Mermaids, and other denizens of the deep are to treat with due respect **Our Most Distinguished Subject.** **And** we further direct all Landlubbers and Mariners who have not crossed our Domain, to treat the aforesaid with the respect due to One of Us.

Arctic Ocean

North Pacific Ocean

North Atlantic Ocean

Equator

Indian Ocean

South Pacific Ocean

South Atlantic Ocean

Given under Our Hand at our Court, on board the   R.M.S. TRANSVAAL CASTLE

on the Equator, this 19 th day of November   19 65

Neptunus Ocean Rex

Captain.

Antarctic Ocean

PATTERSON

UNION-CASTLE produced ornate souvenirs of the Crossing the Line ceremony.
The crew were not exempt!

Then along a bit further to the trampolines. One section of the beach is sectioned off and they have laid out a dozen trampolines, all quite safe and sound. The boys wanted a go, and I plucked up courage and also had a go. It was hilarious and I started to jump up and down like the others. Then I wanted to do something different and so fell on my knees and bounced up again on to my feet. Didn't fancy the idea of bouncing back on my rear and then standing up, but finally decided to do it and found I couldn't get back on my feet again. So there I was bouncing on my bottom, unable to stop. Nearly had hysterics. Tried to do it again and it was a bit better but I got very hot and felt exhausted. We had 10 minutes on there and then fell on to seats at the side of the section. It was great fun and I wouldn't have missed it.

Then we came back home and collapsed with a cool drink. The car we hired was a Japanese one, a Toyota, very good and nippy. Have you heard of it? Held six of us with a slight squeeze. Then decided to go out for a meal and went to a lovely placed called the Seahaven round in the Yacht Basin, for dinner and dancing. Good food, lots of plonk and we all rolled home utterly exhausted but having had a super day.

I'm on duty all day today and it's such a contrast after yesterday. Still, can't have everything. This morning had a bit of a nasty shock when I came into the Bureau at 8.30. Opened my drawer beside my chair and out walked an enormous cockroach. It was about 4 inches long, and I showed John and we rushed to the back of the Bureau and shouted for Ernie. He's the "family retainer", and he rushed in, grabbed the drawer and took it away to empty all the contents on the floor of the alleyway. It wasn't there, of course, so now I sit here wondering where the hell the thing is, and whether it is going to walk out again just yet. I was quite frightened - it was a nasty sight first thing in the morning! John wasn't much better either - he ran away too. All adds to the general excitement of the day. What with the Africans chipping the paint off the ship's side, the typewriter and two telephones, life is not quiet here. The lulls are lovely though, at present it must be African-resting time as it's absolutely quiet. Won't last for long, but then it will be my lunchtime. I feel content with life. Take care, and see you soon.
Love, Ann

Cape Town, 4th April 1967
Dear Mummy and Daddy

Thank you for the letter on Sunday. I haven't managed to write you a letter before this because we have been pretty busy here, and I am now sick of the sight of passenger telegrams and mail. It is sailing day tomorrow and we are all looking forward to 4 o'clock sailing time.

I had Sunday evening off and a crowd of us went out for a meal to the Troubadour coffee house, which cooked beautiful steaks and salad (uncooked) in a rather beatnik guitar-playing atmosphere and folk singing. Quite interesting! Monday morning I went into town and met Mrs. V.d.B. at 11.30 and we had coffee in Stuttafords. Then back to her home for lunch. She said that they had been very touched to receive an Easter card from you - so thanks. We had been talking about glass and china, and she mentioned that she had bought an ashtray in Copenhagen on one occasion when she went on a cruise before the war in, guess what, the ARANDORA STAR! I fell off my chair at this, and said that you had been an Engineer on that ship and all that. There seems to be no end to the coincidences I witness with that family. There was another one today, but that is another story. Mrs. V.d.B. was on the last cruise before the war, because they were turned back before getting to Helsinki and war was announced just after they got home.

Please Daddy, can you write out a list of your naval career for me - I'm dying to know if you happened to be an Engineer on the ARANDORA STAR when she was. Isn't it strange? She is the niece of Leonard Dewey, the man who helped start the Blue Star company - do you know him?

Anyway, I had lunch and then was packed off to bed again for a couple of hours. Lovely. Then Sir (the Archdeacon) gave me a lift back to the ship, and I pottered around for a while. I have ordered some grapefruit, and will be bringing that as my contribution to the rations, apart from <u>anything else</u>. (glug, glug .... hic, ...). You haven't said what smelly things you would like - if you think of it can you let me know in your LP letter. Last night I went to the Sable Room again. Today I am on duty again and an older lady came along to embark early this morning and gave me her ticket. Guess what (here I am about to relate the second coincidence)? Her address in England, which we always need on the ticket, was c/o Miss Read, of Windsor. Remember her, Personnel Officer, I.C.I. Paints Division, etc.? So I told the story of the V.d.B's, their friend Miss Cowdray who works for Sir, and my connections with Miss Read. Small world again. Isn't it fantastic how these things seem to happen just by knowing the V.d.B.'s?

Now to other things. I have heard from Davey, who is definitely coming to meet me on 17th April. So I should be home normal-type time on the Monday evening in the Mini-Rolls. Hooray. Davey will be on leave and doesn't yet know what ship he will be going back on, but he should be able to tell us more on the 17th.

I've had a letter also from Angie (Palmer) saying they'd had Mr Ian Smith and wife up and down coast, lovely couple. They had to keep reporters and photographers at bay to begin with, and Ian Smith had drinks with Davey Haynes in his cabin, she said. She's just got promotion to Assistant Purser! She was also amazed that I was the only Purserette on here this Voyage.

That is just about all the news I can think of for the moment, so I shall finish this off tomorrow before we sail.

Wednesday
This is terrible: the mail for passengers is enormous and I feel so weary. Soon we sail, hooray. See you soon.

Take care of yourselves, and don't go putting your feet through any ceilings this time after papering!

See you soon. Love, Ann

Extract From The Ship's Deck Log

R.M.S. Edinburgh Castle
COMMODORE W. S. BYLES, R.D.

SOUTHAMPTON TO CAPETOWN via LAS PALMAS

VOYAGE 123   April 28 to May 10, 1967

Date	Distance Run	Speed	Latitude-Longitude	Wind force	Temperature at Noon Air Sea	Itinerary
28-4-67				NE2	58° 50°	1300 Departure Southampton. 62 First Class and 381 Tourist Class Passengers on board Calm sea. Fine and clear
29-4-67	473	23.9	44°35N 08°53W	ExN6	57° 55°	0100 Vessel rounded Ushant and entered Bay of Biscay 1900 passed Cape Finisterre and left Bay of Biscay Cloudless with horizon haze
30-4-67	547	22.5	35°55N 12°36W	SE2	60° 53°	1030 Divine Service in First Class Lounge, Commodore officiated. Calm sea. Cloudy, fine and clear
1-5-67	489	21.9	Las Palmas		68° 63°	1130 arrived Las Palmas. 1700 departed Las Palmas 47 First Class and 367 Tourist Class Passengers on board
2-5-67	408	21.9	21°47N 17°46W	Variable	70° 69°	Rippled Sea. Few clouds, fine and clear
3-5-67	545	22.1	12°42N 17°28W	N2	70° 66°	0636 passed Cape Verde, Dakar, the most westerly point of Africa. Calm sea. Cloudy, fine and clear
4-5-67	543	22.3	05°06N 12°53W	Lt. Airs	83° 85°	0600 passed Company's N'bound vessel Good Hope Castle Cloudless, fine and clear
5-5-67	533	22.2	02°09S 07°47W	SE4	83° 82°	0420 Vessel crossed Equator in DR Longitude 09°12W Cloudy and clear
6-5-67	523	22.7	09°12S 02°40W	SE4	80° 79°	Cloudy, fine and clear
7-5-67	530	22.16	16°32S 02°22E	SE5	72° 71°	1030 Divine Service in First Class Lounge, Commodore officiated. Moderate sea. Cloudy and clear
8-5-67	510	22.16	23°20S 07°43E	SSE5	70° 68°	Cloudy, fine and clear
9-5-67	498	21.43	28°32S 13°51E	SE4	64° 64°	Moderate sea. Few clouds fine and clear
10-5-67	377					0700 Estimated Time of Arrival Cape Town (S.A.S.T.)

DISTANCE 5,976 Miles   ....   AVERAGE SPEED 22·00 Knots

Extract From The Ship's Deck Log

R.M.S. Edinburgh Castle
COMMODORE W. S. BYLES, R.D.

CAPETOWN TO SOUTHAMPTON via LAS PALMAS

VOYAGE 123   May 24, 1967, to June 5, 1967

Date	Distance Run	Speed	Latitude-Longitude	Wind Force	Temperature at Noon Air	Sea	Itinerary
24-5-67		At Capetown			68°		1736 Departed Capetown Fine and clear 85 First Class and 484 Tourist Class Passengers on board
25-5-67	402	21·38	28°54S 13°12E	SxE3	64°	64°	Moderate swell. Cloudy and clear
26-5-67	562	21·55	21°55S 06°20E	SSE5	77°	68°	Vessel rolling to moderate swell. Cloudy and clear
27-5-67	542	22·58	14°37S 00°45E	SE5	72°	77°	Moderate sea and swell. Overcast and clear
28-5-67	540	22·50	07°15S 04°30W	SSE3	78°	79°	1030 Divine Service in First Class Lounge. Commodore officiated. Slight sea. Sunny and clear
29-5-67	556	23·7	00°09N 10°04W	SE3	81°	79°	1140 Vessel crossed the Equator in DR Longitude 09°50W Cloudless, fine and clear
30-5-67	546	22·75	07°42N 15°08W	Light Airs	84°	85°	Calm sea. Fine and clear
31-5-67	540	22·50	16°05N 17°32W	NNW4	74°	72°	0740 Passed Company's S'bound Mail Vessel S.A. Oranje 0835 passed Cape Verde, most westerly point of Africa Few clouds, fine, slight haze
1-6-67	531	22·13	24°46N 16°33W	NE5	69°	66°	2300 Arrived Las Palmas Overcast, fine and clear
2-6-67	381	20·70	30°54N 14°22W	NxE5	68°	68°	0348 Departed Las Palmas 99 First Class and 484 Tourist Class Passengers on board Sunny and clear, few clouds
3-6-67	518	22·34	39°02N 11°10W	NxE5	66°	62°	2330 Passed Cape Finisterre and entered Bay of Biscay Moderate sea. Cloudless, fine and clear
4-6-67	516	22·43	47°04N 06°54W	NxE3	59°	58°	1030 Divine Service in First Class Lounge, Commodore officiated. Slight sea. Cloudless, fine and clear 1700 Vessel rounded Ushant, left the Bay of Biscay and entered the English Channel
5-6-67	331		Southampton				0700 Estimated Time Of Arrival at Southampton Docks

DISTANCE 5,965 MILES   - -   AVERAGE SPEED 22·21 KNOTS

R.M.S. "EDINBURGH CASTLE"
COMMODORE W. S. BYLES R.D.
VOYAGE 123
LEAVING SOUTHAMPTON 28TH APRIL 1967

Near Las Palmas
Monday 1st May (King Harold's Day)
Dear Family

Hullo. Things are fine here and we are slowly approaching the island. It is quite near now and in fact we are pottering around in circles trying to do nothing as far as I can see.

The sea has been lovely and calm and life is very pleasant. I think I am probably in a slightly alcoholic haze after last night, but everyone else says it is pleasant this voyage. Friday sailing day was quite restrained and we sailed a little late, because the P&O "CHUSAN" had priority for some reason and went first. We passed her later that afternoon and sent rude messages apparently. The new girl, Irene, is excellent and good fun. She is coping very well and it is so much better to have another girl down the other end - it saves a lot of worry. The five girls get on very well in fact, much better than the others last voyage. I just sit on the fence anyway, and get on with most people so it didn't affect me, last voyage, but things are much more comfortable now.

Saturday was nice: had my hair piece put on after work and then went to the Cocktail Party. We have just over 60 First Class passengers so it seems very empty up here. More time to gossip though.

Yesterday I kept my hair on, so couldn't go to Church, because last time the Chief Purser laughed at my hat perched on top. Father accused me of being a heathen then roared with laughter, so I didn't mind.

Then at lunchtime there was a party in one of the Engineer's cabins, which lasted an hour or two. Collapsed into my little bed and slept until 4.15. I like Sundays. Then tea, Bureau 4.30 til 5.30 (nothing too strenuous) then letter writing and preparing for another party. Us girls decided to give a party, so that all the new people could meet one another. That was thoroughly successful - it lasted through dinnertime (we had food sent up to the cabin) until 9.30. Then the Nursing Sister invited us round to her house for Irish coffee. She is Irish and knows just how to brew it, so you can imagine how good it was. I like it. Then we went back to another cabin and the others played cards. I just watched and drank and had quiet zizzes in a large armchair. Lovely way to spend an evening.

We are now in Las Palmas and it is hot and sticky. We officially went into whites on Saturday evening, which we all thought was terribly early in the voyage. Still, it is just right for working in and now it is hot enough.

Cannot think of anything more. Oh yes, we have on board 2 Ford drivers and a Ford Corsair. You may have heard that the WINDSOR CASTLE is to race a Ford car from Cape Town to the UK, to prove that our sea route is the quickest way to get from Cape Town to UK. Ford accepted the challenge as part of a publicity stunt and in fact sent the car out with us, with the drivers, to wait for the sailing of the WINDSOR. That really is the only item of interest.

See you soon. Take care. Love, Ann.

AT SEA, MONDAY 8TH MAY

Dear Mummy and Daddy,
It is 9.45 a.m., the Monday before Cape Town and I have absolutely nothing to do. We have just over 40 pax. and they cause us very little bother at the Bureau, in fact they come here after breakfast usually just to chat about the previous night. They really are a good crowd. Our two Ford drivers are the nicest ones. They are great fun and have attached themselves to our crowd.

At the Dinner Dance the other night the Chief Engineer asked Vicky and me to join his table, and so there were twelve of us all, including Eric and Ken, our drivers. Eric is the slightly noisier one of the two, and they both have a fine sense of humour. We had a super time that evening. We did the Black & White Minstrel act and that was fairly successful. Vicky and Jeannie composed a ditty about Eric and Ken and we sang that and they were thrilled to bits. It is going to be so quiet without them. They leave Cape Town on Wednesday with the WINDSOR CASTLE at 4.p.m. Their route takes them through the wildest parts of the country and the Sahara, and they are supposed to arrive in Southampton on the Sunday before the WINDSOR docks. They say that they probably have a fifty-fifty chance of beating the WINDSOR. If they are home on the Sunday, apparently they have been booked to appear on the Palladium Show as an odd appearance. So look out for them on 21st May. Their journey from CT/UK is being covered by an ATV team, and their progress is being reported on Sportsview twice a week on Wednesday and Fridays, so do look at it for me.

Tuesday now.
As before, there is nothing to do so here I am again typing to you. On Sunday I went to a party at lunchtime, slept as usual afterwards, did a little nothing in the Bureau, and then had a rather large party at my home. Everybody came, including Ken and Eric. They are very complimentary and are also good company so you can imagine how hilarious it is sometimes. They talk non-stop and Vicky and I can't always get a word in edgeways. They have really made this voyage marvellous, and how terrible it's going to be when they leave us tomorrow. Last night was the Prizegiving and Farewell Dance and that was rather enjoyable. They bought a bottle of Champagne and Vicky and I drank it between us, because they are "on the wagon". Eric says his has only 3 wheels at the moment, and is in a precarious state, but apparently they are used to doing this before they start on a rally or long drive.

Tomorrow they will be having a Press Conference and all that, I gather, and then they hope to take Vicky and me out to lunch. We are all keeping our fingers crossed. Then of course at 4 o'clock they are off. Ken lives in London and Eric lives in Barnsley, Yorkshire, and they each own a large Ford garage. So after the race and all the goings-on at your end, they will each be going back home and that will probably be the end of the story. Nice though!

Please could you keep a big eye open for all paper cuttings and any adverts about them, now and after they get home. I would be very grateful. I went to look in the car yesterday and it is absolutely packed with things, but comfortably so, and very carefully.

Well, it is now Cape Town and nearly lunchtime. Thanks for the letter this morning, and I'm glad you liked Davey's flowers

Life is rather hectic today as you can guess. Eric and Ken went over to the WINDSOR for a reception and lunch. They had planned to take us out for lunch, but that is off now. So as soon as I'm free and off duty, I shall go over there. There won't be much time to see them before they leave. Eric gave me a lovely present yesterday evening (a super powder compact) to remind me of him. I've been given maps and schedules and been promised a postcard from up-country. I gather the Daily Express is covering their trip, so please can you try and get copies for me?

<u>Later</u>
Well, we went over to see the men off and it was all rather enjoyable, and touching. We were in uniform, Vicky, me, Colin and Jeannie, and we felt part of it. There were dozens of cameramen including ATV, so look out for me on the telly. I'm serious! We're longing to see the papers tomorrow. There were hundreds of people around and it felt rather nice to "belong". Life is certainly going to be much quieter without them. I'm on duty tonight and intend to write a letter to Davey and then go to bed early. It will make a change. More later. Love, Ann

Port Elizabeth
13th May, Saturday
Dear Family

Mummy - happy Mother's Day. Didn't realise it was tomorrow until yesterday, so it was too late to do anything about it. I am well, but extremely tired at the moment. We all went out in a big crowd last night and got back very very late. Had a jolly good evening though. I slept this afternoon and now feel a bit dopey.

There is not really any news to tell. Life is jogging along very quickly and well, although it is quite cool and we are still in blues and beginning to wish that we had a second dress! We are following the progress of Eric and Ken in the newspapers and Vicky and I are keeping scrapbooks. Have quite a lot in them already, and several pictures

None of us have appeared yet, and in fact we hope they don't, but we intend to go and see if the paper people will let us see the proofs of the pictures which were taken at the docks. I suppose we were in a little bit of limelight and some pictures were taken of the men wearing our hats, as a joke. Several photos were taken, so somebody must have one we can see.
Really that's about all the news. I'm quite busy at work, happy, tired and quite enjoying life.

Did the car pass the MOT test all right I wonder. I kept my fingers crossed. Hope you haven't had any more snow at home. Isn't it freak weather.

Have my new shoes come yet? Hope so, cos I'm falling out of the others, all of a sudden.

I wonder what you have done to my bedroom. I feel inquisitive about it, but I suppose I can contain my soul in patience. Must go, we are just about to sail. Love, Ann

Durban 16th May
Dear Family

Thanks for the letter yesterday. I am sorry about the car - why did it suddenly pack up? Was this before the MOT? It's a terrible thing to happen. Money to be spent too!!!

If this letter starts off by sounding a bit funny, it's probably the effects of the sun. Although I am on duty all day until 5.30, I took my lunch hour up on the sun deck and almost fell asleep. Now I am glowing well and have pink knees and don't feel completely conscious. Oh well, it was super. If this is winter, you had better emigrate.

We went into whites for arrival yesterday and things felt much better. Oh yes, big excitement yesterday morning. A telegram from Eric and Ken. It said "Arrived Salisbury 7 p.m. OK, it's all go ain't it inform all concerned love Morecambe and Wise." I felt thrilled to bits. We have been following their progress (as I said before) with tremendous interest and our scrapbooks are quite full.

The latest thing however is that three countries will not now let them drive through, because they started their journey in South Africa, so Ford have had to plan to airlift them and make them wait at the end of the amount of time they would have taken to drive through, plus a penalty hour or two. News is coming through quite slowly and reports are not always accurate so we shall just have to wait and see. It's all rather exciting anyway.

Another bit of excitement. I got my picture in the paper. How about that then. You remember I told you about the dozens of photographers at the start of the race in Cape Town, and Vicky, Jeannie, Colin and I were all there in the centre of things. Well, just one photograph has appeared in print with any of us on it, and there is Colin and me, with my back to the camera, standing beside the car and Eric, talking to one of the Ford people. There I am, plus hat and hair. The Quartermaster on here saw the picture first and rushed over to tell me, and since then one or two other people have come up and said "Wasn't that your picture with the Drivers?". So - fame at last. I will show you the picture when I get home - it's stuck proudly in my scrapbook at the moment. Quite honestly although it's a large picture, there are lots of people in it, but certainly I am very recognisable. There you are - that's something to tell the neighbours about. I wonder if you have looked at the ATV film yet, or even if they have screened it yet. You must look out for me - we all smiled at you. I imagine the UK papers might have reported the start of the race, and will let it drop until they reach say France and Lydd and then en route to Southampton.

After all that news, there isn't anything else to say. I'm well, happy, the sun is shining, the sky is blue, I cannot type very well, and I'm certainly not overworked this afternoon. Tonight I hope to be going out with the usual crowd for a meal and dancing so that will be fun. It's not a bad life - I'm lucky. But you might keep an eye open for a nice job in The Times or Telegraph ....

I'm surprised you haven't heard from Davey. He has just started a shore job with Union-Castle in Southampton, as a sort of Staff Chief Officer. He starts today and is quite looking forward to it. He has asked for leave when I get home and that has been agreed apparently. He says he is saving Green Shield stamps for you Mummy!

Well, it seems to be tea-time, so I think I shall stop and take a little refreshment. More tomorrow if there is time and anything to report. Take care. Love, Ann xxx

Port Elizabeth, 19.5.67
Hullo there

There really hasn't been any news to tell you. I keep wondering how the car is, and whether by now things have improved. How nasty to think it is going to cost real money to repair. Most un-British. I wonder how the decorating is going and what you have done.

Today we are back in blues again - it is quite surprising how the temperature drops so suddenly round the Coast this time of year. Mummy, while it was hot enough for sunbathing in Durban, it is still winter everywhere else and is decidedly chilly. Cape Town and PE were quite cool - it isn't hot all the time. But at least the sun shines.

I have the day off on Tuesday in Cape Town so I suppose and hope I will be going to see Mrs Van der Byl. It is always best to have the day off in Cape Town the day before we sail, I think, because there is always so much mail and chaos, it's nice to be out of it.

Had a letter from Doreen thanking me for the birthday present. Hope Dorothy is feeling better now. Are they going to sell a dog? Love to Elaine and Derek. See you soon. Love, Ann xxx

Monday 22nd May

Dear Family

Thank you for the letter yesterday. Great dramas at this end - we went to an SOS call the evening before and didn't dock at Cape Town until 5.p.m. so I didn't get the letter until then.

Thank goodness I know now what happened to the car - it sounds an expensive event. But how nice of Uncle Geoffrey to loan you his little Anglia - you just persevere with driving a "roller skate"! I wonder how long it will take to get repaired. It is certainly a major event, or tragedy for that matter.

You certainly seem to be gallivanting around, despite the lack of transport. Don't suppose that will ever change.

Thanks for the news of the drivers. We have just heard that they won the race, by an hour or so. Naturally we are pleased, but it seems a bit of an anti-climax now because of the long flight they had to take across those 3 African countries. It disqualified them as far as we were concerned. Still, it was fun while it lasted. Keep up the good work with the newspaper cuttings.

That is nice news about John and Biddy - I immediately thought "Oh, I will be an aunty", then remembered I will only be a second cousin to "it". Oh well, never mind.

I like the news about your Weather Satellite, seeing it in orbit in the heavens after your work on it - that is something to be proud of I reckon. I boasted about it here, saying my Father had just seen his weather "spacecraft" in orbit, the first one ever. You're right, it is thrilling.

Oh yes, the drama on Saturday night. We had the Derby then, just so that the Coastal passengers couldn't complain that we never did anything for them. It is a big work-up for us. However, it went off quite well - they all enjoyed it, and after it finished I went up to the Cocktail Bar with some of the First Class passengers. Had a drink and then about 11.15 someone rushed in (a drunken pax.) shouting that we had turned round and were going to the assistance of a small coaster that was on fire. He was a bookie, and added that he was going to make a lot of money from salvage. I was just about to leave anyway, so I went home and collected my coat and went right up to see what was happening. Met the others on the way so heard that it was true. We all stayed up on the Boat Deck and drank the Chief Engineer's brandy to keep warm (you remember, brandy and Canada Dry = B & C's!), and watched the coaster. We were about 3 cables length away (show-off) and simply stood by in case of them abandoning ship and to protect her, as she was without light. The flames were shooting up and we could see people rushing around with torches. We barely moved along, backward and forwards on the off-side of the coaster, in a terrific sea and swell, with a gale blowing. We stood by until daybreak and then another little boat took over and we shot away as fast as we could, which wasn't very fast in fact because of the gale.

It was raining and misty and we couldn't see any land. When we got to Table Bay there was a 50/50 chance that we would get in, because of the wind, but in the end we did. It was pelting with rain and blowing still, and there were lots and lots of people waiting on the quayside wondering what had happened; Father had lots to write about and I didn't stop until 8.50 p.m.

It was all quite interesting and so I have enclosed a newspaper cutting about it (the picture was taken by our Photographer on board) and a note written by Father. You might be particularly interested Daddy.

I seem to have written quite a lot about that episode but there is not much other news. I had a letter this morning from Davey's mother - nice of her. Davey is well and is working in Southampton.

That is about all for the moment - more tomorrow if there is time. I am seeing the Van der Byls tomorrow and they are taking me out for the day. Several of us are invited to the Mount Nelson Hotel tomorrow evening for dinner by one of our passengers, so that should be interesting if nothing else.

See you soon - take care of yourselves. Love, Ann xx

Cape Town, 24th May 1967
Dear family

It's half an hour to sailing, thank goodness, and it can't go quickly enough. We all always feel like this every sailing day from Cape Town, so we just pray for 3.30 when "they" all have to say goodbye to their friends and we get a bit of peace.

Just odd things. I have got some grapes this time and the plonk you wanted me to get this time for a change. Cigarettes will be organised in due course, and that is just about everything.

Yesterday was a lovely day. The weather changed completely and the sun shone, the sky was blue, there was no wind at all and the country looked all clean and nice. I had a very quick hair cut at 10 o'clock, and the Van der Byls picked me up at 10.30, so it was quite a rush.

We went out north of the city and towards Paarl. Stopped at the bottom of a Pass to look at the Huguenot Monument which was lovely, then went up and over the Franschoek Pass. Super view from the top, including a vineyard called Bellingham which is a wine we drink out here, rather frequently. Rather heavy Rosé, but rather good. Then down the other side of the Pass and along a stream track to a quiet place for a picnic lunch. And some lunch: hot thick vegetable soup from an enormous Thermos, warm newly baked meat pasties, cheese and apples, and then hot coffee from another Thermos. All this in a highly civilised manner from a white cloth on a table and chairs.

Set off again to complete the circle (almost) back towards Cape Town. Went through the fruit growing area called Elgin and other places and then over another Pass called the Sir Lowry Pass which gave a fantastic view over False Bay. We could see the whole of the Cape Peninsula right from Table Mountain (the back of it) to the Cape Point. Then back along the straight road to the ship. Lovely drive, with a stop for tea on the way.

Had a quick doze and then changed and out again to the Mount Nelson Hotel. That is one of the biggest ones in the city, owned and run by Union-Castle, and very staid and slow. However, one of our rather nice First Class passengers asked a crowd of us to dinner there so how could we say no. There were 14 of us in the party altogether. We had a jolly good meal though it wasn't particularly outstanding. About 11 o'clock the hostess for the evening decided to go out to the Sable Room where we could drink and dance (which we couldn't do at the Mount Nelson). We all went there until about 1 o'clock when we came back to the ship for a night-cap and fell into beds. That was so kind of Mrs Jameson (yes, the whisky family) to take us out. So that was a super day off and one I thoroughly enjoyed.

See you on 5th June. Take care of yourselves.

Can't think of anything more at the moment - I will probably remember just after we sail when I can't do anything about it. Oh well. I'm well, quite happy, and feeling a little warm and weary at the moment. My legs ache. That reminds me, have my shoes come yet please? Hope so - I'm falling out of these literally, at the moment. See you soon. Love, Ann xx

31st May 1967
Dear Family

This is just your usual note to read on Tuesday morning, when I will be asleep in bed probably and you will be getting Daddy off to work or just getting a cup of tea and having a lie-in. It's my "peep from the deep". (Did you like that?)

The sun is shining, the wind is blowing quite strongly, and the flying fish are flying around madly. It's a lovely day. We passed Dakar about 7.30 this morning and there is a ship to be seen on the horizon. We must be about in line with Timbuktu. This sort of day makes it all worth coming to sea for.

We have had a good voyage home so far. The ship started to roll as soon as we finally left Cape Town (at 6 o'clock in the end, because of engine problems) and didn't stop until Sunday morning. My table lamp fell off my dressing table twice - each time I thought we had stopped rolling and had put it back in its place and over it went again. Most unusual, but apparently it was because of the wind being behind us and pushing us all over the place. Time of year and all that. Anyway, Sunday morning we went to Church and the sun came out for the first time and the ship stopped rolling and it became very hot and sticky. It was a super day and we all got lots of suntan in the afternoon.

The Chief Engineer Stan Harron had a rather fine party that evening - Black Velvet (Champagne and Guinness) or Golden Velvet (Champagne and beer). All quite lethal, although I simply drank neat Champagne. Much more in my line. We had super eats there, and I had to go and have a little rest at 9.30 p.m. Then they woke me up and we all went down to the Leading Hands Recreation room to play darts. At least, the men played darts. We drank Pepsi-cola and I began to wake up a bit. Then it was dancing to finish up, then bedtime. I like Sundays at sea.

Last night was Dinner Dance Night and wasn't bad, but I suppose we were spoilt outward bound when we thoroughly enjoyed it. It was so hot last night, even in the air-conditioned splendour of the Dining Saloon, and we all felt a bit hot and sticky. Still the dancing and the music was good and so I enjoyed it.

I am playing Deck Tennis in the evenings after work now and getting exhausted. But I am determined to get some sort of exercise and I like this way of doing it. We have a regular four now and I think I am improving a bit - I'm not very good but at least I'm enthusiastic, and I make a lot of noise. The others are all better than me so I reckon I get the best out of it all.

Can't think of anything more for the moment, so I'll add to this tomorrow and post it off at Las Palmas.

Well, we are at Las Palmas, thanks for the letter. I had quite a few: 5! Lucky me. Thanks for the news - you suddenly seem much nearer, thank goodness. I'm still pink and glowing from the sun yesterday, but it's not too painful - serves me right.

Soon be home now. Hooray. Have another cup of tea, I won't be awake yet!
Love, Ann xx

Extract From The Ship's Deck Log

R.M.S. Edinburgh Castle
CAPTAIN A. A. FREER

SOUTHAMPTON TO CAPETOWN via LAS PALMAS

VOYAGE 124

June 16 to June 28, 1967

Date	Distance Run	Speed	Latitude-Longitude	Wind force	Temperature at Noon Air	Temperature at Noon Sea	Itinerary
16-6-67				NE2	70°	60°	1300 Departure Southampton. 79 First Class and 446 Tourist Class Passengers on board. Calm sea. Fine and clear
17-6-67	465	22·68	44°43N 08°43W	NNE3	69°	60°	0015 Vessel rounded Ushant and entered Bay of Biscay. 1700 passed Cape Finisterre and left Bay of Biscay. Cloudless with horizon haze
18-6-67	575	23·00	35°36N 12°45W	NNW4	66°	66°	1030 Divine Service in First Class Lounge, Commodore officiated. Overcast, fine and clear
19-6-67	466	20·44	Las Palmas		68°	69°	1130 arrived Las Palmas. 1700 departed Las Palmas. 51 First Class and 439 Tourist Class Passengers on board
20-6-67	423	22·75	21°28N 17°32W	NE5	74	63	Cloudless, fine, slight horizon haze
21-6-67	547	22·79	12°20N 17°26W	SW4	86°	78°	0500 passed Cape Verde, Dakar, the most westerly point of Africa. Cloudy, fine and clear
22-6-67	539	22·46	05°00N 12°32W	SE4	85°	84°	Moderate sea. Few clouds, fine and clear
23-6-67	520	21·67	02°02S 07°30W	SE3	79°	73°	0400 Vessel crossed Equator in DR Longitude 09·00W. Cloudless, fine and clear
24-6-67	531	22·13	09°16S 02°25W	SE4	78°	76°	Cloudy, fine and clear
25-6-67	528	22·47	16°16S 03°00E	SSE2	68°	63°	1030 Divine Service in First Class Lounge, Commodore officiated. Cloudy and clear
26-6-67	519	22·09	23°06S 08°36E	SxE3	63°	65°	Moderate sea. Cloudy, fine and clear
27-6-67	494	21·48	29°32S 14°10E	S5	59°	59°	Moderate sea. Few clouds fine and clear
28-6-67	337						0700 Estimated Time of Arrival Cape Town (S.A.S.T.)

DISTANCE 5,944 Miles   ....   AVERAGE SPEED 21·98 Knots

Extract From The Ship's Deck Log

R.M.S. Edinburgh Castle
CAPTAIN A. A. FREER

CAPETOWN TO SOUTHAMPTON via LAS PALMAS

VOYAGE 124   July 12, 1967, to July 24, 1967

Date	Distance Run	Speed	Latitude-Longitude	Wind Force	Temperature at Noon Air	Sea	Itinerary
12-7-67			At Capetown		63°		1615 Departed Capetown Fine and clear 56 First Class and 338 Tourist Class Passengers on board
13-7-67	443	22.49	28°14S 12°57E	SE6	63°	61°	Rough sea. Few clouds, fine and clear
14-7-67	553	22.57	21°03S 06°37E	SE4	65°	62°	Fine and sunny. Slight horizon haze, moderate sea
15-7-67	557	22.74	13°43S 00°41E	S'ly 3	68°	67°	Overcast and clear
16-7-67	552	22.53	07°15S 04°55W	SxE3	76°	76°	1030 Divine Service in First Class Lounge. Master officiated. Few clouds, fine and clear
17-7-67	557	23.21	00°58N 10°34W	SE3	78°	66°	0900 Vessel crossed the Equator in DR Longitude 09°30W Fine and clear
18-7-67	546	22.75	08°24N 15°50W	S'ly 3	80°	80°	Few clouds. Fine and clear
19-7-67	550	22.96	17°39N 17°39W	N3	83°	80°	0545 passed Cape Verde, most westerly point of Africa Few clouds, fine, slight haze
20-7-67	531	22.13	25°43N 16°11W	NW4	72°	68°	2000 Arrived Las Palmas Fine with horizon haze
21-7-67	363	19.95	31°27N 14°13W	NxE4	74°	70°	0030 Departed Las Palmas 64 First Class and 341 Tourist Class Passengers on board Fine and sunny, horizon haze
22-7-67	534	22.25	39°57N 10°53W	NxE4	71°	67°	1830 Passed Company's S'bound Mail Vessel R.M.S. Windsor Castle Cloudless, fine and clear 2200 Passed Cape Finisterre and entered Bay of Biscay
23-7-67	476	20.70	47°17N 06°42W	N4	64°	64°	1030 Divine Service in First Class Lounge. Master officiated. Few clouds, fine and clear 1700 Vessel rounded Ushant, left the Bay of Biscay and entered the English Channel
24-7-67	315		Southampton				0700 Estimated Time Of Arrival at Southampton Docks

DISTANCE 5,977 MILES   - -   AVERAGE SPEED 22·10 KNOTS

R.M.S. "EDINBURGH CASTLE"
CAPTAIN A. A. FREER
VOYAGE 124
LEAVING SOUTHAMPTON 16TH JUNE 1967

Friday,
Hi
It was nice to speak to you again this morning. We were in whites and are now changing at noon to blues. I can't keep track, we change so often. Still, it's cooler now so it doesn't matter. No more news. See you in July, take care. Sailing soon. Love, Ann

Las Palmas, Monday 19th.
Dear Mummy &Daddy

It is only 11.30 in the morning and yet we are here and being turned to come alongside our berth. It's the first time we've got here so early for a long time. It's very noisy down here in the Tourist Class Bureau end again but it's quite amusing. Had my hair trimmed on Friday evening after work and Brian also washed and set it for me, so that made a nice change. He is very good to me in that way. We finished work in good time on Friday so I could go to the Tourist First Night Dance. It wasn't very successful as usual, because nobody ever wants to dance.

Saturday was hectic and my feet ached by 5.30, and then there was more standing at the First Class Cocktail Party. Met several nice people. Then we had Tourist Bingo between films. After that I went to the First Class Dance and quite enjoyed that. Sat with some lovely people, including an American lady and her young daughter. The daughter has suggested I visit her next voyage when she hopes to have an apartment in Cape Town.

It's all chaos at the moment here because we have just arrived and everyone wants to know everything all at once. I'll write some more a bit later. And I'm hungry too, and want my lunch.

That was this morning. Now it is 3.45 and I'm munching Smarties, again down the slum end, without a soul around (except the Shopkeeper who gave me the packet of sweets). Everyone has gone on a tour of the town.

I finally had my lunch, closed the Bureau and had an hour off just now to go pottering. I went on the Dance Deck to look at the stalls there, which usually have Toledo-type jewellery, and lovely tablecloths etc. But they are so expensive. Elaine wanted me to get her one some time, but perhaps you will tell her that I shall wait until they sell some cheaper ones. The one I thought she might like was £6, and that was a special reduction for me.

The P&O ship "ORCADES" has just sailed and she looked quite a sight (nice) as she was tugged round and away, music blaring away.

Can't really think of any more news to tell you - there just isn't any. I wonder how Mummy's leg is now. And whether the car is better and behaving herself again. I wonder if the weather is still good. We went into blues at noon just before sailing but went back into whites on Saturday night for the Cocktail Party and now it is a bit warmer and muggier (isn't that a nice word?). The sun isn't really shining but at least it is fairly hot here. Oh yes, everyone liked my new bombshell earrings, and the dress too. I'm very glad we found that dress, although it took some doing.

Must finish now - time to get this to the post at the other Bureau. Take care. Love, Ann xxx

R.M.S. " Edinburgh Castle"
UNION-CASTLE LINE

23rd June 1967

Dear Miss Williams,

We are holding the Childrens Fair at 10.30 a.m. on Saturday and we would be very pleased if you can come.

From Ann Hesford, on behalf of all the children

The duties were varied

Day before Cape Town, at sea, Tuesday 27th
Dear familio

I've got nothing to do at present, believe it or not, and this is quite unusual for the Tourist end. Work has been going down quite well, although it never seems to end until 5.30 each day. We are on the go the whole time here, or I am at least. So often I seem to be the only one here, and it makes things a bit hectic. Still, the coast is almost here and then I shall get some time off. I shall be going shopping on Wednesday afternoon and I also have the evening off, so that will make a break.

I have just been chatting to my young friends. They can just about see over the counter, but they always seem to be at a loose end at this time of day and come and prop up the counter and chat, or show me their toy cars and things. It's rather nice.

Now I've just had a cup of Russian tea (remember the dress day in London and lunch, Mummy?) and feel even better.

The voyage has gone quite well, and the evening Entertainments have been quite enjoyable. We had a free evening the other night and attended the First Class Dinner Dance which was quite enjoyable. But it's just not the same as the ORANJE, when us girls were allowed to dress up and wear our own clothes. Those were the days ....(my goodness, I'm beginning to sound like you two!).

Well, that was all hours ago. Suddenly everyone woke up, went for their afternoon tea, and decided to visit us. Still, they were most excited about getting to Cape Town. This evening I washed my hair, and now I've just got changed ready to go for drinks with Jeannie. This is Farewell Dance night, with Prize Giving first, so that will be my fling for the evening.

Tomorrow will be an early start of course and how we dislike that. The only consolation is letters. I shall post this tonight, without waiting to see your letters, so I can reply to that later on.

The ship is rolling, and I have my heater on. It's all rather snug, and very civilised! I suppose I shall have to have a little brandy to keep me going. Lovely life. Must think about leaving it some time or other. I hear there were bad gales at home - hope you are all right, as usual it's a bit worrying when we're so far away. See you soon anyway. Do tell me all the news, and do take care. Love, Ann xx

Port Elizabeth,
Friday 30th June 1967
Dear family

Thank you for the letter in Cape Town the other day. It is 9.30 a.m. and I haven't had any letters here at all. And it was my turn to get up early to do the mail.

Well, that was $1\frac{1}{2}$ hours ago. Now I have had a letter from Davey, and I have the morning off so I can write to you. The weather is cool and I can't be bothered to go to town - I shall only spend money. My washing is now up to date, and so my conscience is clear! I enjoyed your C.T. letter.

Yes, I remember the Canterbury visit we all made, and didn't we go to Maidstone then too? I seem to remember the River there and a market and lots of earrings. Do you? Goodness, that dates me! I liked the sound of your Sunday. I like hot weather in our back garden, especially with tea and drinks on the lawn. Have you got the new garden shade yet?

My sunbed is excellent by the way. It has been used for a time just about every day when it was hot. Worth every penny. Daddy, I liked the cryptic message at the end of your letter about decorating. Oh dear, has M. been at you again? What is it this time?

Oh yes, yesterday morning I was drinking my coffee and listening to the wireless. The Morning Service was announced, and guess what. It was Archdeacon Van der Byl conducting it from St. Barnabas Church, Cape Town. How about that. I heard him introduce the Service and then I had to go, but what a surprise.

Please could you let me know what spirits to bring home this time, and Blue Grass/Old Spice. I want to keep you stocked up. The wine order you may leave to me, with confidence I might add. This time I think I shall go a bit reckless. Yum. (You can stop licking your lips - I won't be home just yet!). Odd information - I went for a Chinese meal on Wed. night in Cape Town, nice. Take care. See you soon. Love, Ann

East London, Sunday 2nd July
Dear Mummy and Daddy,

Thank you for the letter this morning and now I feel extremely curious about how you are enjoying your weekend. I didn't think you were going and then suddenly I get letters from you and Davey talking about the weekend in Sidmouth. I wish I was with you all. I hope the weather is good because it's quite a nice place, isn't it? Isn't Mr. H nice? I can imagine you two men getting on very well together.

Mummy, are you better now? I heard that you went to the doctor and you said that you had some tablets. I hope your leg is better and your stomach too. I'm glad you went to the doctor anyway. Yes, you did tell me about Aunty Grace breaking her wrist and I seem to remember saying Oh what a change. Still, I hope she is enjoying her holiday. I seem to remember you saying that she had six new dresses too.

Now where did I get to with telling you about what I had been up to. Life seems a little slow these days, and round the coast I would rather be at home. I told you I went shopping in Cape Town last Wednesday afternoon and managed to get a small blue handbag to go with my new dress. It is quite small, with a definite handle, and looks rather good with the shoes and earrings. My outfit is now complete. I think. In the evening went out for a Chinese meal, to a rather nice place called the Green or Yellow Dragon out near Mouille Point Lighthouse. All hung with lanterns and Chinese music (?) in the background and eating out of bowls with chopsticks (I was cowardly and used the tiny china spoons they sometimes use). Thursday was sailing day and so no time off.

Then it was Friday and Port Elizabeth. I had the morning off but it was cold and my time off seemed very short. So I wrote letters and kept warm and chatted to Vicky and drank hot beef tea. Pleasant way to spend a morning. Vicky is leaving at the end of the trip, because she reckons she has had enough. I can quite see her point but she wants to have a change, and she has quite a good job lined up she thinks, although she will have a holiday first. I had to work on Friday afternoon but then I had the evening off. There seems to be a ritual now of making up a party to go to the Skyroof restaurant for dinner that evening. It was the Chief Engineer's birthday the next day so it was a sort of celebration. We did justice to the occasion. I had got a bottle of cheap champers in an ice bucket in my cabin for when we got back. When we eventually got back on board (we had a lovely time there as the food and band are excellent) I put my key in the Yale lock, and guess what, it snapped off. Just like that. We had hysterics almost, especially knowing about the Champers behind the locked door, so the men all put their shoulders to the door and pushed.

The lock broke and so did the door frame. We all fell in and picked up the lock which had come clean away from the door frame. Ernie has a spare key to my cabin but of course at that time of the morning he wasn't around. However, we managed to cope with the champagne and surprisingly only one person woke up (John B-I, so we gave him some Champagne and told him to keep quiet).

Everyone else must have been overcome, after a party we all attended at 7 o'clock that evening, even before we went out. (I got the sequence wrong there somewhere). Next morning I got the lock put back firmly on to the door frame and tried to apologise and explain to the Chippies just what had happened to cause my lock to be broken so thoroughly. Tee hee.

I worked yesterday morning but was off after lunch. Managed to get myself in a car that was going for a drive along the coast road and that was lovely. The sky was blue, the sun was trying to shove out some heat, and the sea was throwing itself onto the shore with all the force it could manage. There are lots of rocks around the coast, interspersed with very sandy areas, and this causes the sea to fly up and spray goes everywhere. With the sun on it, it looked like lots of rainbows everywhere. It is a very uninhabited area - used mostly in summer, when people come down here to their summer homes which are beginning to be built around the town. The surfing is excellent apparently - we saw several people in the water, although it must have been terribly old. The weather is so cold, the temp. is only in the 40's, or was this morning. Not Outspan weather at all. Last night was Dog Racing and it was terrible because none of the passengers wanted to join in, or showed any signs of being interested. I give up.

This is just about my doings up to date - I don't seem to have any time off during the next few days. I shall get the things you wanted this time from the Shop. By the way I bought myself a nice black leather handbag, which I have been meaning to buy for a long time. All for now. Take care of yourselves - and tell me all! See you soon. Love, Ann x

Durban, Tues. 4th 12.45
Dear family

Thanks for the letter yesterday Mummy. What is Daddy doing these days, is he working away somewhere? Couldn't think why he would call in to Elaine's "on his way home".

I'm glad the films have come back - they seem to have taken a long time, don't they. Hope I get them before we leave Cape Town. I am on duty both days here so life seems very dull and unfair. Still I shall have a day off here next voyage. We have to take it in turns not to have the day off in Durban. Next time I have thought of going to a Game Reserve. There is rather a fine one about 5-6 hours driving away from here. If I can organise a car, I shall try and get some others interested. Don't think I shall bother about Johannesburg then. So much to do, and so little time to do it all! Of course, I've seen quite a lot already, so I can't complain.

Yesterday Irene went to the Indian Market and bought something for me. I asked her to get me a large laundry basket and she did. It's rather large - like an Ali Baba pot almost. Can't yet think where I'm going to keep it, but never mind. Cost me all of 14/- !!!

That is just about all there is to tell you. It's cold and wet, and I think I have a cold - ugh. Oh well, tomorrow we will be homeward bound. I'm looking forward to hearing all about "the weekend". Take care, see you soon. Love, Ann x

P.E., 7th July
Dear family

Guess what: I have just managed to decipher D's last 2 paragraphs! And that has taken me all day! It's now 5.05p.m. and we sail at 7.00 p.m., ages away yet. Thanks for the letter this morning. Davey also sent one and said you had a good weekend. I'm glad about that, and I'm looking forward to your comments. I laughed about Aunty Doris being speechless - I bet she is dying of curiosity! Roll on Cape Town and letters.

In Durban, to bring you up to date, I had a telephone call from the 2nd Officer Dave Hawker, on the RICHMOND CASTLE, ex S. A. ORANJE, and he invited himself to dinner. After that a crowd of us went to the pictures and saw "Two for the Road", which was very funny, filmed by Chris. Challis! Super photography and locations! I boasted about us knowing him and his family from Longford.

We sailed late from Durban and for the first time ever saw Durban at night from the Indian Ocean, with all the lights twinkling. It was beautiful. Then it was East London and work all day, sailing at 5, so that wasn't too bad. Then a passenger party after sailing - and guess who I met - the singer Dick Haymes and his wife Wendy. They seem quite pleasant. Have you heard of him - you must have done? She comes from Wraysbury, so we had a chat about Wraysbury and Harmondsworth.

This morning I hired a Mini and drove, with the Nursing Sister, to the country. We were going to a Wildlife Park, but couldn't seem to find it, so just drove on. Came to lovely mountains, plateau, river and cliff-type rocks. Tiny "hotel" (joke) in middle of nowhere, so had coffee and sandwiches. Lovely drive through Van Staden's Pass; then big rush home for work at 1.30. So on it goes.

I have Sunday off, so I'm looking forward to going out for the day. Hope it comes off. Normal day at sea tomorrow - how nice. See you soon, take care, write legibly. Love, Ann xx

Cape Town, Monday 10th
Dear Daddy,

Thank you for the lovely letter. I was longing to get it and hear all about the summit meeting! And to think that I could read all your writing too. Wonders will never cease (I hope).

Yes, I remember B & B at Chard - I made Davey drive through there last time so that I could see the river running down each side of the street - remember? I liked the bit about the Haynes Hydrographic Section - it made me laugh.

Having just removed two tiny splinters from one finger, I feel able to continue this letter, don't know where they came from. Just found another one. My goodness, I must be a chip off the old block or something. Well, I've just been for some tea and now feel able to continue, again. Can't remember where I got to with the tales of the Edinburgh Forests (joke ?, like Vienna Woods, you know). Did I tell you I went to a Cocktail party on Saturday night on here and met Dick Haymes (and wife) who is a well-known crooner/singer? I think I did.

Yesterday was my day off and was I looking forward to it. Flew out of the Bureau at 10 o'clock and went over to the CAPETOWN CASTLE. My dear old ship is just near us here in the docks and is sailing tomorrow. So I went over there just to have a look round and discovered all sorts of people on there that I knew, and didn't know were on her. Floated back here for drinks and lunch.

Then had a sleep for half an hour and then off for a lovely trip up Table Mountain. The weather was perfect, with a few clouds, very high up, miles above the Table. We walked a long way along the top, over the other side facing Cape Point direction. The view is superb and the Mountains in the distance looked just as I like to see them - very solid and grand, and very awe-inspiring. Got very tired walking and with all that fresh air so we had coffee in the chalet at the top then caught the cable car down, just as the sun was beginning to set - that was about 5.45.

Then more time to drink and laugh, then we went out for a meal. It was a steakhouse in the city, with a difference. It was a wooden-built little house, beautifully varnished inside, with odd copper things and bottles hanging around, and the waitresses (all two of them) were the strangest I have seen for a long time. They had pale lilac coloured knitted jersey mini-dresses (with long sleeves) just half-way down their thighs, gingery hair, long lilac dangling earrings, and long white boots! They looked interesting, because they were quite well-made girls. All the men were fascinated, of course. Like a lot of places here, you take your own wine, which I think is a very good idea. They usually chill it for you, while you are having your first course.

Today is family day here and everything is closed and the city has gone to Sea Point they tell me. Strange how we always manage to get the holidays here, which don't earn us any leave whatsoever.

We had a very large party of school children on here from Cape Town/Durban/CT. Their leader was pleasant, and during the voyage gave Colin and me each a brooch badge which was what they all wore - very nice it is too, and a nice thought on their part. However, when we docked here yesterday morning their leader came up to us again and gave us each a little parcel and said thank you for what we had done. Inside was a Parker Jotter pen, inscribed with their motto in Afrikaans (something about friends in distant parts). Wasn't that kind of them?

Just now, one of the seven Davids who used to be on the ORANJE appeared. He is now on the RICHMOND CASTLE and we met them the other day somewhere up the coast - can't remember where, but I told you about it at the time I think. I'm off duty soon so I shall take a walk round with him to his crate and have a look round there.

I have organised some fruit to bring home and the wine order has gone in, so I feel as it I am now homeward bound - thank goodness. I'm looking forward to getting home - I think I'm bored too much here. Seem to be reading an awful lots of books these days. Seen any good jobs in the Daily Telegraph lately? Hey, ho, time to close the Bureau almost, so I shall post this off I think. See you soon. Take care and don't work too hard. Love, Ann xxx

Cape Town
12th July 1967
Dear Mummy and Daddy

Well it's finally sailing day Cape Town and goodness is it cold. I am sitting in the Tourist Bureau jumping up and down for keys, but it is so chilly this morning that I have just put on my little red vest! This is under my navy uniform dress of course. The last few days have been unusually warm and everyone suspected all sorts of odd things might happen. Today it has changed and we are back to winter. The sun is shining but it is cloudy and the Mountain is covered.

As I told you, Sunday was my day off and I enjoyed it. But the last two days I have been in the Bureau writing letters and reading lots of pages. There is very little else to do. Fortunately I had the evenings off so that was all right.

Monday lunchtime I was doing a meal relief in the First Class Bureau when this man came along, then his friend, and chatted for a while. He then said "Come and have a drink with me, 7 o'clock here". So I said yes. In the afternoon Dave Hawker came over and I went back with him at 6 o'clock to his RICHMOND CASTLE. It seems so small after this, that you can only just see the funnel over the top of the quayside! Anyway, I flew back here just after 7 and met the man and went up to the Cocktail Bar for a drink. Then he said "Come and have dinner with me", so I took a deep breath and said I would. He is a journalist and travels over the world fairly frequently and was quite interesting to listen to. So I got changed and off we went, to several hotels around Sea Point, which I had never been to before, and then to his super 4th floor flat where he cooked a meal! It was quite amusing, especially when his girlfriend (it couldn't have been anyone else) rang up and he didn't quite know what to say to her. I wanted to go home then so off we went. It was quite an amusing/interesting evening anyway, although I wondered what I had let myself in for!

Then it was Tuesday and more reading and letter writing and then time to knock off. Had a little rest and then drinks and out for a meal. Went to a lovely place in the city, with a super band. Apparently they play on the local radio station quite often, and their female singer is excellent. It was Vicky's last night in Cape Town so it was a sort of celebration.

Today it's sailing day and with a bit of luck I might get to bed early this evening. I'm such a gadabout!!!

Now to business. Please could you order me two pairs of stockings Mummy? You have the shade and size slip at home there. Also, please could you order me a half tin of Jacob's Cream Crackers, for Mrs Van der Byl? Ta. She wanted some other biscuits, but I think I shall just get some small packets and take them back with me. It might be a bit difficult to get them to her from the ship. She also wants some stockings, but I can get them when I come home I think.

Big news this morning is John (Ingram). You know his wife Judith is expecting another infant. Yesterday unfortunately she nearly had a miscarriage and the doctor's verdict this morning is that John must stay with her. So he will be signing off and staying home. In many ways he is rather pleased (apart from the reasons for doing so) as all decisions are taken out of his hands. He would like to leave the job but cannot really do so just yet, for financial reasons. So this settles it all for him. Whether this will be the end of his sea career or not no-one knows.

I have just had to dig another splinter out of my thumb this time, it's getting a bit much. It must be my till which is coming to bits or something.

Sitting behind me on the back counter is a pocket of grapefruit. Just think - in two weeks time (or less) we will be eating them together. Isn't it strange. They will be put in cool storage for the voyage home. I hear through the grapevine (joke coming up) that the bulk wine order is aboard, so that is good news. I can see I won't be travelling light when I come home this time.

Well, now it's 3.10 and time I posted this or it will be even more chaotic in a few minutes. See you soon - take care of yourselves. Love to Elaine and Derek and Dorothy & Derek. Any news yet? Love, Ann xx

At sea, Monday, Equator day.
Dear family

This is my usual note to you from Las Palmas, but I thought I would start it early as there are one or two things I might forget if I don't write them down now.

So. It is just after 2 and I feel rather well. The sun is hot and brilliant, I had half an hour's sunbathe before lunch, then a cold lunch and wine. I feel rather well .... We only went into whites yesterday so we feel a sense of release, if you see what I mean, because it is not really pleasant to live in the same dress for about 3 weeks! Still, my cold went (I think I forgot to mention this). I went to the Doc. and he gave me some penicillin tablets, medicine, and said eat this lot. So I did, and in three days I lost my voice, couldn't do any broadcasts, felt most peculiar, and got rid of my cold and felt normal again. It was all quite dramatic.

Leaving Cape Town was nice, and rather amusing. One of the other Castle fruit boats had sailed the day before, broke down a few hours away, and was towed back. An hour before we were due to sail, the RICHMOND CASTLE (the one I went to see) sailed, and broke down in the middle of the harbour. So she had to be pushed back in the quayside. We all crossed our fingers and hoped for the best when it came to our turn. Our tugs were busy with the RICHMOND so we sailed a little late, and it was blowing a bit of a south-easter so we felt lucky to get out easily. But we did.

The next morning, heading for home out of Cape Town, we discovered we had a stowaway. She is about 60 and is quite mad; she has a kind of religious mania and goes about spouting the words of the Lord and handing out small booklets about turning to Christ. One she says is written by her father and the other by her mother. I was blessed twice that first afternoon! She also referred me to Revelations 22, I think it was. (Have I mentioned before, when we have little parties, the invitations are often Biblical references - I believe it is a naval tradition - and certainly fascinating). Anyway, stowaway lady smells strongly of "Vick" so we always know when she is around. Most odd. At the Captain's Cocktail Party she came in, shook hands with him and promptly handed him one of her booklets. He was silenced immediately and barely hid a smile. However, she passed along and he passed it aside. Cor.

One of the films on here the other day was "Showboat". You must have seen it because it is about 30 years old I think. Howard Keel, Kathryn Grayson, Paul Robeson etc. are all in it. Remember? I enjoyed it very much, and I think I might try and get the record if there is a cheap edition going.

My laundry basket is sitting happily in my home nowadays. It is full of sundry things of interest, like a gallon of red wine, a gallon of white wine, a bottle of brandy, 4 table legs, and 2 bottles of Pepsi-cola. A rare mixture. At least it won't fall over. Mind you, you can't even push it anywhere.

Yesterday was Sunday (brilliant girl) and that is the day we enjoy best. We hardly seem to open the Bureau at all - just till Church time, then it is coffee time before we open again, then lunchtime and we don't open until 4.30 p.m. So I went up for a pre-lunch drink on deck, then sunbathed until about 2, then cold lunch, very considerately organised by one of the crowd, including wine, and what else but a nap and rest in the remainder of the time. Lovely way to spend a day at sea.

Then last night was Vicky's leaving party. It was an enormous success. It was also the day of the Darts Match, Leading Hands v. Officers, so at 10 o'clock we will trooped down to their establishment. I don't play, but I drink and support everyone, and dance with the rest of the people not playing. Finally surfaced (of a sort) near midnight and started to try to clear up the mess in the alleyway. Most of it was left til the morning.

We have been putting the clocks back half an hour every night until Saturday (such a funny idea to do it in half -hours) but we could have really done with a bit more last night.

Tonight is a birthday party for the First Engineer's wife which should be fun. Tomorrow is Dinner Dance night (and hair-up night) and then it will be Las Palmas and nearly home. More a little later then.

At Las Palmas, Thursday night.

Thanks for the letters, now you all seem so much nearer. See you soon. As usual, when you read this I shall be tucked up in bed (I hope!). Don't call me - I'll call you!!! Love, Ann xx

R.M.S. EDINBURGH CASTLE

First Engineer Officer Robbie Robertson, front left, and Mrs Robertson with shipmates

Extract From The Ship's Deck Log

R.M.S. Edinburgh Castle
COMMODORE W. S. BYLES, R.D.

SOUTHAMPTON TO CAPETOWN via LAS PALMAS

VOYAGE 125   August 4 to August 16, 1967

Date	Distance Run	Speed	Latitude-Longitude	Wind force	Temperature at Noon Air	Sea	Itinerary
4-8-67				WxS3	56°		1300 Departure Southampton. 120 First Class and 479 Tourist Class Passengers on board Few clouds. Fine and clear
5-8-67	463	22·05	44°37N 08°23W	Variable	64°	66°	0006 Vessel rounded Ushant and entered Bay of Biscay 1715 passed Cape Finisterre and left Bay of Biscay 2130 passed Company's N'bound vessel Pendennis Castle Calm sea. Cloudy, fine and clear
6-8-67	547	21·88	36°02N 12°23W	NNW4	68°	69°	1030 Divine Service in First Class Lounge, Commodore officiated. Low swell. Cloudy, fine and clear
7-8-67	496	21·38	Las Palmas		73°	69°	1224 arrived Las Palmas. 1700 departed Las Palmas 99 First Class and 478 Tourist Class Passengers on board
8-8-67	414	22·50	21°40N 17°35W	NNE6	75°	70°	Rough sea. Overcast and clear
9-8-67	533	22·20	12°45N 17°35W	NNW3	82°	83°	0600 passed Cape Verde, Dakar, the most westerly point of Africa. Cloudy and clear, occasional showers 0821 Passed Company's N'bound vessel Good Hope Castle
10-8-67	530	22·08	05°16N 13°07W	WxS5	77°	79°	Moderate sea. Cloudy and clear, occasional rain
11-8-67	525	21·88	01°54S 08°07W	SExS3	71°	71°	0545 Vessel crossed Equator in DR Longitude 09°20W Slight sea. Fine and clear, horizon haze
12-8-67	516	21·50	09°01S 03°17W	SExS4	72°	73°	2030 Passed Company's N.bound vessel S.A. Oranje Moderate sea. Overcast and clear
13-8-67	534	22·25	16°21S 01°51E	SExS5	66°	66°	1030 Divine Service in First Class Lounge, Commodore officiated. Moderate sea. Overcast and clear, rain
14-8-67	504	21·91	22°48S 07°32E	SE5	62°	64°	Rough sea. Cloudy and clear
15-8-67	497	21·61	29°10S 13°24E	SE6	62°	62°	Moderate swell, rough sea. Few clouds fine and clear
16-8-67	384						0700 Estimated Time of Arrival Cape Town (S.A.S.T.)

DISTANCE 5,943 Miles   ....   AVERAGE SPEED 21·93 Knots

Extract From The Ship's Deck Log

R.M.S. Edinburgh Castle
COMMODORE W. S. BYLES. R.D.

CAPETOWN TO SOUTHAMPTON via LAS PALMAS

VOYAGE 125   August 30, 1967, to September 11, 1967

Date	Distance Run	Speed	Latitude-Longitude	Wind Force	Temperature at Noon Air	Sea	Itinerary
30-8-67			At Capetown		63°		1645 Departed Capetown Overcast and clear 63 First Class and 494 Tourist Class Passengers on board
31-8-67	449	22.23	28°19S 12°39E	SE5	70°	60°	Rough sea. Few clouds, fine and clear
1-9-67	565	22.60	21°09S 05°57E	SE5	73°	64°	Moderate sea, vessel rolling easily. Fine and clear.
2-9-67	545	22.71	14°10S 00°06W	SE5	66°	67°	Moderate sea. Overcast and clear
3-9-67	540	22.5	06°42S 05°13W	SExE5	71°	73°	1030 Divine Service in First Class Lounge. Commodore officiated. Vessel rolling easily, Overcast, occasional rain
4-9-67	542	22.48	00°24N 10°45W	SSE3	77°	72°	0940 Vessel crossed the Equator in DR Longitude 09°18W Low swell. Overcast and clear
5-9-67	532	22.17	08°00N 15°23W	S4	86°	80°	Moderate sea, few clouds. Fine and clear
6-9-67	535	22.29	16°21N 17°39W	W3	83°	84°	0730 Passed S'bound Mail Vessel S.A. Oranje 0743 passed Cape Verde, most westerly point of Africa Slight sea. Few clouds, fine and clear
7-9-67	528	22.00	24°57N 16°25W	NE4	72°	70°	2300 Arrived Las Palmas Moderate sea, low swell. Cloudless and clear
8-9-67	369	20.49	30°49N 14°30W	NNE5	74°	73°	0348 Departed Las Palmas 101 First Class and 503 Tourist Class Passengers on board Rough sea. Cloudy, fine and clear
9-9-67	519	22.00	39°06N 11°24W	NxE5	71°	70°	1925 Passed Company's S'bound Mail Vessel R.M.S. Windsor Castle Rough sea, fine and clear
10-9-67	514	22.35	46°58N 06°52W	NE3	64°	65°	0020 Rounded Cape Villano and entered Bay of Biscay 1030 Divine Service in First Class Lounge. Commodore officiated. Slight sea, overcast with haze, mod. visibility 1745 Vessel rounded Ushant, left the Bay of Biscay and entered the English Channel
11-9-67	333		Southampton				0700 Estimated Time Of Arrival at Southampton Docks

DISTANCE 5,971 MILES - - AVERAGE SPEED 21·86 KNOTS

R.M.S. "EDINBURGH CASTLE"
COMMODORE W. S. BYLES R.D.
VOYAGE 125
LEAVING SOUTHAMPTON 4TH AUGUST 1967

Sunday at sea
Dear M & D

Wish I was with you. I'm longing to hear how Friday evening went. I enjoyed planning all the bits and pieces and was glad you enjoyed the surprise. I'd love to have been there. Hope you had a good time. News items: we have to do the Newspaper ourselves now, which means getting up at 6 a.m. Nasty. Just like the old days again. Ernie has been forbidden to do it for us, so off we go again. That settles it as far as I am concerned, I can't stand much of this 6 a.m. lark! Today was the first day and my turn. Ugh. Still, it was Sunday and we had the afternoon off. The weather was splendid and I am positively glowing with health now. Oh yes. Sailing day Mr Cook appeared, said his usual words of nothing, then said to me "We've had several glowing reports of you recently." Wasn't that nice! Didn't like to tell him that he had better make the most of my services while he can!

Tomorrow is Las Palmas day and I am having some time off. I intend to go shopping, cause I want to buy a leather coat. Ann Dunne knows where to go for one, and will take me I hope. So how about that! I feel a bit extravagant, but it will be so much cheaper than at home. By the way, do you want brandy again this time, or something else? By the way, my mac. is not on board so I have given it up for lost. I <u>do not</u> understand.

Tomorrow Mr. Bernard Cayzer joins us, til Cape Town, so there should be all sorts of happenings. Oh well. It's started already. It is obviously going to be one of those voyages. Roll on 11th September. Hope you have a good holiday. I will be thinking of you, as usual of course and wondering just how much wine you're seeing and trying! Enjoy it all anyway, and take care. Love, Ann xxx

Monday at Las Palmas
Dear Daddy

Just wanted to say thank you for the letter just now. It was such a surprise! I felt very lucky getting two letters here. About the wine, I knew you were pleased about me getting it, apart from you actually saying so. But the money is quite unnecessary, and anyway £5 is too much! Shall I get the same again this time? Including the Champagne? I shall do that quite happily. Seems ages away yet.

It was a good leave, wasn't it? I did enjoy the party especially. I'm looking forward to 11th September now.

Right at this moment all is humming in preparation for "our Bernard". He should arrive in 30 minutes. Must post this now. Take care. Love, Ann

Cape Town, Wednesday
16th August 1967
Dear Mummy and Daddy

Thanks for the letter this morning. It was very cheering, as I had been waiting for letters for days now.

By now you will be leaving piles of clothes everywhere I can imagine, getting ready for tomorrow. It seems strange to think of you getting ready to go - I can see it all happening. There doesn't seem to be any rush to write to you of course but I thought you would like to know the oddments of this voyage so far.

Things looked lovely going past the Isle of Wight - seeing lots of places I had seen the previous week, right from St. Catherine's Lighthouse, Oratory, Tennyson's Monument, and the Needles. I rushed on deck just in time to see all this. It was awful leaving Southampton because I didn't really want to go.

Anyway, things went as usual until Las Palmas. Then chaos reigned and suddenly cleared. Bernard was due to arrive at 2.30 p.m. and was half an hour late, so we were all on our toes. We had cleared the Bureau, and nothing was in sight, except us, and I have never seen it look so tidy. It never will again either. The gold braid mustered in the Bureau Square, and Bernard then arrived. He ignored the Bureau and took to his cabin, and we hardly saw him for 24 hours. Then the next day he came and introduced himself to us individually - said he hadn't seen me before - had I been with the Company long. Yes, I told him, I had. Oh, he said. (He was one of the people we had to meet during interviews, as well as Sir Nicholas Cayzer, think they liked to give us the 'once over'.) Because of his arrival however, the Purser stopped shore leave for us so I couldn't go and look at leather coats. I think I might try and buy one on the way home if I can.

New page, new subject. We have dancing lessons most evenings now after dinner, for half an hour. Originally we (about 10 of us) wanted to learn a few new cha-cha-cha steps, but now it has turned into a formation team, because the Dancers want to do a Demonstration on the way home (us, that is, not them). The matter caused us some amusement. What will happen remains to be seen. At the Dinner Dance last Friday we all naturally got up to do the cha-cha-cha. Rather amusing, because we were all doing the same steps.

I think I told you that we have to do the News on here now. The morning after the Dinner Dance was my News day, and what with the 6 o'clock start I didn't feel too bright. Still, we get the afternoon off until 4 o'clock so that makes up for it. The sunshine was super on Sunday and for the few days before the Equator so I have got quite brown, for me.

I took some dictation from Bernard Cayzer the other day and he seemed pleased with my efforts. He came and shook hands this morning and said goodbye and good journey home. Nice of him. As you can imagine he had his nose politely into absolutely everything on board, including our cabins too, one morning, and everyone will now have to wait until we get home for his complaints or otherwise. At last he has gone, and everyone can relax and breathe more freely again.

Oh yes, on Saturday night we passed the ORANJE and I rushed up to the Bridge and guess what, I spoke to one of the mates (Phil) on the VHF. We spoke for several minutes and he told me that Cozette is leaving this voyage. She is the tall blonde Hostess, Austrian mother, blue eyes, remember the photographs? It was nice to chat to him anyway and rather peculiar. Very odd, this modern science, it's marvellous what you can do with machines, isn't it.

After that I rushed down below, changed into my yellow dress and yellow sunglasses (made a yellow hat too) and rushed back up top again for a quick dancing lesson then down again for Frog Derby Night. Sunday night I had a party, didn't have to go to Entertainment, and then we all went down to the Leading Hands Darts match, plus Father and Mr. Bernard. Both made speeches, and Mr. Bernard bought drinks all round. Rather a splendid gesture!

Monday it started to get rough and we didn't get much chance to go on deck and so felt sorry for ourselves. The work piled up and so did the sea. Monday night was Farewell Dance night and we rolled all night, I didn't sleep well at all and then I had to get up to do the News. It was dark and cold and I felt very sorry for myself. Still, the sea calmed down and the work piled up and I finally finished at 7 o'clock. Then it was a drink and dinner and a little Tourist Dancing. Then shower and bed, nice and warm and time to put on nail polish, read and sleep. We docked on time and then there were letters, hooray. Lovely.

Oh yes, the other night someone had an emergency operation for appendicitis and caused history, because they have never had an operation on here before. Apparently the preparations were hilarious because the table kept rolling about at first and things couldn't be found. The woman was surgeried however and is now fine and in hospital here.

The Quartermaster is complaining furiously about me typing so I shall have to stop I suppose. He does go on. He's laughing now at the thought of me writing about him.

Must stop now, post this and go for lunch and off. Love, Ann.

Cape Town, Wed. 16th (contd.)
Dear Family

This is going to be a continuation of the first one (what a logical mind I have!) because more has happened since I ran out of space on the last aerogramme. I finished work at 1.30, had a quick lunch, then Sheila (McGregor) and I went over to the WINDSOR CASTLE, where I saw Derek Mason. We had a nice chat for half an hour (he used to be on the ORANJE) and then left there to go to town. We both bought 2 LP records (cheap ones, of course) and felt satisfied. Then there was a cloudburst and the gutters of Adderley Street positively roared with rainwater. We were soaked within seconds running for a taxi to get us home. But triumphant at last, we made it, plus basket, flowers (sweet peas - reminded me of home of course) and records. Time for a quick cup of coffee then back to work (well, sort of). Did a little typing, chatted a bit, wrote this and generally did nothing in as efficient a manner as possible. Hey ho, time for a little something before dinner, Bureau being closed, then dinner, and open again until 9 o'clock. Nice orderly existence. I shall keep this until P.E. and finish it then, as there is no rush to post it off, so you will get two ports' news at one time. (On reflection, that apostrophe looks good, doesn't it?)

Port Elizabeth, Friday 16th
Well, I'm in my cabin after an unexpected day's work, trying to catch up with this note. But this morning I got a letter from Elaine (first in almost 2 years!) and what news! I jumped out of bed shrieking "I'm going to be an aunty" and just had to tell everyone. Even at that time of day they were quite appreciative. Cor. I hear you are pleased. What an understatement. I am thrilled to bits for them and for us all. Isn't it super news.

Just to keep things in sequence I ought to mention leaving Cape Town. We left on Thursday at 10.30 a.m. and it was raining and there was a rainbow over the city, and no sign of the Mt. Then we started rolling furiously and didn't stop until P.E. My cabin was in a state of siege and absolutely everything had to be cleared off the surfaces. Bottles went into my wardrobe drawer, flowers in the basin, record player Sellotaped down well, clock flat on the rug on the daybed, and everything else in drawers. I didn't sleep much at all, because I thought I might fall out of bed, and nobody enjoyed that evening. Irene even fell off her chair in the Dining Room at lunchtime which caused a bit of a stir. She just sat there and laughed. After lunch we went back to work and staggered around.

Then I had to go up to the Commodore and get a note from him. Whilst standing at the door before leaving him, there was a big lurch and we both staggered and everything around us started moving. Then I did my good deed for the day. Guess what I caught? You won't - it was the budgie in the cage! Father has this blue budgie which has been with him for 14 years and it sits on the desk near him. This was a heavy cage but it moved with the ship's roll, and as I was standing nearby I just held my arms wide and caught it! It all happened so suddenly we didn't have time to think and the poor bird must have wondered what was happening.

He soon settled down again and we picked up lots of cigarettes, ornaments and coffee cups, and carried on. Wasn't that a strange thing to happen. My deed for the day - catching the Byles Budgie!

Even when we had to put some new pax. lists up on the Notice Board I had to sit on the carpet in the Square to do it. The Board would only have fallen over if they had been put upright, so I sat down to the job. I thought that was a bit outside the realms of Bureaucratic duties! Then a bit later it was Boat Drill and that finished the afternoon.

That evening it was too rough for Dancing so we had Frog Racing. There was a Ladies Race, and I entered and won it. Then there was a Finals Race with the four winners and do you know what - I won that too! How about that. Next morning here we were, in P.E. It poured with rain absolutely all day and night. It was my day off, but Irene is ill so I had to change with her. At first I was upset because I was going to the Addo Elephant Park, but the tour was cancelled due to the weather, so it didn't matter so much. Must go next trip. Finished at 5.30 and then home to music and chats. Drinks before dinner, and after dinner, it's surprising how people congregate together whilst we are in port, then finally off to the Dance in the Lounge. It was quite fun and the party finally broke up at about midnight. So it was quite a reasonable day. But the rain. And it was cold and I had to wear my red vest, and I haven't had my cabin heater off for about 3 days. I have the porthole open and the wind comes roaring in but that's the best way to ventilate the room really.

I feel so pleased about Elaine's news. What a nice piece of news for you to go on holiday with. Hope you got my missive on holiday day too.

Odd information. One of our First Class passengers coming out was a Mr Ken Wood, who is the Kenwood Chef food mixer man. It's his name! He was one of the backers financially, by coincidence, of Sheila Scott, who flew from Cape Town to London alone, remember? Mr Wood had his wife and daughters with him, and one daughter was very popular with the male Officers!

Oh yes, John Bokor-Ingram came on board on Wednesday evening and we had a long chat. Invited to a party at his home downcoast. He is quite happy now, having resigned. That is about all the news for now. More next time. See you soon now. Love, Ann xx

At sea, Monday 21st August 1967
Dear family,

Here we are at sea, it's before dinner, and we ought to be in Durban. It's a long tale so here goes.

Saturday evening we eventually left P.E. 2 hours late. That was annoying but I was given the evening off so I went to bed. The next morning we arrived at East London at an unearthly hour and I was up at 6.15 to help do the mail. Very very cold, but sunny.

Irene was ill still so I had to work in the morning. It was freezing cold, vest, cardigan and gloves weather, although still sunny, and then they said I could have the afternoon off. I rushed through lunch; then changed and left the ship. Went along to the beach nearby and walked and walked, all along the beach front. Eventually got to the Aquarium (well, that's what they call it - it isn't actually rated as one of the major tourist attractions of the place - they haven't any here for that matter, except for the Pineapple Research Station) and there was a splendid little swimming pool, complete with little mini-penguins, having a <u>whale</u> of a time. Some were sitting on the maypole-type thing in the middle, preparing for action, and some were in action, in the water. It was quite amusing to watch them preparing to jump in, but not quite having the courage to do so the first time they thought of it.

Then round a few yards to another pool, bigger this time, where there were some seals swimming around. It was obviously warmer under the water than on top or out of it, so I didn't see much of them but I took some pictures. Then along a bit further past the aquarium towards the end of town (they call it a city) and here the surf was blowing off the sea and I started to get damp.

The sea was really rough by this time, with a tremendous wind, which pushed me back 2 steps with every 3 I took (you see what I mean, anyway). I thought I would have got too wet going any further, so I turned back. But it was a splendid sight to see all the sea, waves, surf, rocks etc. causing havoc all along the coast. It took me about 40 minutes to walk along as far as I did, and it took about 15 minutes to get back, so you can imagine the strength of the wind; I met the hairdressers and some others back near the ship, so we went for a cup of coffee.

I suppose I should explain that the East London Docks are in the Buffalo River, beside the railway lines, beside a lovely beach, beside 2 hotels. And it's deserted in winter, packed in summer. Anyway, we had coffee, then set off again across the railways. There was a lovely big engine, the sort I call a cow-catcher, with a "shover" in front, you know the sort, and the others decided to take a picture of me pushing it, or pretending to. Unknown to me, while I was feeling terribly brave and standing in the track, pretending to push the thing along, the engine driver spied us, smiled to himself and the others, and let off a clanking noise. I nearly jumped out of my skin, and the others roared with laughter. The engine driver thought it was a huge joke, and so did I afterwards. The train hadn't moved, and wasn't going to, but he made it make this noise. We finally got a picture!

Although we were due to sail at 5 p.m. the powers-that-be decided it was too rough, even after sunset, and again later that night, so we left at 6.30 a.m. this morning Monday. So we have had a day at sea, irritated at the thought of being here when we could be in Durban. Thank goodness my day off is Tuesday. With a bit of luck I should be able to get away. I'm determined to.

However, at lunchtime today I went on to the Bridge. I suppose we were about a mile or 2 away from the coast, which was hilly and wooded, and now and again you could see native huts, round and thatched, on the top of hills, or in sheltered valleys. The sun was shining from a cloudless blue sky, and the water was sparkling. Suddenly Dick gave a shout, and we rushed to the wing of the Bridge in time to see some porpoises jumping in front of the ship. Then we saw a shark, yes really, because I saw its fin. One of the most odd things that I saw was the actions of some birds. They were flying around, about 30 feet above the water, when suddenly they must have spied some fish below them. They suddenly dive-bombed down into the water and disappeared from sight. It was usually 2 or 3 at a time, and they moved at a tremendous speed. It was obvious that they got what they wanted, in the fish line. So that made quite an interesting jaunt to the Bridge. I like being invited to go up there, because you can see so much.

We are due to arrive at Durban about 10 o'clock this evening and that will probably be a prolonged business. Still, I suppose it is better than going in tomorrow morning. It is probably going to be a very late night though, with docking, mail and passengers.

Well, I hope you prospective grandparents (tee, hee) are well, and have had a good holiday. I keep thinking about you and wondering what you are doing, and how you are enjoying it. See you soon anyway, take care of yourselves. Love, Ann

Durban Wednesday 23rd August

Dear prospective Grandparents

This is its Aunty writing to you again. I know I posted the last letter to you when we arrived here, which was at 11.30 p.m. on Monday night. That was a terrible hour to arrive, especially as we had the Bureau open at 9.30 and just had to sit around and wait for them to get us alongside. Still, they finally managed it and there we were. We closed the Bureau at Midnight and I just went straight to bed. Lots of passengers got off, but lots didn't but they got off first thing on Tuesday (yesterday). Thanks for the letter here - I can imagine everything so clearly when you tell me about the things that happen at home. But I heard from Davey that you got the telegram safely. I think you could quite safely post my letters much later than you do. I thought that telegram would perhaps be a big surprise and you would like it, so I fixed it. I was dying to be there when it arrived, actually, so I could see your reactions. And I'm glad the other films have arrived. I had given them up for lost, so that was a very nice surprise. Apart from that, I had forgotten what the pictures were of.

So where were we. Oh yes, Tuesday morning, opened shop at 8.30, then worked (sort of) until 10 o'clock. Then off for the whole day! Irene was back at work and things were almost back to normal, so I got my day off. You couldn't see me for dust at 10 o'clock. Two of us hired a Mini and I had already made up my mind that I wanted to go to the Oribi Gorge, many miles down south. We got the Mini and then had a quick coffee and set off. I had put on my yellow dress that morning, and guess what - the Mini was primrose yellow too! It's name was Zeus, wasn't that nice.

We took the N2 Road south, and it was a lovely blue sunny day. The road was straight and fast for some time, between hills, then we got to the sugar cane fields, everywhere you could see, for miles, on the hillsides, with occasional gaps where they had built the native kraals where the workers lived. There was a little narrow-gauge railway line, running all over the place, which obviously carried the cut cane in the season. At present they were beginning to cut it down, and we saw loaded railway trucks in Halts further along the line. The lines (real ones) went along the side of the sea and the beaches were quite deserted, so we had lovely views between hills. Sometimes the road got inland, but most of the time it was beside the sea.

Stopped suddenly once because the native women were sitting weaving baskets and things on the roadside. They had mud-hut stalls behind them and just sat on the grass outside weaving and gossiping. One dirty baby crawled around in the mud and looked happy. I bought a waste paper basket which was beautifully made. Very plain but tasteful, I think is the expression! Then on further towards a place called Port Shepstone. It has a Lighthouse that we passed the night before. There we turned right and took to the foothills. A few miles later we saw the right sort of signposts and this is when we went on safari again. It was a tiny track cut into the side of the rocks, and the path went round what I called a canyon. It was a sort of gorge, but was the route of a river. It wasn't dangerous or anything, but just full of bends and unexpected views across the gorge.

The road descended to the river bed, mostly dried out, the track forked here and we could have gone across the river by ford, but we carried on straight and then crossed it by a proper bridge. Then we started climbing again and that was interesting. Got to the top of the other side of the gorge and went across fields of more sugar cane.

This eventually brought us out on to a track which led to the Oribi Gorge Hotel. We went there and discovered our canyon was only a sort of off-shoot of the Oribi Gorge. The Hotel had a big garden and sunshades, and big overhanging trees of flowers of gorgeous colours (do you see what I mean). A man announced that the land was all owned by some Major and if we wanted to see the views of the gorge we had to pay a couple of shillings and take the car. So we did. Went off along another track, just sand, and came to Pulpit Rock, Baboon's Castle, and a little waterfall which was obviously very big and noisy at times, and then round to the end of the escarpment to look at the gorge from the other end. The river took a peculiar turn there and it was an obvious horseshoe, the view being called the Horseshoe Bend. Having seen all the views we could, we went back to the hotel for tea and cream cakes. They were lovely.

Then off again back further along the circular route to civilisation. This involved going over a real Mountain Pass (with capital letters) and it was a bit of a race against the light by this time. We stopped in a sugar cane field to take a picture of the sun setting over the hills, then drove as fast as possible round the Pass. Got back to Port Shepstone just by dark and then it just meant the motor road back home. Got back by 8 o'clock feeling exhausted.

In the evening went out for a meal and felt too tired almost to enjoy it. Back home rather late because there was a cabaret show on at the place we went to. But it was a super day and we gave Zeus back rather reluctantly this morning. So that was the story of Durban and now I must post this off. See you soon.

Well, 5 o'clock sailing is now 7 p.m. We hope. Love, Ann x

Cape Town 28th August 1967
Dear grandparents to be

Thanks for the letter yesterday, although I still don't know how you are and where you are. I'm glad you liked the telegram, I enjoyed the surprise of planning it.

There really isn't much news to tell you at present. We left Durban late, at 7.15 p.m. instead of 5, so it was dark and lights were twinkling. Being Commodore Byles' last voyage we expected and got a big send off, with lots of noise. On the Thursday morning we got to East London at 8.30 which was a very nice sort of time to arrive, and I managed a short sunbathe after lunch, as the sun was very hot. Had a short nap on a sunbed. Departure was just at sunset, at 5 o'clock, and the tugs really went to town there - lots of noise and hoots, and the pilot boat did its bit too. The Signal Station on top of the hill above put up a flag message saying "have a good voyage " and we hoisted "thanks very much" back to them. Whistles all round and away we went, sun setting behind us. I had tested the whistles an hour before we sailed, just to make sure everything was all right, which gives me a tremendous sense of power! Little things please little minds, and all that.

Next morning was P.E. Lovely day again, worked only until 9.15 then let off and Sheila and I went shopping. Had a good old look-around the town, which isn't very big, but it's got some nice shops. Big wide street, Army band marched past at one point (very noisy and unmusical), hot sun, not too many people, and lots of bargains. More bits to go in the Ali Baba pot. We were supposed to sail at 7, but it was foggy instead, so we didn't leave until 9.30 p.m. Then we had a good send off, night time or no night time.

R.M.S. EDINBURGH CASTLE sailing from Cape Town (Photo Ian Shiffman)

UNION-CASTLE
BADGES OF RANK

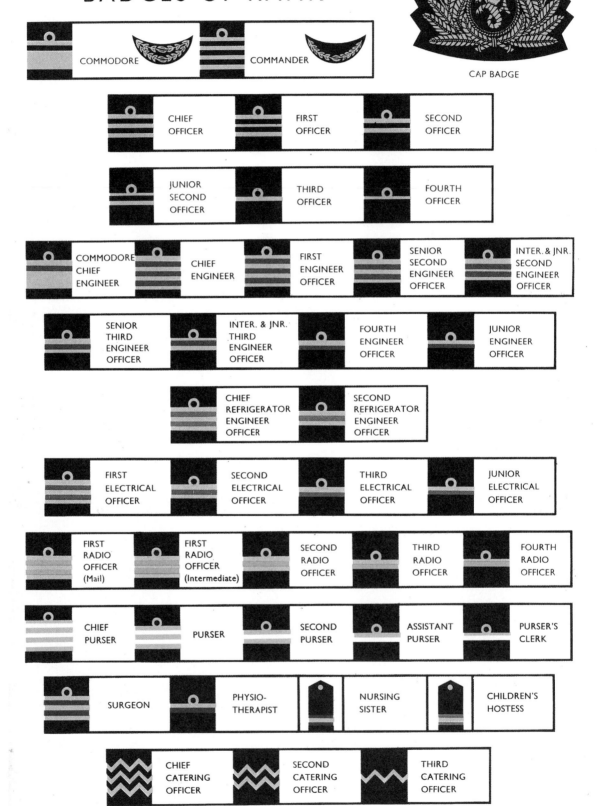

CAP BADGE

COMMODORE

COMMANDER

CHIEF OFFICER

FIRST OFFICER

SECOND OFFICER

JUNIOR SECOND OFFICER

THIRD OFFICER

FOURTH OFFICER

COMMODORE CHIEF ENGINEER

CHIEF ENGINEER

FIRST ENGINEER OFFICER

SENIOR SECOND ENGINEER OFFICER

INTER. & JNR. SECOND ENGINEER OFFICER

SENIOR THIRD ENGINEER OFFICER

INTER. & JNR. THIRD ENGINEER OFFICER

FOURTH ENGINEER OFFICER

JUNIOR ENGINEER OFFICER

CHIEF REFRIGERATOR ENGINEER OFFICER

SECOND REFRIGERATOR ENGINEER OFFICER

FIRST ELECTRICAL OFFICER

SECOND ELECTRICAL OFFICER

THIRD ELECTRICAL OFFICER

JUNIOR ELECTRICAL OFFICER

FIRST RADIO OFFICER (Mail)

FIRST RADIO OFFICER (Intermediate)

SECOND RADIO OFFICER

THIRD RADIO OFFICER

FOURTH RADIO OFFICER

CHIEF PURSER

PURSER

SECOND PURSER

ASSISTANT PURSER

PURSER'S CLERK

SURGEON

PHYSIO-THERAPIST

NURSING SISTER

CHILDREN'S HOSTESS

CHIEF CATERING OFFICER

SECOND CATERING OFFICER

THIRD CATERING OFFICER

B. 6541261

PRINTED IN ENGLAND

Tugs, the S.A. VAAL, a Clan Line ship down the line, the Pilot and finally us. We all gave tremendous whistles and the sound echoed all round the coast and the hills behind. Still a bit foggy but we got underway and did about 12 knots to the tune of the fog horn all night. I went to bed early and had to get up for the News at 6 the next morning. It was clear by that time, just, so we set off as fast as possible to make up time, and in case the fog came down again.

Saturday downcoast is our day at sea, and it was beautiful this time. The sun shone brilliantly down from an almost cloudless blue sky, the water sparkled and vaguely in the distance one could see the top of the mountains along the coast. Lots of birds around, and I even saw an albatross, but it was only a small one. Lots of small boats and bigger tankers around, which gave the drivers something to do up top.

Had a sleep in the afternoon to make up for my early rise (mind you I always go back to bed for half an hour when I finish just after 7) and felt fine in the evening. It was Derby night and strangely enough we all enjoyed it. Wore my yellow dress, sunglasses, and trimmed a yellow picture hat with white roses. Quite a sight! I was on the Tote table taking money. Afterwards there was a party in Colin's home and that was good. Mrs Byles was there too - she is quite fun, and is rarely serious.

Next morning was 6.30 arrival Pilot Cape Town. Ugh. Felt very sorry for myself most of the morning. Oh yes, we had gone so fast during the day before, anticipating fog at nightfall, that we got to Table Bay and dropped anchor at 1 a.m. that morning. I know, because we were in Colin's cabin still, and listened as it fell in the water! I digress! The day improved and so did I. Then I finished at 5.30 and had a headache. Had a rest in bed, took some tablets and felt a bit better.

Then Doctor, Jeannie, Sheila and I went to John Ingram's party, at his home in Cape Town. Had a lovely time there, talking shop with all sorts of Union-Castle people. Big coincidence coming up: John has frequently talked of his friends the Bullocks, Tony and Rosemary. They come from Hillingdon way, which I knew vaguely. Last night they were at the party. Walked into the room and Rosemary immediately said "I know you". We were in the same year at Bishopshalt! How about that! She worked for British Eagle as an air hostess, and actually recommends it. Cor. Her husband left Union-Castle Purser's staff just before I started, but I have often heard his name mentioned. They have been married for nearly two years, and she has a 4 week old baby. We had a long gossip about everyone we could remember at school. Thoroughly enjoyed the party. We got there at 7.45 and left at 10 (it was a cheese and wine party).

Back home, discovered another party up top, so we all went up there, and started to help someone celebrate a birthday. The birthday came and we all enjoyed the celebration.

Today was work again, well a sort of work. We have few people on board and they don't bother us, so we chat and read books. Very pleasant but extremely boring. Lunchtime today I went off at 1.30 and fed my face. Then one of the Engineers and I took a taxi round to the Old Harbour. It was a super hot day and so we walked round and looked at tugs, and boats, and boat building, and cleaning and water and sky and it was lovely. Then round to another little harbour and there were the fishing boats unloading and the fish loaded into metal trays, and put in a frig. train-carriage-thing. It was a very fishy smelling place, but fascinating. All on a very small scale of course.

But the funny thing was that in the centre of the little harbour were about 10 seals, basking in the hot sun. They looked so funny, lying there, with as much of their bodies out of the water as possible.

Then we went to the Cafe for coffee and watched the tugs leave, they are so manoeuvrable. Got back here in time to start again at 4, until 5.30. It's that now so I shall finish this and post if off. See you soon, take care. Love, Ann xxx

Cape Town, 30th August
Dear Family

As usual, it's terribly close to sailing time, and I must rush this and try and cope with the cash customers too.

Yesterday was a super day. The Van der Byls collected me at 10.15 and off we set in the car, round the Table Bay to a place called Bloubergstrand. Had cup of coffee and hot scones, jam and cream, there and felt thoroughly piggish. The view was superb across the Bay, and the sun was shining on the water and the tide was in and the sea was sparkling, with just a haze at the bottom of the Mountain. It's a classic view, wonderful.

Then we went north, towards a place called Darling, its only claim to fame being the fields surrounding the town. These are cattle grazing fields usually but in the Spring they are a carpet of flowers, of all colours, and people drive up for miles to see them. We went into the fields, and walked around, and drove, and saw blue, red, pink, orange, white and black flowers. They were beautiful and just like a carpet. The hills sloped away and in the distance we could see the high mountains. Some fields were just a mass of blue, and these were lupins, which are planted to make the ground fertile apparently and also happen to look super. Along the side of the roads, in the ditches, were wild arum lilies. Got damp feet taking pictures, but I think they might be worth it.

Then on up hill and down dale, with long mountainous views all around, towards the sea. Had usual high standard picnic lunch beside the sea at a tiny place called Yzerfontein. There was absolutely no-one around and all the little holiday homes were closed up. The sea rushed in, and the sun shone, we fed ourselves, and then they rested and I collected shells. There were hundreds all over the tiny beach, and I found a crab in a rockpool.

Then we set off home again, slowly, and it was nice. The view was still superb, and finally we got back to their home up the side of the Mountain. Then it was time for a cup of tea and a rest. Then people came in for drinks and then we had early supper. They had a Bible Study Reading meeting, so the Archdeacon ran me back to the ship, feeling rather exhausted with so much fresh air.

We are due to sail very shortly, so must go. As it is Commodore Father's last voyage, we are dressed overall, and apparently it looks nice. We are all going on deck for this last departure. (Las Palmas won't count, being at dead of night).

Hope you had a good holiday. See you soon, take care. Love, Ann xxxxxxxx

P.S. I have decided it is about time I resigned from this job, so I shall speak to Mr. Cook when we get back to the UK. xxx

At sea, Monday 4th Sept. 1967
Neptune Day
Dear family

Just to keep up the tradition of sending you a letter from Las Palmas for us all to read on Tuesday, here's the latest Williams Ocean News.

Starting with departure Cape Town, where I left off with the last letter: it was a super departure. We closed the Bureau, and all rushed round giving out coloured streamers. The sight from the Tourist end was fantastic - so colourful and rather moving, as lots of people held streamers with their friends on the quayside and they gradually broke. As you know, it is Father's last voyage and we hoped for something special in the way of a send off from Cape Town. We got it! We got ourselves turned round and out of the harbour entrance and then the noise started. The tugs usually sound 3 whistles, then we do, and the Pilot "peeps" and that's that. This time, there were all sorts of wailings from the tugs, loud rude noises from our whistles, and the PENDENNIS CASTLE started whistling and hardly stopped for breath until she ran out of steam. We almost did too but used another whistle as well. The Portuguese ship nearby whistled, the Blue Star ship whistled, and two little tugs crept out from the Old Harbour where they live and whistled, the little fishing vessel waiting to enter harbour whistled, and the noise was terrific and deafening and lovely. We finally got the Pilot off, much later than usual, and still the noise went on, until we were well away. It was very touching and very thrilling.

That night was nice - we all went to the bioscope and saw the latest James Bond film called "You only live twice". You've probably heard the music and song at home already. Very amusing and exciting. Next night was Cocktail Party night and I had my hair done specially. The weather was still chilly and we were still in blues. Met several nice people; one man has since offered me a job in Cape Town in his big department store (he owns it). Next night was Tourist Cocktail Party and guess what, I met a lady who I had met last year on the ORANJE, and strangely enough she lives in a flat in Cape Town over Rosemary Bullock's (the girl I used to go to school with). Isn't it all weird?

Then we finally went into whites; today it's warm and a bit sticky, but gosh it's nothing like as hot as it can be. Yesterday was the usual nice sort of Sunday. Church (nice hymns) and then drinks at lunch time with another ex-ORANJE passenger, with others, then shut-eye until 4.00 p.m. because there was no sun, then hair-do time, and at 6.15 we all had to muster for a picture with the Commodore. Then he had a big party and we all got a bit 'rotten' on Champagne cocktails. Lovely. Then dancing lessons at 8.30 until 9.30, then down to the Leading Hands club for the usual Darts match. Managed to get in bed by Cinderella, or shortly afterwards anyway. And that's that. Tonight is a big party, so more news tomorrow.

Tonight is Las Palmas and we are almost there, and the time is 9.45 at night, a dreadful time to get anywhere. I feel tired, but I actually think I may get ashore tonight and how I am looking forward to it! I have been invited by one of the pax. and he is rather nice, and so is the crowd I expect to go with, to the Reina Isabel Hotel, which is owned and run by Union-Castle. There should be a floor show too, so I am keeping my fingers crossed. It all sounds too good to be true.

To continue the news. Tuesday night was Dinner Dance night and I was asked to join the Purser's table, with Sheila, and we had rather a good time. Good pax. and nice music, and I had shortened my mess dress and felt rather as if I had a new dress - isn't it funny how things like that make a difference?

The do went off very well and I enjoyed it. Us girls are having a party tomorrow night at 10.30 p.m. and are making flowers and things, because we are calling it a 'happening' and are pretending to be flower children. Just proves we are not so far behind the times, despite the gap between us and civilisation!

Yesterday at sea the French Navy gave us a Review, or something like that. A whole convoy went past, including a 14,000 ton aircraft carrier, carrying helicopters, and sundry battleships and things. All quite exciting, we missed them by yards, and they went both sides of us. I imagine they knew what they were doing!

Lots of people lining the side rails, all gazing in wonder and awe at all the ships. In fact life is quite amusing now, what with it being Father's last voyage. Unfortunately he seems to be a bit under the weather most of the time and a bit confusing to talk to, but I think it must be very upsetting for him at the moment. It's a good job Mrs Byles is here, because she tries to keep him organised. But there are so many parties, and I have been to lots, 2 or 3 each evening, pax. and Officers, and it is all very social.

Now I must post this off, and wait for my evening to start. It will be so nice to get on land again too.

See you soon. Love, Ann.
P.S. Don't call me, I'll call you!

R.M.S. EDINBURGH CASTLE

Left to right, Master at Arms, The author, Commodore("Father") and Mrs Byles, and Purser Collin Dellar

As my last voyage on active service draws
to its close, I feel it imperative that I should
thank my ship's company, one and all, for their loyal
and efficient service. There comes a time when we
must all retire; my quotation comes from the pen
of Charles Lutwidge Dodgson, known to us as Lewis
Carroll:

> "'You are old, Father William,' the young man said
> 'And your hair has become very white;
> And yet you incessantly stand on your head -
> Do you think, at your age, it is right?'

> "'In my youth,' Father William replied to his son,
> 'I feared it might injure the brain;
> 'But, now that I'm perfectly sure I have none,
> Why, I do it again and again.'"

It is your service, affection and help that
have been the greatest things to me - and I cannot ignore
the beautiful presents which you have given to myself
and my wife. Perhaps at my age these things have passed, but for
you "I must go down to the seas again" and the "call of
the running tide is a wild call and a clear call which
cannot be denied".

And so as I go into retirement my wife joins
me in wishing you all the reward of service willingly given,
and such remuneration as your Union may from time to time
decide!

                    W. S. BYLES
                    COMMODORE

9th September 1967

R.M.S. EDINBURGH CASTLE

Retiring Commodore Bill Byles and his Officers

Extract From The Ship's Deck Log

R.M.S. Edinburgh Castle
CAPTAIN D. W. SOWDEN, R.D.,R.N.R.

SOUTHAMPTON TO CAPETOWN via LAS PALMAS

VOYAGE 126   September 22 to October 4, 1967

Date	Distance Run	Speed	Latitude-Longitude	Wind force	Temperature at Noon Air	Temperature at Noon Sea	Itinerary
22-9-67				W2	65°		1300 Departure Southampton. 143 First Class and 465 Tourist Class Passengers on board Cloudy fine and clear
23-9-67	465	22·14	44°40N 08°38W	SSW3	65°	65°	0030 Vessei rounded Ushant and entered Bay of Biscay 1657 Passed Cape Finisterre and left Bay of Biscay 2015 Passed Company's N'bound vessel Pendennis Castle Moderate sea. Cloudy and clear, occasional rain
24-9-67	551	22·04	35°55N 12°22W	SxW4	74°	72°	1030 Divine Service in First Class Lounge - Master officiated. Moderate swell, vessel rolling to NNW'ly swell. Cloudy and clear, occasional rain showers. 0730 Passed Company's Vessel Clan MacGowan
25-9-67	490	21·58	Las Palmas	SW1	75°	°	1154 Arrived Las Palmas. 1534 departed Las Palmas 131 First Class and 469 Tourist Class Passengers on board Fine and clear
26-9-67	449	22·45	21°04N 17°40W	SW3	74°	71°	Slight sea. Fine and clear 1210 Passed Company's Vessel Clan MacIlwraith
27-9-67	520	21·67	12°24N 17°23W	NW3	78°	84°	0527 passed Cape Verde, Dakar, the most westerly point of Africa. Slight sea. Overcast and clear 0821 Passed Company's N'bound vessel Good Hope Castle 1215 Passsed Company's vessel Clan Finlay
28-9-67	539	22·46	04°53N 12°47W	WW3	78°	80°	Rippled sea. Cloudy and clear, occasional rain
29-9-67	524	21·83	02°07S 07°36W	SE4	75°	75°	0418 Vessel crossed Equator in DR Longitude 09°C8W Slight sea. Cloudy and clear
30-9-67	528	22·00	09°07S 02°17W	SE4	74°	72°	Moderate sea, low SE'ly swell. Overcast and clear
1-10-67	538	22·42	16°30S 02°55E	SE5	65°	69°	1030 Divine Service in First Class Lounge - Master officiated. Rough sea, heavy swell. Overcast and clear
2-10-67	499	21·70	23°06S 08°16E	SE5	63°	64°	Moderate sea, moderate SE'ly swell. Overcast and clear
3-10-67	502	21·83	29°42S 13°24E	S3	62°	62°	Moderate SSE'ly swell, slight sea. Cloudy and clear
4-10-67	340						0700 Estimated Time of Arrival Cape Town (S.A.S.T.)

DISTANCE 5,945 Miles   ....   AVERAGE SPEED 21·92 Knots

Extract From The Ship's Deck Log

R.M.S. Edinburgh Castle

CAPTAIN D. W. SOWDEN R.D., R.N.R.

CAPETOWN TO SOUTHAMPTON via LAS PALMAS

VOYAGE 126   18th October, 1967 to 30th October, 1967

Date	Distance Run	Speed	Latitude-Longitude	Wind Force	Temperature at Noon Air	Temperature at Noon Sea	Itinerary
18-10-67		At Cape Town			76°		1554 Departed Cape Town Cloudy, fine and clear 30 First Class and 409 Tourist Class Passengers on board
19-10-67	467	22·78	27°56S 12°39E	S3	65°	62°	2050 Passed Company's cargo vessel Rotherwick Castle Slight sea. Overcast, cloudy and clear
20-10-67	576	23·04	20°19S 06°16E	SE3	75°	66°	Slight sea. Cloudy and clear 1625 Passed Company's cargo vessel Roslin Castle
21-10-67	555	23·13	13°08S 00°13E	SE3	75°	66°	Slight sea. Overcast, fine and clear 2000 Passed Company's cargo vessel Clan Ranald
22-10-67	545	22·71	05°56S 05°22W	ExS3	76°	74°	1030 Divine Service held in First Class Lounge. Captain officiated. Slight sea. Overcast and clear
23-10-67	549	22·88	01°26N 10°47W	SE3	81°	80°	0733 Vessel crossed the Equator in DR Longitude 09°41W Slight sea. Cloudy and clear
24-10-67	536	22·23	08°44N 15°56W	Var.Lt.Airs	83°	83°	Rippled sea. Cloudy and clear. Occasional rain
25-10-67	544	22·67	17°21N 17°50W	NE3	82°	83°	0500 Passed Cape Verde, most westerly point of Africa 0545 Passed Company's S'bound Mail Vessel S.A. Oranje Moderate sea. Cloudy and clear
26-10-67	526	21·93	25°56N 16°17W	NNE3	75°	74°	Slight sea. Cloudy and clear 2048 Arrived Las Palmas
27-10-67	366	20·00	31°41N 14°08W	N3	71°	73°	0100 Departed Las Palmas 93 First Class and 449 Tourist Class Passengers on board Moderate sea. Few clouds, fine and clear 2340 Passed Company's cargo vessel Clan McCleod
28-10-67	530	22·08	40°11N °06W	NW4	65°	67°	0750 Passed Company's cago vessel Rochester Castle Vessel pitching heavily to moderate sea. Cloudy and clear 2130 Rounded Cape Villano and entered Bay of Biscay
29-10-67	502	22·92	47°46N 06°14W	WNW4	56°	58°	0110 Passed S'bound Mail vessel R.M.S. Windsor Castle 1030 Divine Service in the First Class Lounge. Captain officiated. Moderate sea. Cloudy and clear with rain 1045 Passsed Company's cargo vessel Clan McIntyre 1500 Vessel rounded Ushant, left the Bay of Biscay and entered the English Channel
30-10-67	279		Southampton				0700 Estimated Time Of Arrival at Southampton Docks

DISTANCE 5,975 MILES - - AVERAGE SPEED 22·02 KNOTS

128

R.M.S. "EDINBURGH CASTLE"
CAPTAIN D. W. SOWDEN, R.D., R.N.R.
VOYAGE 126
LEAVING SOUTHAMPTON 22ND SEPTEMBER 1967

Las Palmas
Monday 25th September
Dear Family and newyellowbed,

I miss you all! However, we are now at LP and trying to get over the shock of being here so early. We were alongside at 12 noon and are due to leave at 3 p.m. It's never been heard of for decades, I should think.

Later

It's 2.30, I have had a quick lunch and been for a walk on the quayside. It is lovely and hot and super out there. Took your cine camera too and took some feet of film. I think I am beginning to get the hang of it now - hope so.

To start off with the news or happenings since I last saw you all. Wednesday work finished at 4.15 which is unheard of so Davey and I went out for a super meal in the evening and that was that. Thursday work went well too, but after I got back to my cabin about 6 one of the Junior Engineers, who is now on leave, came in and said would I like to go out that evening, if I wasn't doing anything else. I wasn't, so I changed quickly and joined him and two other Engineers in his car. We went to a pub in the wilds of Hampshire for wine, which was specially brewed there - I had cherry wine - and then back to his home where his mother had cooked a big meal for us all. Then we all went out to another 2 country-type pubs, all wooden, brasses and Great Danes, and had big schooners of sherry straight from the wood. Cor. Going along one of the lanes there was a glint from the side of the hedge and what should appear but a rabbit. It ran out into the road and wouldn't get off. It ran ahead of us for ages, and John finally got out and chased after it. It ran faster and weaved from side to side of the road and I have never seen anything so funny as us driving along a tiny lane at about 15 mph chasing a man chasing a rabbit! The rabbit suddenly realised he would be better on the other side of a hedge and that was that. It was hilarious we thought. Back to the ship for a reasonably early night.

Next day was sailing day and a bit hectic, specially down in the Tourist end of the ship. Had a letter from Davey just to say have a good voyage, and a lovely card from Elaine, Derek and thingi saying Bon Voyage. Wasn't that nice of them.

Friday night was busy typing and had to attend First Night Dance. Saturday was First Class Cocktail Party night and hair do. Sunday night I gave a party and we had a Musical Quiz.

It's minutes to sailing time, and I have not got time to add more to this. I have a cold, which is getting better rapidly now that we are in whites and the weather is good. The sea is calm and so most things are fine. I am taking a little film. I feel fairly well. Mr. Cook was very friendly to me the other day too.

Take care, see you soon. Love, Ann x

At sea, Saturday 30th September 1967
Dear family,
Another reading of the Epistles of the EDINBURGH CASTLE starting at the second chapter.

I'm having rather a super voyage so far; lots of people seem to know now that I am leaving and many have said they are sorry. But to start at the beginning. I told you I caught Irene's cold on Thursday and for about 3 days my voice was terrible, and then I had a cold for one day, and felt very sorry for myself. I gobbled tablets and cough mixture and improved rapidly. Being down the Tourist end, you need your voice so much, and it was all a bit annoying, apart from feeling ill. But by Monday I was all right. Although I started that letter to you in good time, somehow it got finished in a rush, so I'm sorry if it seemed a bit peculiar. This one will be different, I hope, and that is why I am starting it now, while there are still several days to go.

Odd news items anyway. We have a Hereford bull on board on the Forward Deck as cargo. He is going to be sold in Cape Town. Large animal apparently.

We were in blues on Sunday and went into whites on Monday, which wasn't soon enough for any of us. I can never understand why the Deck bods are allowed to have the say about what us 'moles' wear, it's always too hot so soon down here.

I wrote from Las Palmas to Miss Roper asking if she could try and sell my hat and buttons and things like that. I had spoken to her on the Friday sailing day and she said she probably could, so that's one less worry.

The new Captain is Capt. Sowden, who was on the CAPETOWN CASTLE last year when I was. His wife is here too, which is quite interesting. They always call the Purserettes "Twinklefingers", which is a bit odd.

The voyage has been hot, and lovely weather-wise, as well as otherwise. We saw porpoises the other day but I didn't manage to get them filmed, but I will. The cine camera is in use fairly often, and I took a lot of film at the Crossing the Line ceremony yesterday. Some of our pax. I have seen many times before. Isn't it strange how you know people again. Some people were on the ORANJE last year. Some people were on the SAAMTREK tour party that were here 2 voyages ago from Cape Town to Durban and back. They remember Colin and me, and that's rather nice.

One couple I recognised and couldn't think why, and then I talked to them at the Cocktail party and discovered why I knew him. He is the England cricketer Mr. Lightfoot, who travelled on the ORANJE last year with Basil D'Oliveira, Rumsey, Newman and Scott. Remember me telling you about them? He asked me not to say anything to anyone about him, because he didn't want to be roped in for the cricket match or anything like that.

The social round on here is tremendous. We have had a party or two every night, apart from the Entertainments.

We left Las Palmas at 3.30, which was so funny really, and Jeannie had a party then that evening. Tuesday was Cocktail Party Night this end, and Colin had a party on Wednesday. Thursday was the big night Tourist Class with Fancy Dress, Dancing and Fish and Chip Supper on Deck and I met a nice lady passenger who bought me a drink. The next day she gave me a present - a silver Commemorative Sir Winston Churchill Crown piece, in a little case, as a thank you. Wasn't that thoughtful of her. Remember when we went to see Churchill's body lying in state in Westminster Hall, Daddy, after queuing for miles and hours? Had to pay our respects, didn't we. Wasn't that a lovely present. I thought it was.

Tonight is Derby Night, so more of that another time. I told you about the Tote we run, called Hoppit & Coppit (Port Said) Limited - motto "It pays to stay with the firm that stays to pay". I love that name!

At sea, Tuesday 3rd October.

Well, tomorrow is letter day and land again. How nice. Thought I had better keep up to date with this letter, then I can post it and not be far behind with the news.

Saturday night was Derby Night, as I said, and quite fun. That is the night us Purser's staff all dress up and I wore my yellow dress, and had made a big yellow, white and green buttercup hat, with long white ribbons to tie in a bow under my chin. Very fetching! Party before dinner with hairdressers, so the evening went well.

Sunday was the best day of the week, as usual, with Church and Sunday afternoon off. It always seems a nuisance to go back to the Bureau just for a hour afterwards, but I suppose we must be decent about it. In the evening there was another party, and then I had the evening off (Sheila did Bingo for me) and went to the bioscope (Magnificent Men in their Flying Machines again) until 10, then down to the Leading Hands Club for the usual Darts Match. The clocks altered that night, and I was on the News, so the night was altogether too short. Slept in the afternoon so that made up for it. Then another pax.-type party, and Bingo and early to bed, with another hour off the clocks. Nasty business. Then today, working all day, not very busily, and clearing up ready for tomorrow. Tonight is our Farewell Dance, and that should be nice. It usually is. So more news tomorrow, or Thursday.

Oh yes, have you managed to get my new black shoes from that shop in Slough? I'm looking forward to hearing the tale of what happened. Another thing, Mummy, please could you make a hair appointment for me in the Village, just to have my false piece fixed on, afternoon some time of Saturday 4th November, providing we are still going to The Orchard? Thanks very much. Take care, seen you soon. Love, Ann xx

Cape Town, 5th October
Dear family,

So much for that. Now we are in Port Elizabeth and it's Friday. It's my day off and am I looking forward to it, as it is going to be very full. But to get up to date first with Cape Town. We arrived as usual at 7, after being up for the Pilot just after 6. The tablecloth was over the Mountain so it was not ideal filming weather and I only took a little, just so that "we had arrived in South Africa". We all worked that morning until lunchtime. Then I changed and went over to the WINDSOR CASTLE to see Derek. He was pleased to see me and we chatted for quite a while. Then I met Sheila (our Hostess) in the Square and we left and went to town to window-shop. At least, that is how it started. I was looking at the price of bracelets, because I rather fancy the idea of one in gold chain, with pearls in it. I saw a super one in a shop for £7.10.0 which is quite reasonable, considering, but I don't know how much they are at home, do you? Anyway, it was a lovely one, but I didn't buy it, because I wanted to think about it some more. So I bought a record instead: Caterina Valente and including "The Breeze and I". She is very popular out here and most shops have her records. That afternoon in Cape Town there was apparently a "hippy" wedding, in the City Gardens. Didn't see any sign of it, but it sounds interesting. It was to be a real wedding too. Had dinner on board and then John Ingram appeared and stayed to chat. He is very happy now and much more settled down out here.

Then it was Thursday morning and sailing at 10.30 a.m. That is a good time to sail, because we can get all the work done by our usual closing times in the Bureau. Very organised. Bingo at 5.30 p.m. then a free night, because there were 2 showings of the film. Went to bed early to get ready for today.

Oh yes, some passengers from Cape Town are a group of 52 Volkspele singers/dancers. They are a group, like our country dancing teams in England, who go round the country giving demonstrations, all dressed in their local national costumes, like the Voortrekker ones us girls wore on the ORANJE for Republic Day last year, do you remember? Theirs are all nylon, and rather vicious-looking colours, like purple or yellow, but some are white nylon with black velvet short capes, and they look nice. Their ages range from 20 odd to 60 odd. The men wear costume, but nothing startling. They are all travelling to Durban with us, and they are giving a demonstration on Saturday night of singing and dancing. Should be fun I reckon. Saves us putting on an Entertainment anyway.

Today I hope to go to see the dolphins this morning, to take some film. This afternoon Sheila and I are determined to go to the Elephant Park, the trip we couldn't do last voyage, and this evening I am going out to the Skyroof Restaurant with the usual crowd, which should be a super last-time event. It doesn't feel much like a last trip in some ways, because I can't quite believe that I am leaving, it's like having your head in a cloud of cotton wool. Oh well, must away, only 2 minutes duty left, then up and away.

Saturday morning

Cor, I had a super day yesterday, one I shall never ever forget. Sheila and I left the ship just before 11 and went to the Aquarium. I filmed the snakes, and birds, and then we went into the dolphin tank ring. Filmed a lot of their performance and it was lovely. The sun was quite hot, the sky was blue and clear, and it was nice to be on holiday. Met the photographer and we all sat together.

Home for a quick lunch, then off again, with Peter the photographer, to the Addo Elephant National Park. It's an organised 2 coach tour which runs every Friday, mainly for ship's pax. We left at 2 o'clock and set off northwards, towards the Mountains. It was flat land at first, built up for the first 2 miles, then scrubland. Then suddenly it was wooded and hilly and up over one range of hills, we were on the top of a plateau and looking down into the valley was green and lovely and wooded and mountainous in the distance. We passed a few fields, covered in anthills, quite big ones, about a foot high. Then over the last hills and over a funny railway line and we were there: the sign said "Welcome to Addo Elephant National Park", and we went through a gate and on for about 2 miles to the entrance-type house. It was one of the feeding places of the elephants and what do you know, there were about 8 elephants!

The whole park is about 16,000 acres and one section is fenced off for the elephants, with these specially cleared feeding/viewing spots at intervals around the fence (safely inside of course). So to see this crowd right at the start, obviously just waiting for me, was marvellous. We all took film, just in case they decided to move, and it was quite interesting. The baby played around mum, dad looked on angrily and aunty and uncle pottered, and the other two youngsters tried to fight and knock dust off each other. Then we were invited into the restaurant for tea and biscuits, which were very welcome. (The drive was 35 miles and took more than an hour, our driver being rather cautious.) That was the only civilisation we saw, because then we went off in our coach (small one, 12 of us in it) along the sand road tracks round the fence and off across paths. First things we saw were lots of ostriches! How about that. Just standing around for us, in the middle of nowhere. Then on further to where we saw eland, springboks, wildebeest, and lots of scrubland and hills and blue sky and misty mountains far away. Then we went on much further and finally came to a lake, and guess what we saw there - 2 hippopotamuses. They were blobs in the water at first but then one submerged and came up blowing bubbles and then (all of which I was filming) of all things, he yawned the most enormous yawn! It was so funny and I only hope it comes out on film. (contd.) Love, Ann

P.E., Saturday 7th Oct. 1967
Next Instalment of yesterday's super day:

So the hippos yawned and I hope it all came out on film. Then we went back towards the entrance of the park and suddenly an ostrich ran out across the road in front of the coach, closely followed by a guinea fowl. Then came another ostrich and they all rushed off into the bush. I thought they must have been ostracised by the rest of the herd!

By this time it was about 5.30 or later so we still had to get out of the Park and drive back. We got back onto the national road (laugh!) finally and then back home by 7.10. Normally the tour is due to end at about 6 at the ship, so you can tell we had seen a lot, apart from our cautious driver. I was exhausted, mostly from fresh air and excitement, which was a pity, because I was due out again at 8 o'clock. So I had a quick rest for 15 minutes and felt better. Kept seeing elephants and ostriches in my mind, all running about. Oh yes, on our way back past the original elephant feeding spot, we noticed that the keeper had put a huge pile of oranges down by the water trough, to attract them there. Most of the crowd were there, but just while we were watching, one large elephant came thundering down a far distant hillside, obviously not wishing to be left out of the feast. He must have covered about 1 mile in as many minutes. It was so funny. That was something I didn't film. Then we came home, as I said, and it was dark and the coach bumped about so much that I couldn't even sleep.

That evening we went in a crowd to the Marine Hotel, Skyroof restaurant, which is a favourite place for most of us. That is the one high above the city with the lights far below and away. Very good band and food. Unfortunately my tummy isn't my friend today, and I seem to have caught the bug that many have got - known as chef's complaint. The chef is dirty and not liked, and is blamed for most things. Today is cool and overcast and makes me glad I was off yesterday. My next day off is Durban on Tuesday and then we plan to visit a game reserve which should have lions and giraffe. Cor, I can't believe it, and I am trying hard not to get too excited about it in case something happens. But it didn't on Friday, so maybe my luck will hold.

Odd thing I meant to tell you before. The last Sunday at sea Church Service we had was a bit rough going sea-wise and hymn-wise. All was progressing well, Father was conducting things strongly and was only occasionally glancing at his wife, whom he calls Treasure. He does this very openly too and is quite amusing about it. However, this particular morning, came the time of the Reading of the Lesson and the Staff Commander got up, started reading and do you know what it was all about? Something along the lines of "Lay not up treasure for yourself on earth, because treasure will be yours in Heaven". You'll probably know the Lesson I mean; it was so funny, sitting in the front two rows as we Officers do, to listen, and then try and control our laughter. Everyone looked at Father and Father looked at nothing, and we all tried not to look at each other. Wasn't that nice though. I don't know who chose that lesson, but it was a laugh on Father anyway.

Joke - Sunday church variety. Why do we always say "A-men" and not "A-women"? Well, we always sing hymns and not hers, don't we!

I rang Mrs Van der Byl on Wednesday night and chatted. I have the Tuesday off in Cape Town and they said they would love to have me. Being very cheeky, I then asked if we could try and arrange a visit to a winery, somewhere like KWV (my brandy people) or something similar, near Cape Town. They loved the sound of that idea, and will try and arrange it between now and then. Aren't I lucky? They have spoken about it before now, as they haven't been there either, so I expect something definite will be done about it. Hope so. Keep your fingers crossed.

That must be all for now. More news when there's more news. Take care of yourselves, and mind that arm Mummy. Love, Ann

Durban, 10th October (Tuesday)
Dear prospective grandparents,

(I like the sound of that, don't you?) Thanks for the letter yesterday. I did enjoy it.

Wednesday
Didn't have time to write anything more then so I shall continue now. Nothing happened at East London except me working hard (well, sort of) and we left there on Sunday at 6 o'clock eventually. Had a Quiz that night, then music and bed. The Bandleader, Trevor, is jolly good and often plays my favourite tunes or plays something of his own choice for me. That night he played "Annie get your gun" film music, then "Snow White and the 7 Dwarfs" and then "The Mikado", so that was a good evening's music. Monday we got here at 9 o'clock which was a very nice time to arrive anywhere, because there was time for a normal breakfast, time to sort the mail and look round and watch us get alongside. I was on duty all day and evening which was a bit of a nuisance. My day off was Tuesday and I planned to go to the Indian Market apart from the Game Reserve. But yesterday was Kruger Day and the Market was due to be closed, so I managed to rush ashore in my lunchhour, with a bit extra.

I got a taxi and went to the Market and had a super time looking round. I felt a bit brave walking round on my own, because there are never many white people around that area. But I scurried around and bought lots of bits and pieces, that you will just have to wait to see. Got back to the ship and changed quickly ready for more Bureau. One of the things I bought were some Chinese wind chimes, I'm sure you know the sort of thing. I know the real things are made of glass, but these are lightweight metal and they tinkle rather well. Anyway, I brought all my goodies down to the Bureau and gloated for a while. I hung the wind chimes up and couldn't find a breeze. Decided to blow every now and again but it got exhausting. Then the Bosun arrived on the scene and blew it for a bit. He went away and about 10 minutes later the Lamptrimmer arrived, presented the compliments of the Bosun, and handed me an empty sprayer, the really old sort with stirrup-pump-type handle and tin on the end! He thought that would do the job better.

After all that, I decided to move the chimes and so I put them in the breeze from one of the blowers and they tinkled all the rest of the afternoon. Nice.

Also bought a tiny black wooden elephant, plus tusks. In one shop they had some beautiful carved sandalwood chests, in about four sizes. The prices were the worst part - the biggest one was £40. At least, that was the starting price. They were lovely, and I would have liked to buy one of those, but my price would have been more like £10. Must visit some antique shops when I get home - I fancy a big oak chest.

We have been in whites in Durban and the weather is lovely and warm. Not too hot at all, but very nice and pleasant, and the sky is blue. Lovely day.

However, yesterday was animal day. Left the ship about 11.30 and went through the town towards Pietermaritzburg, which is west of Durban. In the suburbs of Durban all the jacaranda trees were in bloom and they looked beautiful - purple and graceful. There was a slight breeze and they waved gently, against a background of blue sky and white houses. That made my morning straightaway.

Then out of Town along the national road, through places like Cato Ridge, Camperdown etc. which are scenes of famous Boer War battles long ago (you can almost see spears and hear guns booming out over the land). 40 miles out of Durban, having gone through the sugar cane fields, and over the hills, we came to the turning for the Natal Lion Park and in we went.

It was a 4 mile track to the real entrance and then we were there. Looked round in fear and trembling but couldn't see a thing that looked dangerous so we went in. It is a huge park set amongst the hills, and there is a circular drive of 12 miles around these hills, ending on one hillside with a specially fenced lion park. So we set off along the drive and it wound its way through trees, and scrubland, with lovely views, lots of cactus plants and weird looking ones at that, and then bounding springboks and impala (apparently) around the place. Also saw 2 zebra blending in very well with the background, champing away at the side of a hill. Then suddenly in a bend in the track, there was an ostrich. He was just sitting there, beside the track, blinking away. I felt brave and got out of the car to film him, leaving the car door open of course, and even then he didn't move. Then we threw some bread at him, and he stretched his neck out and gobbled it down. I'm sure I saw it go down his neck and make him gulp when it got to his tummy! He just wouldn't move though and the comment was that maybe the sand was too hard! Then the bread was put out of his reach so he got up and ate it. Film at last, and then we fed him from the car, feeling terribly brave. Actually, I'm sure they are quite tame but it looked good.

Further on we saw lots of big black ostriches trotting around the hillside. Finally we got to the Lion Park and the barbed wire fence doors were opened and in we went. Almost immediately we saw a large Mum lion devouring an enormous chunk of raw meat. She was thoroughly enjoying it too. Aunty sat further back and chewed hers. All round the park were other lions, mostly tearing meat to bits and eating it. Ugh. Got some good film though. The park is run by Chipperfields, the Circus people, and so the lions were not quite as dangerous as they might be. Still, it was all very interesting. Finally left there, stopped for tea on the way back beside a lake. Suppose I must stop - no more room. Love, Ann

Another aerogramme

This is just to finish off the tale about animal day, although you won't get it at the same time. Tea on the way back was at a place on the side of a hill, beside a lake, with lots of birds and fish and chickens around the place. Also chocolate cake with fresh cream on top of it, and tea. Lovely. Back home for a rest, then out for a meal at Seahaven restaurant, which goes in for seafood, set as it is in the yacht basin, with lights twinkling all around. I had paella (first I had a shrimp cocktail) and that was jolly good. I love my tum. Today is embarkation day and there are some rather rude people getting on to go to Cape Town. Still, it could be worse. More later.

Port Elizabeth, Friday 13th October
All that seems days ago now, and far away. Not much seems to have happened lately, mostly because I have been on duty I suppose, and there hasn't been time for much to happen. We left Durban in a torrential rainstorm, so I couldn't take any film. The sea was rough and we rolled and bounced in a most unusual fashion out of the harbour, past the Bluff, and into the Indian Ocean and round to East London. So that was goodbye Durban.

At lunchtime, though, just before we sailed, I went into the Ocean Terminal, which is our berth, and said goodbye to the shopman there. He has a curio shop including jewellery and he is always very nice, and he gives us a slight discount if he can, even on tiny things. Anyway, I went over to see him and suddenly I noticed a gold and pearl bracelet, just exactly what I wanted, and just like the one I had seen in Cape Town. So I bought it.

He gave me a considerable discount, he said specially because it was my last voyage, so what option did I have. And I am thrilled with it. I am not really a necklace-wearing person and the bracelet is ideal with my pearl ring. So that was me satisfied, apart from being poorer.

Thursday was East London and thank you for the letter. I don't like the sound of your arm troubles Mummy. Pity you can't arrange to get out more too. I am glad you have got my new shoes. Thank you. It will be nice to come home to a new pair of shoes, especially with my new handbag just waiting for me. I am going to be poor but well dressed, I can see that. I wonder if anyone will want to marry me for my money? Keep the Land of Hope and Glory going too. More music coming up on 30th October, I can assure you. Did I tell you I have bought another Caterina Valente record, which includes "The Breeze and I" on it? Well, I have.

Yesterday I had a card from Davey, with Chinese writing on the front of it. Couldn't understand it at all. Then inside it said "I must have your answer by Tuesday"; this was followed by more Chinese, written in thick pen by Davey. I got all my spies out finding out if anyone spoke Chinese or could just read it, but no-one can. It's infuriating so he just won't get an answer by Tuesday. It's really very amusing. Anyhow, this morning, lo and behold (I like that phrase, don't you?) who should embark but two Chinese girls! Never ever have I known any Chinese people travel on these ships, and when they do, goodness me they choose this one and I happen to have a card with Chinese writing on it that I can't understand.

So I got all excited and got the card out and showed it to them. Their Father looked at it for several minutes, then raised his head, grinned and said "I'm terribly sorry, but this is Japanese and I cannot understand it." Oh, I didn't know whether to laugh or cry or what. Actually we all laughed and just gave it up. So I am back to square one all over again. Never mind.

I think that is just about all the news for here and now. Tomorrow we are at sea for the day and in the evening there is the Frog Derby which could be quite fun if it is like the usual Coastal ones. We have so many passengers on here, there must be some cheerful ones amongst them.

So that's all the news for now. Take care of yourselves and do get out and about. See you soon. Love, Ann xx

Cape Town, Monday 16th Oct.
Dear family and friends (yes, that's you two),

Thanks for the letter on Sunday. There has been nothing much to report yet so that is why I haven't written for a day or two. I enjoyed reading all your news. I can just imagine Dot and Derek and the baby business. I wonder whether the dogs were included during the talks at their home - how interesting it all is. You must be having a quiet laugh yourselves. Mind you, babies are worth waiting for - look how long you had to wait for me - wasn't it worth it! ??

I'm glad Elaine is well, and Derek - that is going to be interesting soon isn't it. Glad I'm going to be home soon. I didn't know you were all going to Brian's wedding - you must tell me all about it. I'm glad about the shoes from the Curtess man - made me smile, that did. Thanks for doing that bit of business Daddy.

About the Orchard Restaurant in Ruislip, please can you book for 6, I think, you two, us two and them two, if you see what I mean. If Elaine and Derek want to come too, good, that's fine by me. It's all on me as a birthday (mine) treat for you. (Apart from that, I want to wear my long dress again, and generally dress up, don't you?)

Now for my odd items of news. Well, Saturday was a day at sea and Derby Night. Sunday morning we arrived in Table Bay and collected the Pilot as usual at 6.20 a.m. and just as I looked out of my porthole, the sun popped up and the Mountain looked splendid - all rose and grey in parts, and more beautiful than I have seen it for a long time. No time to film it unfortunately, because of the Mail. I'm getting no concessions this voyage - it's bit mean I reckon, but never mind. Anyway, grumbles aside, I rang Mrs Van der Byl in the morning and they will be collecting me at 10.15 on Tuesday so that is all settled. I had to work for the rest of Sunday until 9 o'clock in the evening, so you can imagine I was ready for my little bed when I got there. Monday I was again on duty from 8.30 this time, and during the morning I wrote letters and chatted to people who passed by.

I felt rather discontented with the sight of the Tourist Class Bureau Square and had a sudden nice thought. I decided that I wanted to go out to lunch. I asked Sheila if she fancied going out for a very quick lunch and she said yes. So at 1.30 I flew out of the Bureau, changed hurriedly, grabbed the camera and ran out for a taxi with Sheila, clutching a bottle under one arm. We went round to the Harbour Cafe and then I had peri-peri prawns, plus salad and rice and odd bits and pieces, plus the bottle of wine between us. It was super and was much better because it was such a surprise. After getting through that lot we rushed outside and filmed madly then grabbed the taxi again back home. It was quite hot but overcast and a bit nasty really, a sort of Berg Wind-type day. Still that was that. Finished work at 6 o'clock and had a pleasant sort of evening pottering and getting to bed quite early for me.

Wednesday

Well, yesterday was my day off and it poured with rain absolutely all day. You couldn't see the top of the Sanlam building, let alone the Mountain. Ugh. Still, I was off at 10 o'clock and they picked me up at 10.15. Went back home and had coffee in comfort then went out towards Stellenbosch. Couldn't see a single bit of Mountain which was extremely annoying, because it is really beautiful round there. Still, we went to a super hotel called the Lanzerac Hotel, which is somewhere I have been before ages ago, and had a cheese and wine lunch. It was in one of their special dining rooms, with a bar (a large lazy parrot sat in a golden cage on the bar). The choice of cheese was enormous and we had a bottle of Lanzerac red wine to go with it of course. I saved the bottle because it is just like my table light that is a Rose bottle. I wondered if you would be able to drill this bottle for me too, please Daddy. Anyhow, we worked our way through an excellent lunch and felt rather pleased with life. Clutching bottle, we disembarked and staggered round to the front entrance.

A lady who had been sitting near us at lunch was apparently staying at the hotel and she invited us into her rooms if we would like a look round. So we did and guess what was in her room - you won't, a four-poster bed, complete with splendid drapings. Cor. Mrs Van der Byl told me that after her wedding in England (she is English), she and the Archdeacon spent their honeymoon weekend at the Hind's Head Hotel in Bray. They had a four-poster room there, with the ancient wooden floor all polished but uneven.

Anyway, off again and this time round the mountains and into Paarl, to the KWV cellars. We went on the 3.45 tour and were shown round the cellars. Ymm. They are enormous warehouses storing the barrels containing red and white wine, sherry, port, muscatel etc. The smell was lovely, and varied from warehouse to warehouse, although it was only a faint sort of aroma all over. The barrels were huge, and the 5 biggest contained 50,000 gallons each. They were works of art in themselves, apart from the contents. They only cellar the stuff there - it's made out on the farms and sent to be exported and wholesaled in Africa.

All very interesting, then we went back to HQ and sampled 5 sorts! Us three just sat there happily and thought of all the wine we had had that day. Super. We were given cookery books and leaflets and pictures and left in a lovely daze, still with pouring rain outside.

Then back to the ship and "au revoir" all round. Had a rest then out for dinner and dancing in the evening for the last time in Cape Town. Sad really. Can't believe today is the last day. Must post this off - take care - see you soon. Stoke up the fires and get the chrysanthemums blooming. See you all on 30th October. Put that arm in a sling Mummy and keep her quiet Daddy. Take care. Love, Ann xxx

At sea, Monday 23rd October 1967   Aerogramme - Paquebot
Dear Family   Posted at Sea

Just thought I would try and catch up with the oddments of news, while I can still remember them. It's been rather hectic since we sailed on Wednesday. We have some super passengers, one you may remember me mentioning - Mr. Crossley, he is the chicken sexer, that I have met twice before. Others are friends of the Van der Byls, two lots, and the husband of one works at I.C.I.'s Plastics Division.

Thursday, day one, I was on the News, which was a bit of a blow, but I coped. It was also Father's Wedding Anniversary and they had a party at 11.30 to which we were all invited. So that was the start of a nice day. Then lunchtime was our special sort, cold meat/salad/wine in one cabin, which goes down very well. Had a sleep in the afternoon and felt better. Bingo between bioscope in the evening then bed. Thursday was Cocktail Party night First Class in the Cocktail Bar (there are only 30 pax.) and I met some more nice people, from Scunthorpe. Friday was Tourist Class Cocktail Parties and Dancing and that was fun. Saturday was Frog Racing and then suddenly it was Sunday.

I had planned a big party for Sunday night before dinner and had invites printed and sent out. Bought extra wine in Cape Town to cater and got lots of food from the Catering bods. Church in the morning, then usual sort of lunch, quick sunbathe (sun was out for a change) then decorating of the alleyway. Got the wine on ice in a bath, the place decorated all nautically (it looked lovely) and then hair-do and change. All ready by 6.45 for the first guests. And they poured in and it was a super party, everyone said. Mr. Bain presented me with a parcel on behalf of everyone else, which was embarrassing. I was also given a Union-Castle Line House flag, wonderful.

I think we all drank a lot of wine and then we staggered down to Dinner and then had more wine. Lovely. Then a quick Quiz and then the Crew Darts Match as usual. Felt rather 'rotten' at the end of the evening but it was all absolutely wonderful.

Now it is Saturday before docking and everything is so different. We are in blues today and it feels like the beginning of the end. I have had a super time on the voyage since Cape Town: cold lunches, wine, champagne parties, food aplenty, little sleep, being allowed to play truant from the Bureau and generally having a whale of a time. Had a lunchtime session for some of the crew like my favourite Master-At-Arms (he gave me some beautiful pearls), the Butcher called Willie whose picture was in the Daily Telegraph supplement (remember ?), and the Carpenter (who gave me a lovely wooden carved standard lamp stand with brass feet and handle, that he had made specially for me).

Now it's Sunday morning and only one day to go. After typing the above, I felt sick and had to rush away. Felt quite nasty for a while, but went to bed for an hour at 6 o'clock and felt better after that. It was my day for the News, so I had been up at 6 a.m. so that was probably why I felt tired and sick.

(Last night we had Irish coffee just before 9.15 Prize giving, and that was rather fine. I felt much better.) The Dance had to be cancelled, because we are rolling and pitching terribly. Ugh.

Did I tell you about our lion tamer and his wife? Met them at the cocktail Party and they are going to Billy Smart's winter quarters at Winkfield and have invited me to come along there and ask for them if I want to. They expect to be performing at Smarts Christmas Show in London. Strange the people you meet, isn't it. We also had a Polish man from Chipperfields, but he missed the ship in Las Palmas.

I must finish this and put it in the box. It seems so peculiar to think that this is the last letter to you from the ocean greyhounds. Hey ho, it's been great fun but how I am looking forward to a holiday and being at home.

As usual, I was going to say 'don't call me, I'll call you', but this morning when you read this I shall have to get up early for the dentist. Nasty. Never mind. This is the last letter from me as one of the Lavender-Hull Mob! See you soon.

Love,
Ann

THE END

Traditional South African Dishes

Most of the typically South African dishes originated at the Cape which, of course, was the first part of the country to be occupied. Some dishes came from Holland with the first settlers, some from the East brought by the Malays and some from France, introduced by the Huguenots.

The best of these dishes are to be found in the country districts, and if you ever happen to hear of a Dutch Reformed Church fête don't miss it, for that is the most likely place to buy the dishes, which I am about to describe, prepared to perfection.

Pickled fish, a dish of fish and onions in a curried sauce, is delicious on hot summer days for it is served cold.

Gesmoorde snoek is a kedgeree of smoked or salted snoek with potato and tomato served on rice. It is a favourite fish dish in many Cape homes.

Sosaties, which are sometimes served at a braaivleis (barbeque), are skewered pieces of lamb or mutton which have previously been soaked for about three days in a sauce of curry and other spices. They are grilled over the coals.

Boerewors, also popular at a braaivleis, is a strongly spiced beef sausage, usually home-made.

Bobotie is a minced-meat casserole dish which comes from the East.

Bredes come in various forms—tomato, green bean, dried bean or water-plant with a mutton stew, and, if well prepared, they can be very tasty.

Hoenderpastei is a delicious chicken pie traditionally served with yellow rice and raisins.

Boerebeskuit is a rusk made from a milk bun and it is traditionally served on farms with the early-morning coffee.

Mosbolletjies, served sliced and buttered for tea, is a bun flavoured with raisin-juice and aniseed.

Soetkoekies are crisp, spicy biscuits that will keep for a long time.

Melktert has an almond-flavoured custard filling set in very light pastry and they are served hot or cold.

Koeksusters are made of plaited lengths of dough fried until they are crisp and then dipped into hot syrup. They melt in the mouth.

Oblietjies, a Huguenot delicacy, are thin, crisp, rolled pancakes with a cinnamon flavour.

And lastly is **biltong,** not to everyone's taste, but revered by almost all South Africans. It is the raw meat of game, beef or ostrich which had been laid in a spiced salt brine and then hung in the wind to dry.

67

Some of the pleasures of South Africa

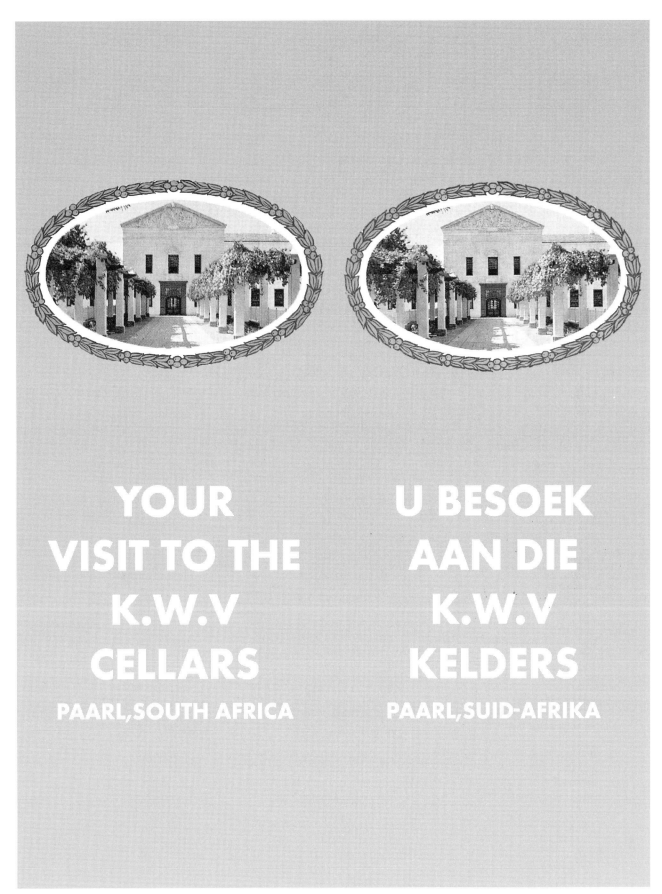

YOUR
VISIT TO THE
K.W.V
CELLARS
PAARL, SOUTH AFRICA

U BESOEK
AAN DIE
K.W.V
KELDERS
PAARL, SUID-AFRIKA

And somewhere to get the wherewithal to wash them down

CREW LISTS

MAIL SERVICE	Transvaal Castle *Left Southampton* *12th November* *for South Africa*
Master	N. Lloyd
Staff Commander..	R. Lofts
Chief Officer	M. Turner
Second Officer	B. Fry
Junior Second Officer ..	C. Brown (Extra)
Third Officer	D. Dudley
Fourth Officer	R. Hobson (Cadet)
Cadet	W. Ferrier
Carpenter	J. Wilson
Boatswain	L. Walker
Masters-at-Arms	L. Langley
	C. Cordall
First Radio Officer	R. Brew
Second Radio Officer ..	H. McColl
Third Radio Officer	I. McKinnon
Fourth Radio Officer ..	R. Wilson
Surgeon	R. Seymour
Nursing Sister	Miss A. Dunne
Physiotherapist	—
Chief Engineer	A. Mailer
First Engineer	W. Patrick
Senior Second Engineer ..	A. Martin
Int. Second Engineer ..	R. Blenkinsop
Junior Second Engineers..	C. Meek
	J. Hill
	A. Stewart
Senior Third Engineer ..	J. Oakman
Int. Third Engineer	D. Keen
Junior Third Engineer ..	J. Inkersole
Senior Fourth Engineer ..	C. Mears
Junior Fourth Engineer ..	D. Garland
Junior Engineers	J. Carruthers
	J. Smith
	G. Baker
	G. Liesching
	G. Du Toit
	T. Brown
Chief Refrigerating Engineer ..	A. Gurd
Second Refrigerating Engineer ..	R. Bintcliffe
First Electrician	D. Thorpe
Second Electrician	F. Thomas
Third Electrician	C. Rayner
E.R. Storekeeper	C. Pyne
E.R. Leading Hand	J. Reid
Chief Purser	M. Bain
Purser	A. Hodge
Purser Catering/Chief Catering Officer	D. Wickenden
Second Purser	J. Ingram
Second Purser Catering/Second Catering Officer	W. Woods
Third Purser Catering/Third Catering Officer	A. Quarrie
Assistant Pursers	A. Doidge
Purser's Clerks	G. Musgrave-Brown
	M. Irwin
	Miss M. Telford
	Miss A. Williams
Junior Purser Catering/Junior Catering Officer	N. Brown
	N. Clarke (Spny.)
Hostess	Miss A. Oelofse
Children's Hostess	Miss A. Ackrill
Chief Barman	F. Hubbard
Storekeeper	M. Gunner
Linen Steward	A. Lydford
First Class Head Waiter.. ..	—
First T/C Steward ..	W. Jackson
Tourist Class Head Waiter ..	R. Furness
Bandleader	J. Gray
Laundryman	A. Burroughs
Chef	V. Moakes
Baker	A. Brohamer
Butcher	H. Cooke
Shopkeeper	S. Lewin

EXTRA SERVICE	Capetown Castle *Left Southampton* *12th January* *for South Africa*
Master	R. M. Wright
Chief Officer	W. McFarland
Second Officer	P. Laister
Extra Second Officer ..	H. Jones
Third Officer	I. Bell
Fourth Officer	R. Belcourt
Cadets	S. Hands
	M. Andrews
Carpenter	D. Perry
Boatswain	W. Arnold
Master-at-Arms	G. Lees
Master-at-Arms	R. Brady
First Radio Officer	J. Eager
Second Radio Officer ..	J. Tuck
Third Radio Officer	D. Campbell
Fourth Radio Officer ..	J. Glenn
Surgeon..	I. Soutar
Nursing Sister	Miss M. Herd
Nursing Sister	Miss M. Kooymans
Chief Engineer	H. Stuart
First Engineer	P. Boon
Snr. Second Engineer ..	D. Taylor
Int. Second Engineer ..	D. Pothecary
Jnr. Second Engineers	R. Skillen
	D. McLeod
	R. West
Snr. Third Engineer ..	V. Stoodley
Int. Third Engineer ..	B. Coates
Jnr. Third Engineer ..	E. Reilly
Snr. Fourth Engineer ..	R. Smith
Jnr. Fourth Engineer ..	J. Nicholson
Jnr. Engineers	D. Batchelor
	P. Coetzee
	M. Wilson
	G. Bunn
	S. Vandal
	R. Cockburn
First Electrician	T. Coates
Second Electrician	C. Pugh
Third Electrician	M. Berridge
E. R. Storekeeper ..	F. Southwell
Leading Hand	G. Walcroft
Purser	R. Funnell
Chief Catering Officer.. ..	S. Beckett
Second Purser	G. Donald
Assistant Purser	A. Edwards
Assistant Purser	I. Fisher
Second Catering Officer	C. Williamson
Third Catering Officer	G. Cary
Purser's Clerk	Miss A. Williams
Purser's Clerk	Miss M. Fisher
Purser's Clerk	Miss C. Vroons
Purser's Clerk	C. Brown
Children's Hostess ..	Miss G. Nash
Chief Barman	P. Spanner
Storekeeper	H. Matthews
Linen Steward	S. Bain
First Pass. Steward ..	L. Jenner
Head Waiter	A. Barkhuysen
Head Waiter	R. Quaife
Bandleader	T. Jones
Laundryman	G. Higgins
Chef	L. Creed
Baker	S. Tilsed
Butcher	A. Kickham
Shopkeepers	P. Hall
	C. McDonald

CREW LISTS

S.A. Oranje — Mail Service — Left Southampton 29th April for South Africa

Master	J. Smythe
Staff Commander	P. Eckford
Chief Officer	K. Barry
Second Officer	R. Milne
Extra Second Officer	J. Inniss
Third Officer	D. Russell
Fourth Officer	C. Sandall
Cadet	W. Ferrier
Carpenter	H. Hale
Boatswain	E. Wheeler
Masters At-Arms	R. Carson
	H. Clarke
First Radio Officer	G. Kilminster
Second Radio Officer	W. Eckersley
Third Radio Officer	D. White
Fourth Radio Officer	F. Barritt
Surgeon	R. Willoughby
Nursing Sister	Miss C. Richards
Physiotherapist	
Chief Engineer	R. Crook
First Engineer	W. Findlay
Snr. Second Engineer	S. Mason
Int. Second Engineer	W. Deacon
Jnr. Second Engineers	G. Blakey
	C. Godfrey
	V. Hamilton
Snr. Third Engineer	M. O'Hara
Int. Third Engineer	K. Richardson
Jnr. Third Engineer	D. Hunt
Snr. Fourth Engineer	K. Amor
Jnr. Fourth Engineer	I. Templeton
Jnr. Engineers	F. Clarke
	J. Cook
	D. Garth
	—
	—
	—
Chief Refrig. Engineer	A. Gurd
Second Refrigeration Engineer	A. McLeod
Third Refrig. Engineer	D. Smith
First Electrician	G. Forrester
Second Electrician	A. Moir
Third Electrician	J. McCulloch
E.R. Storekeeper	K. Pearson
E.R. Leading Hand	W. Theuma
Chief Purser	D. Wickenden
Purser	A. Connelly
Purser Catering/ Chief Catering Officer	G. Green
Second Purser	B. Cooper
Second Purser Catering/Second Catering Officer	D. Padmore
Third Purser Catering/ Third Catering Officer	A. Quarrie
Assistant Pursers	B. Thomas
	D. Mason
	—
Purser's Clerks	Miss A. Palmer
	Miss A. Williams
	—
	W. Fleetwood
Junior Purser Catering/Junior Catering Officer	—
Hostess	Miss C. Cordwell-Green
Children's Hostess	Miss J. Nevard
Chief Barman	F. Nicolas
Storekeeper	A. Gilmour
Linen Steward	C. Handley
F/Class Head Waiter	K. Mackay
First T/C Steward	R. Smith
T/Class Head Waiter	C. Roche
Bandleader	D. Pearce
Laundryman	W. Cronin
Chef	C. Alves
Baker	J. Leslie
Butcher	L. Nicholson
Shopkeeper	K. Hann
Housekeeper	

S.A. Oranje — Mail Service — Left Southampton 23rd September for South Africa

Master	J. Smythe
Staff Commander	P. Eckford
Chief Officer	K. Barry
Second Officer	D. Haynes
Extra Second Officer	T. Inniss
Third Officer	D. Hawker
Fourth Officer	R. Duthie
Cadets	W. Walker
Carpenter	H. Hale
Boatswain	E. Wheeler
Masters-at-Arms	C. Wroe
	H. Clarke
First Radio Officer	G. Kilminster
Second Radio Officer	W. Eckersley
Third Radio Officer	R. Beech
Fourth Radio Officer	J. Turbefield
Surgeon	R. Willoughby
Nursing Sister	Miss P. Sargent
Physiotherapist	
Chief Engineer	R. Crook
First Engineer	W. Findlay
Snr. Second Engineer	S. Mason
Int. Second Engineer	J. Nessling
Jnr. Second Engineers	G. Blakey
	V. Hamilton
	R. Lorimer
Snr. Third Engineer	M. O'Hara
Int. Third Engineer	D. Hunt
Jnr. Third Engineer	K. Amor
Snr. Fourth Engineer	J. Heard
Jnr. Fourth Engineer	C. Meadon
Jnr. Engineers	J. Cook
	H. Knott
	T. Roberts
Chief Refrig. Engineer	D. Laycock
Second Refrig. Engineer	J. Wade
Third Refrig. Engineer	D. Smith
First Electrician	G. Forrester
Second Electrician	W. Pearce
Third Electrician	J. Penston
Fourth Electrician	—
E.R. Storekeeper	K. Pearson
E.R. Leading Hand	W. Theuma
Chief Purser	D. Wickenden
Purser	A. Connelly
Supny. Purser	—
Purser Catering/Chief Catering Officer	G. Green
Second Purser	B. Thomas
Second Purser Catering/Second Catering Officer	D. Padmore
Third Purser Catering/Third Catering Officer	J. Fry
Assistant Pursers	A. Doidge
	D. Mason
Purser's Clerks	Miss A. Williams
	Miss A. Palmer
	D. Howden
Junior Purser Catering/Junior Catering Officer	N. Nussey
Hostess	Miss C. Cordwell-Green
Children's Hostess	Miss J. Nevard
Chief Barman	P. Beech
Storekeeper	S. Bain
Linen Steward	C. Handley
F/Class Head Waiter	K. Mackay
First T/C Steward	L. Jenner
T/Class Head Waiter	C. Roche
Bandleader	D. Pearce
Laundryman	W. Cronin
Chef	C. Alves
Baker	J. Leslie
Butcher	L. Nicholson
Shopkeeper	K. Hann
Housekeeper	—

CREW LISTS

Mail Service	S.A. Oranje *Left Southampton* *11th November* *for* *South Africa*
Master ..	J. Smythe
Staff Commander ..	P. Eckford
Chief Officer ..	K. Barry
2nd Officer ..	D. Haynes
Extra 2nd Officer ..	D. Youles
3rd Officer ..	D. Hawker
4th Officer ..	J. Merrett
Cadet ..	W. Walker
Carpenter ..	H. Hale
Boatswain ..	E. Wheeler
Masters-at-Arms ..	C. Wroe
	F. Harrison
1st Radio Officer ..	G. Kilminster
2nd Radio Officer ..	W. Eckersley
3rd Radio Officer ..	R. Beech
4th Radio Officer ..	J. Turbefield
Surgeon ..	R. Willoughby
Nursing Sister ..	Miss P. Sargent
Physiotherapist ..	—
Chief Engineer ..	R. Crook
1st Engineer ..	W. Findlay
Snr. Second Eng. ..	S. Mason
Int. Second Eng. ..	P. Swift
Jnr. Second Engs. ..	G. Blakey
	V. Hamilton
	J. Acors
Snr. Third Eng. ..	M. O'Hara
Int. Third Eng. ..	D. Hunt
Jnr. Third Eng. ..	K. Amor
Snr. Fourth Eng. ..	J. Heard
Jnr. Fourth Eng. ..	C. Meadon
Jnr. Engineers ..	J. Lutton
	H. Knott
Chief Refrig. Eng.	D. Laycock
2nd Refrig. Eng. ..	G. Walker
3rd Refrig. Eng. ..	D. Smith
1st Electrician ..	G. Forrester
2nd Electrician ..	W. Pearce
3rd Electrician ..	J. Penston
4th Electricians ..	—
E. R. Storekeeper	K. Pearson
E. R. Leading Hand	H. Spicer
Chief Purser ..	D. Wickenden
Purser ..	A. Connelly
P.C./C.C. Offr.	G. Green
2nd Purser ..	M. Hackett
2nd P.C./2nd C.Offr.	D. Padmore
3rd P.C./3rd C.Offr.	J. Fry
Assistant Pursers ..	D. Mason
	A. Doidge
Purser's Clerks ..	Miss A. Williams
	Miss A. Palmer
	D. Howden
Jnr. P.C./Jnr. C.Offr.	N. Nussey
Hostess ..	Miss C. Cordwell-Green
Children's Hostess	Miss J. Nevard
Chief Barman ..	P. Beech
Storekeeper ..	J. Glintenkamp
Linen Steward ..	C. Handley
F/Class Head Waiter	K. Mackay
First T/C Steward	L. Jenner
T/Class Head Waiter	C. Roche
Bandleader ..	D. Pearce
Laundryman ..	W. Cronin
Chef ..	C. Alves
Baker ..	J. Leslie
Butcher ..	L. Nicholson
Shopkeepers ..	K. Hann
	R. Randall
Housekeeper ..	

Mail Service	S.A. Oranje *Left Southampton* *30th December* *for* *South Africa*
Master	J. Smythe
Staff Commander	P. Eckford
Chief Officer	K. Barry
Second Officer	D. Haynes
Extra Second Officer	P. Le Caer
Third Officer	D. Hawker
Fourth Officer	F. Holden
Cadet	N. Butterfield
Carpenter	H. Hale
Boatswain	E. Wheeler
Masters-at-Arms	C. Wroe
	F. Harrison
First Radio Officer	G. Kilminster
Second Radio Officer	W. Eckersley
Third Radio Officer	R. Beech
Fourth Radio Officer	J. Turbefield
Surgeon	J. Clarke
Nursing Sisters	Miss P. Sargent
Physiotherapist	—
Chief Engineer	R. Crook
First Engineer	W. Findlay
Snr. Second Engineer	S. Mason
Int. Second Engineer	P. Swift
Jnr. Second Engineers	G. Blakey
	J. Acors
	V. Hamilton
Snr. Third Engineer	M. O'Hara
Int. Third Engineer	K. Amor
Jnr. Third Engineer	B. Maynard
Snr. Fourth Engineer	J. Heard
Jnr. Fourth Engineer	C. Meadon
Jnr. Engineers	J. Lutton
	H. Knott
Chief Refrigeration Engineer	A. Gurd
Second Refrigeration Engineer	W. Trevett
Third Refrigeration Engineer	M. Quincey
First Electrician	G. Forrester
Second Electrician	W. Pearce
Third Electrician	J. Penston
Fourth Electricians	—
E.R. Storekeeper	K. Pearson
E.R. Leading Hand	H. Spicer
Chief Purser	D. Wickenden
Purser	A. Connelly
Purser Catering/Chief Catering Officer ..	G. Green
Second Purser	J. McFadyen
Second Purser Catering/Second Catering Officer	D. Padmore
Third Purser Catering/Third Catering Officer	M. Wicksteed
Assistant Pursers	M. Jones
	A. Doidge
Junior Purser Catering/Junior Catering Officer	N. Nussey
Hostess	Miss C. Cordwell-Green
Children's Hostess	Miss J. Nevard
Chief Barman	P. Beech
Storekeeper	J. Glintenkamp
Linen Steward	C. Handley
F/Class Head Waiter	K. Mackay
First T/C Steward	L. Jenner
T/Class Head Waiter	C. Roche
Bandleader	F. Pearce
Laundryman	W. Cronin
Chef	C. Alves
Baker	J. Leslie
Butcher	L. Nicholson
Shopkeepers	K. Hann
	R. Randall
Housekeeper	—

CREW LISTS

MAIL SERVICE	Edinburgh Castle *Left Southampton* *10th March* *for* *South Africa*
Master	W. Byles
Staff Commander	R. Lofts
Chief Officer	A. Wigham
Second Officer	R. Stearn
Extra Second Officer	G. Holden
Third Officer	D. Grimes
Fourth Officer	C. Marman
Cadet	M. Dowsett
Carpenter	J. Love
Boatswain	N. Ward
Masters-at-Arms	W. Provan
	K. Turner (Actg.)
First Radio Officer	H. Liggins
Second Radio Officer	H. McColl
Third Radio Officer	T. McAnerney
Fourth Radio Officer	J. Foley
Surgeon	M. Macnamara
Nursing Sister	Miss M. Thompson
Physiotherapist	—
Chief Engineer	S. Harron
First Engineer	W. Robertson
Snr. Second Engineer	P. Lovell
Int. Second Engineer	K. Talbot
Jnr. Second Engineers	S. Morrison
	D. Warren
	J. Inkersole
Snr. Third Engineer	D. Burr
Int. Third Engineer	T. Williams
Jnr. Third Engineer	J. Mayer
Snr. Fourth Engineer	R. Gorst
Jnr. Fourth Engineer	C. Smuts
Jnr. Engineers	R. Wright
	J. Taylor
	—
	—
	—
Chief Refrig. Engineer	J. Ringshaw
Second Refrig. Engineer	G. Walker
Third Refrig. Engineer	R. James
First Electrician	T. Stallard
Second Electrician	W. Street
Third Electrician	A. Bennett
Fourth Electricians	—
E.R. Storekeeper	P. Phillips
E.R. Leading Hand	B. Atkinson
Chief Purser	M. Bain
Purser	R. Wynter
Purser Catering/Chief Catering Officer	G. Waugh
Second Purser	C. Dellar
Second Purser Catering/Second Catering Officer	R. Bowen
Third Purser Catering/Third Catering Officer	W. Stewart
Assistant Pursers	J. Ingram
	R. Gascoyne
Purser's Clerks	Miss A. Williams
	P. Edwards
	I. Jenkins
	—
Junior Purser Catering/Junior Catering Officer	R. Warren
Hostess	Miss V. Craig
Children's Hostess	Miss P. Wakefield
Chief Barman	L. Odell
Storekeeper	D. Marston
Linen Steward	C. Bosman
F/Class Head Waiter	M. Walmsley
First T/C Steward	A. Secker
T/Class Head Waiter	T. McIntosh
Bandleader	T. Jones
Laundryman	J. Sumpton
Chef	G. Perez
Baker	S. Thomas
Butcher	L. Newman
Shopkeepers	S. Lewin
	W. Hardy
Housekeeper	—

MAIL SERVICE	Edinburgh Castle *Left Southampton* *28th April* *for* *South Africa*
Master	W. Byles
Staff Commander	R. Lofts
Chief Officer	O. Barnsley
Second Officer	R. Stearn
Extra Second Officer	P. McMillan
Third Officer	D. Grimes
Fourth Officer	R. Kirkpatrick
Cadet	M. Dowsett
Carpenter	P. Bell
Boatswain	J. Perry
Masters-at-Arms	W. Provan
	R. Brady
1st Radio Officer	H. Liggins
2nd Radio Officer	H. McColl
3rd Radio Officer	T. McAnerney
4th Radio Officer	J. Foley
Surgeon	M. Macnamara
Nursing Sister	Miss A. Dunne
Physiotherapist	—
Chief Engineer	S. Harron
First Engineer	W. Maitland
Snr. Second Engineer	P. Lovell
Int. Second Engineer	P. Swift
Jnr. Second Engineers	D. Warren
	J. Webster
	J. Inkersole
Snr. Third Engineer	D. Burr
Int. Third Engineer	T. Williams
Jnr. Third Engineer	J. Mayer
Snr. Fourth Engineer	R. Gorst
Jnr. Fourth Engineer	C. Smuts
Jnr. Engineers	R. Wright
	J. Taylor
Chief Refrig. Engineer	J. Ringshaw
Second Refrig. Engineer	G. Walker
Third Refrig. Engineer	J. Ferguson
First Electrician	T. Stallard
Second Electrician	W. Street
Third Electrician	A. Bennett
Fourth Electricians	
E.R. Storekeeper	P. Phillips
E.R. Leading Hand	B. Atkinson
Chief Purser	M. Bain
Purser	R. Wynter
Purser Catering/Chief Catering Officer	G. Waugh
Second Purser	C. Dellar
Second Purser Catering/Second Catering Officer	R. Bowen
Third Purser Catering/Third Catering Officer	W. Stewart
Assistant Pursers	J. Ingram
	A. Holmes
Purser's Clerks	Miss A. Williams
	Miss I. Dowden
	C. Elliott
Junior Purser Catering/Junior Catering Officer	R. Warren
Hostess	Miss V. Craig
Children's Hostess	Miss J. Bonner
Chief Barman	L. Odell
Storekeeper	D. Marston
Linen Steward	C. Bosman
F/Class Head Waiter	R. Skevington
First T/C Steward	A. Secker
T/Class Head Waiter	T. McIntosh
Bandleader	T. Jones
Laundryman	J. Sumpton
Chef	V. Moakes
Baker	S. Thomas
Butcher	W. Murray
Shopkeepers	S. Lewin
	W. Hardy
Housekeeper	—

MAIL SERVICE	Edinburgh Castle *Left Southampton June 16 for South Africa*
Master	A. Freer
Staff Commander	R. Lofts
Chief Officer	O. Barnsley
Second Officer	R. Stearn
Extra Second Officer	P. McMillan
Third Officer	D. Grimes
Fourth Officer	R. Kirkpatrick
Cadet	M. Dowsett
Carpenter	P. Bell
Boatswain	J. Perry
Masters-at-Arms	W. Provan
	R. Lloyd
1st Radio Officer	H. Liggins
2nd Radio Officer	G. Walker
3rd Radio Officer	T. McAnerney
4th Radio Officer	J. Foley
Surgeon	I. Reekie
Nursing Sister	Miss A. Dunne
Physiotherapist	—
Chief Engineer	S. Harron
First Engineer	W. Robertson
Snr. Second Engineer	P. Lovell
Int. Second Engineer	P. Swift
Jnr. Second Engineers	D. Warren
	J. Webster
	J. Inkersole
Snr. Third Engineer	D. Burr
Int. Third Engineer	J. Mayer
Jnr. Third Engineer	L. Hopkins
Snr. Fourth Engineer	R. Gorst
Jnr. Fourth Engineer	C. Smuts
Jnr. Engineers	R. Wright
	J. Taylor
	—
	—
	—
Chief Refrigerating Engineer	J. Ringshaw
Second Refrigerating Engineer	G. Walker
Third Refrigerating Engineer	F. Ing
First Electrician	T. Stallard
Second Electrician	J. Lawlor
Third Electrician	K. Wylie
Fourth Electrician	
E. R. Storekeeper	P. Phillips
E.R. Leading Hand	B. Atkinson
Chief Purser	M. Bain
Purser	R. Wynter
Purser Catering/Chief Catering Officer	I. Beckett
Second Purser	C. Dellar
Second Purser Catering/Second Catering Officer	R. Bowen
Third Purser Catering/Third Catering Officer	W. Stewart
Assistant Pursers	J. Ingram
	A. Holmes
	—
Purser's Clerks	Miss I. Dowden
	Miss A. Williams
	C. Elliott
	—
Junior Purser Catering/Junior Catering Officer	R. Warren
Hostess	Miss V. Craig
Children's Hostess	Miss J. Bonner
Chief Barman	L. Odell
Storekeeper	D. Marston
Linen Steward	C. Bosman
F/Class Head Waiter	R. Skevington
First T/C Steward	A. Secker
T/Class Head Waiter	T. McIntosh
Bandleader	T. Jones
Laundryman	J. Sumpton
Chef	V. Moakes
Baker	S. Thomas
Butcher	W. Murray
Shopkeepers	S. Lewin
	W. Hardy
Housekeeper	—

MAIL SERVICE	Edinburgh Castle *Left Southampton September 22 for South Africa*
Master	D. Sowden
Staff Commander	R. Lofts
Chief Officer	O. Barnsley
Second Officer	R. Stearn
Extra Second Officer	P. McMillan
Third Officer	J. Grundy
Fourth Officer	M. Dowsett
Cadet	D. Fellowes
Carpenter	P. Bell
Boatswain	J. Perry
Masters-at-Arms	W. Provan
	R. Lloyd
Chief Radio Officer	H. Liggins
2nd Radio Officer	H. McColl
3rd Radio Officer	T. McAnnerney
4th Radio Officer	R. Kenyon
Surgeon	I. Reekie
Nursing Sister	Miss J. Griffiths
Physiotherapist	—
Chief Engineer	S. Harron
First Engineer	W. Robertson
Snr. Second Engineer	A. Simms
Int. Second Engineer	J. Robinson
Jnr. Second Engineers	D. Warren
	J. Inkersole
	B. Hargraves
Snr. Third Engineers	T. Williams
Int. Third Engineer	A. Waldron
Jnr. Third Engineer	S. Rogers
Snr. Fourth Engineer	C. Barnard
Jnr. Fourth Engineer	R. Wymer
Jnr. Engineers	J. Soar
	F. Ing
Chief Refrig. Engineer	J. Ringshaw
Second Refrig. Engineer	G. Walker
Third Refrig. Engineer	R. Shirley
First Electrician	T. Stallard
Second Electrician	J. Lawlor
Third Electrician	K. Wylie
Fourth Electrician	—
E.R. Storekeeper	P. Phillips
E.R. Leading Hand	B. Atkinson
Chief Purser	M. Bain
Purser	R. Wynter
Purser Catering/Chief Catering Officer	I. Beckett
Second Purser	C. Dellar
Second Purser Catering/Second Catering Officer	R. Bowen
Third Purser Catering/Third Catering Officer	W. Stewart
Assistant Pursers	A. Holmes
	M. Irwin
Purser's Clerks	C. Elliott
	Miss I. Dowden
	Miss A. Williams
Junior Purser Catering/Junior Catering Officer	—
Hostess	Miss S. McGregor
Children's Hostess	Miss J. Bonner
Chief Barman	L. Odell
Storekeeper	D. Marston
Linen Steward	C. Bosman
F/Class Head Waiter	R. Skevington
First T/C Steward	A. Secker
T/Class Waiter	T. McIntosh
Bandleader	T. Jones
Laundryman	J. Sumpton
Chef	G. Perez
Baker	S. Thomas
Butcher	W. Murray
Shopkeepers	S. Lewin
	W. Hardy

DRAMATIS PERSONAE

Abbe (Jacqueline) Nevard	Children's Hostess, S. A. ORANJE
Alan Beech	Supernumary Radio Officer, S. A. ORANJE
Alan Holmes ("Twink")	Assistant Purser, EDINBURGH CASTLE
Andrew Quarrie	Third Purser/Catering, TRANSVAAL CASTLE
Angie Palmer	Purserette, S. A. ORANJE
Ann Williams	Purserette
Anne Dunne	Nursing Sister, TRANSVAAL CASTLE & EDINBURGH CASTLE
Anthony Doidge	Assistant Purser, TRANSVAAL CASTLE & S. A. ORANJE
Arthur Wigham	Chief Officer, EDINBURGH CASTLE
Audrey Wakefield	Children's Hostess, REINA DEL MAR
Aunt Grace	Mrs Grace Winks, Aunt to Ann Williams
Aunty Doris (Hart)	Aunt of Ann Williams
Bain, Mr. Marcus	Chief Purser, TRANSVAAL CASTLE
Baker, Mr. A.M.H. ("Boffin")	Superintendent Purser, London Office
Barry Thomas	Second Purser, S. A. ORANJE
Basil D'Oliveira	Test Cricketer, passenger S. A. ORANJE
Bede Cooper	Second Purser, S. A. ORANJE
Bill Eckersley	Second Radio Officer, S. A. ORANJE
Bill Ferrier	Cadet, TRANSVAAL CASTLE & S. A. ORANJE
Bill Fleetwood	Purser's Clerk, S. A. ORANJE
Bill McEwan	Marine Superintendent, Southampton
Bill McFarland	Chief Officer, CAPETOWN CASTLE
Bokor-Ingram, baby Simon	Son of John & Judith Bokor-Ingram
Bokor-Ingram, Mrs. Judith	Wife of John Bokor-Ingram
Brian Madeley	Passenger, CAPETOWN CASTLE
Bullock, baby Alison	Daughter of Tony & Rosemary Bullock
Bullock, Mr. Tony	Ex-Purser, living in Cape Town
Bullock, Mrs. Rosemary	Wife of Tony Bullock
Byles, Commodore W. S.	Commodore, EDINBURGH CASTLE
Byles, Mrs. Freda	Wife of Commodore Byles
Cayzer Bt., Sir Nicholas	Chairman, British & Commonwealth
Cayzer, Mr. Bernard G. S.	Director, British & Commonwealth
Cecilia Vroons	Purserette, CAPETOWN CASTLE
Challis, Mr. Christopher	Cinema Film Cameraman, from Longford, Middlesex
Chris Dadson	Third Purser/Catering, REINA DEL MAR
Chris Fry	Third Purser/Catering, S. A. ORANJE
Chris. Richards	Nursing Sister, S. A. ORANJE
Clare Trevor	Film star passenger, S. A. ORANJE
Colin Brown	Extra/Second Officer, CAPETOWN CASTLE
Colin Dellar	Second Purser, EDINBURGH CASTLE
Connelly, Mr. A. A.	Purser, S. A. ORANJE
Cook, Mr. W. A.	Superintendent Purser, after Mr Baker retired
Cozette Cordwell-Green	Hostess, S. A. ORANJE
Crook, Mr. Ron	Chief Engineer, S. A. ORANJE
Daddy	Mr. Harry Williams, Father of Ann Williams
David Hawker	Third Officer, S. A. ORANJE

David Haynes	Second Officer, S. A. ORANJE
David Howden	Purser's Clerk, S. A. ORANJE
David Macmillan	Ex-Pursers Dept., B&C Project Team on S. A. ORANJE
David Padmore	Second Purser/Catering, S. A. ORANJE
Derek Edge	Friend of the Williams Family
Derek Mason	Assistant Purser, S. A. ORANJE
Derek Owens	Fiancé/Husband of Elaine Williams
Dick Haymes	Singer, passenger on EDINBURGH CASTLE
Dick Stearn	Second Officer, EDINBURGH CASTLE
Don Hunt	Int/Third Engineer, S. A. ORANJE
Doreen Stammers	Friend from I.C.I. Paints Division
Dorothy Edge	Friend of the Williams Family
Elaine Williams	Younger sister of Ann Williams
Eric Jackson (Mr.)	Passenger EDINBURGH CASTLE & Ford Corsair car driver, racing WINDSOR CASTLE from Cape Town to UK
Ernie Savage	Bedroom Steward, S. A. ORANJE & EDINBURGH CASTLE
Findlay, Mr. Bill	Chief Engineer, S. A. ORANJE
Freer, Captain A.	Captain, EDINBURGH CASTLE
Geoff. Green	Purser/Catering, S. A. ORANJE
Glenda Nash	Children's Hostess, CAPETOWN CASTLE
Godfrey Musgrave-Brown	Purser's Clerk, TRANSVAAL CASTLE
Graham Donald	Second Purser, CAPETOWN CASTLE
Harron, Mr. Stan	Chief Engineer, EDINBURGH CASTLE
Hector McColl	Second Radio Officer, TRANSVAAL CASTLE & EDINBURGH CASTLE
Hodge Mr. A.	Purser, TRANSVAAL CASTLE
Ian Bell	Third Officer, CAPETOWN CASTLE
Irene Dowden	Purserette, EDINBURGH CASTLE
Jeannie Bonner	Children's Hostess, EDINBURGH CASTLE
Jim Inniss	Extra Second Officer, S. A. ORANJE
Jim Turbefield	Fourth Radio Officer, S. A. ORANJE
John Bokor-Ingram	Second Purser, TRANSVAAL CASTLE & EDINBURGH CASTLE
John Drago	Cousin of Ann Williams
John Flower	Purser's Clerk, S. A. ORANJE
John McFadyen	Second Purser, S. A. ORANJE
John Sparling	Purser's Clerk, EDINBURGH CASTLE
Katy Thompson	Nursing Sister, EDINBURGH CASTLE
Keith Underwood	Purser, REINA DEL MAR
Kelso, Captain C. Reg.	Captain/Staff Commander, & B&C Project Team Leader on S.A. ORANJE
Ken Chambers (Mr.)	Passenger EDINBURGH CASTLE & Ford Corsair car driver, racing WINDSOR CASTLE from Cape Town to UK
Ken Faulkner	Family friend from Harmondsworth, Middlesex
Ken Wood	Kenwood Chef Mixer inventor, passenger EDINBURGH CASTLE
Lenny Odell	Chief Barman, EDINBURGH CASTLE
Lightfoot Mr.	County Cricketer, passenger S. A. ORANJE
Lloyd R.D., R.N.R., Captain N.M.	Captain, TRANSVAAL CASTLE
Lofts, Mr. Rodney ("Lofty")	Staff Commander, EDINBURGH CASTLE
Maggie Parry	Purserette, REINA DEL MAR

Maggie Telford	Purserette, TRANSVAAL CASTLE
Marian Paget	Friend from I.C.I. Paints Division
Marsha Spanswick	Friend from I.C.I. Paints Division
Maureen Fisher	Purserette, CAPETOWN CASTLE
McIver, Mr.	Cayzer, Irvine & Co.
Mike Hackett	Second Purser, S. A. ORANJE
Mike Irwin	Purser's Clerk, TRANSVAAL CASTLE & EDINBURGH CASTLE
Mike Turner	Chief Officer, TRANSVAAL CASTLE
Milt Bren (Mr.)	Film-producer passenger, S. A. ORANJE
Mr. Collett	An engineer from I.C.I. Paints Division
Mummy	Mrs. Rose Williams, Mother of Ann Williams
Newman Mr.	County Cricketer, passenger S. A. ORANJE
Olive Preston	Friend of Ann Williams
Pat Ashby	Friend from I.C.I. Paints Division
Patsy Lyden	Purserette, REINA DEL MAR
Peter Bazlinton	Second Purser, S. A. ORANJE
Peter Eckford	Staff Commander, S. A. ORANJE
Peter Hall	Assistant to Superintendent Purser, London
Peter Laister	Second Officer, CAPETOWN CASTLE
Peter	Photographer, EDINBURGH CASTLE
Phil. Sargent	Nursing Sister, S. A. ORANJE
Remfry, Mr. Cyril	Union-Castle London Passenger Dept.
Remfry, Mrs. Freda	Union-Castle London Office
Robbie Rutt	Cruise Director, REINA DEL MAR
Robertson Mr. W. ("Robbie")	First Engineer, EDINBURGH CASTLE
Robertson Mrs. W.	Wife of Mr. Robertson
Roger Willoughby	Doctor, S. A. ORANJE
Ron Fenton	Family friend from Harmondsworth
Roper, Miss Thelma	Personnel Officer, Female Staff
Roy Duthie	Fourth Officer, S. A. ORANJE
Roy Funnel	Purser, CAPETOWN CASTLE
Rumsey, Mr.	Test Cricketer, passenger S. A. ORANJE
Scott, Mr.	Test Cricketer, passenger S. A. ORANJE
Sheila Marr	Bishopshalt School friend of Ann Williams
Sheila McGregor	Hostess, REINA DEL MAR & EDINBURGH CASTLE
Smith , Mr. Ian D.	Prime Minister of Rhodesia, passenger
Smythe D.S.C., R.D., R.N.R., Captain J.P.	Captain, S. A. ORANJE
Sowden R.D., R.N.R., Captain D.W.	Captain, CAPETOWN CASTLE
Sowden, Mrs.	Wife of Captain Sowden, S. A. ORANJE
Tony Dyer	Purser, REINA DEL MAR
Tony Edwards	Assistant Purser, CAPETOWN CASTLE
Trevor Jones	Band Leader, CAPETOWN CASTLE & EDINBURGH CASTLE
Uncle Geoffrey (Ashby)	Family friend in Harmondsworth
Van der Byl, Mrs.	Wife of Ven. Archdeacon Van der Byl, passenger
Van der Byl, The Ven. Archdeacon A. F.	Ven. Archdeacon of Cape Town, passenger
Verwoerd, Dr. Hendrik	Assassinated Prime Minister of South Africa
Vicky Craig	Hostess, EDINBURGH CASTLE
Wickenden Mr. D.	Purser/Catering, TRANSVAAL CASTLE
Williams, Mr. Harry F.	Father of Ann Williams
Williams, Mrs. Rose M.	Wife of Harry, and Mother of Ann Williams
Wright, Captain R. M.	Captain, CAPETOWN CASTLE
Wynter, Mr. R.	Purser, EDINBURGH CASTLE

THE UNION-CASTLE MAIL STEAMSHIP COMPANY, LIMITED

OFFICERS IN THE PURSER'S DEPARTMENT

Information for Applicants for a position of Purserette

This Company was formed by the amalgamation of the Union and Castle Lines in 1900. It is a subsidiary of the British & Commonwealth Shipping Company, which also controls the Clan Line and other Companies. Passenger ships of the Union-Castle Line operate between the United Kingdom and ports of South and East Africa.

A Purser's duties are similar in some respects to those of a Bank Manager and a Hotel Manager, and he is generally responsible for the berthing, welfare and entertainment of passengers, and the Purser's staff assist him in these duties.

The pay on joining is £46. 2s. 6d. per month rising to £51. 7s. 6d. per month. There is also a bonus of five days' pay per month while on Articles. A subsistence rate of 15/- a day when on duty on shore and 7/- a day when on leave is also payable.

SERVICE: Purserettes are not eligible for promotion. The appointment is for a maximum period of four years, but they may transfer to the shore staff subject to a suitable vacancy existing in the Company's Offices.

UNIFORM: Officers buy their own uniform. The Company does not hold itself responsible for the cost of an Officer's uniform or equipment if she leaves the Company for any reason whatsoever. Uniform is worn at all times on board ship. The details of uniform required will be supplied on request. The approximate cost of uniform is £60.

INTERVIEW: Applicants are required to attend at the Head Office of the Company for a preliminary interview before being placed on a waiting list for attendance at a selection board.

MEDICAL EXAMINATION: Applicants who have been accepted by the selection board are then required to be passed medically fit by the Company's doctor.

PROBATIONARY TRAINING: There is a course of approximately two months' training in the Company's offices ashore after acceptance.

LIFEBOAT CERTIFICATE: Officers will be required to sit for a lifeboat certificate after six months' sea service.

DISCIPLINE: Purserettes are under the direct control of the Purser and must conform to ship's discipline as required by the Captain and as detailed in the Articles of Agreement which are signed each voyage.

AMENITIES: Purserettes rank as Junior Officers and are berthed in single cabins.

They mess in the First Class Dining Saloon and are allowed use of the decks and public rooms.

LEAVE: Leave amounts to approximately two months per year and is taken between voyages. This includes one day's leave for every Sunday spent at sea, as a seven-day week is worked on board.

The Company reserve the right to recall from leave and transfer from ship to ship should necessity arise.

QUALIFICATIONS:

1. Age between 23 and 28.

2. A standard of education equivalent to G.C.E. with passes in at least three subjects, to include English Language and Mathematics at Ordinary Level.

3. Good manner, appearance and background.

4. Recognised secretarial training. Shorthand and typewriting speeds of not less than 120 w.p.m. and 50 w.p.m. respectively.

CAYZER HOUSE,
2 & 4, ST. MARY AXE,
LONDON E.C.3.

UNIFORM LIST

Bourne & Hollingsworth,
Oxford Street,
LONDON W.1.

		£. s. d.
1	Navy Worsted Dress	8. 8. 0.
4	White Cotton Day Dresses (75/- each)	15. 0. 0.
1	Black Mess Dress	6.19. 6.
2	White Mess Dresses (79/6d. each)	7.19. 0.

2 prs.   Black court shoes with medium heel

2 prs.   White court shoes with medium heel

Gieves Ltd.,
27 Old Bond Street
LONDON W.1.

1   Tricorne Hat with 2 white covers

Monnery's Ltd.,
5 Billiter Street,
LONDON E.C.3.

<u>Uniform Trimmings</u>

1   Company's Badge and Band

8   Medium Merchant Navy Officers pattern gilt buttons

12   Small Merchant Navy Officers pattern gilt buttons

2 prs.   Shoulder Straps (White backed)

2 prs.   "   "   (Black backed)

ACKNOWLEDGEMENTS

I would like to thank Caledonia Leisure & Media Limited for allowing the use of the Union-Castle Line name and logo.

I would also like to thank Captain Reg. and Mrs June Kelso for supplying some of the Crew Lists from "B & C Review", which were missing from my collection, and Mr Ian Shiffman for supplying colour transparencies, acknowledged *in situ*.

I would also like to thank Mr Alan S Mallett for his advice and assistance in bringing this publication to fruition.

My thanks go especially to my wonderful family and friends, and particularly my colleague Mr Leslie Ruecroft, Managing Director of the re-launched Union-Castle Line, who is making my late husband David's dream and plans for the Centenary Voyage a reality.

Ann Haynes
August 1999